The Theology of Vatican II

Revised and Enlarged Edition

Christopher Butler
Auxiliary Bishop in Westminster

DARTON, LONGMAN & TODD
LONDON

First published in 1967 by
Darton, Longman & Todd Ltd
89 Lillie Road, London SW6 1UD

Revised and enlarged edition 1981

ISBN 0 232 51520 4

British Library Cataloguing in Publication Data

Butler, Christopher
The theology of Vatican II. – Rev. and enl. ed.
1. Vatican Council (2nd: 1962–1965)
I. Title
262′.52 BX830 1962

ISBN 0–232–51520–4

Phototypeset by Input Typesetting Ltd, London SW19 8DR

Printed in Great Britain by The Anchor Press Ltd
and bound by Wm. Brendon & Son Ltd,
both of Tiptree, Essex

Contents

Introduction

The second Vatican Council opened on 11 October 1962, and ended in early December 1965. At Oxford in 1966 I devoted my Sarum Lectures to the theme: The Theology of Vatican II. These lectures gave rise to the first edition of the present book, published in 1967. Since 1962 a new generation has come to adulthood, and it seems desirable to offer, in the present Introduction, some brief historical notes to provide a context for the substance of the book. And first, a list of modern Popes:

Pius IX	1846 – 1878
Leo XIII	1878 – 1903
St Pius X	1903 – 1914
Benedict XV	1914 – 1922
Pius XI	1922 – 1939
Pius XII	1939 – 1958
John XXIII	1958 – 1963
Paul VI	1963 – 1978
John Paul I	1978
John Paul II	1978 –

The French Revolution in the closing period of the eighteenth century, followed as it was by the meteoric career of

Napoleon Bonaparte, had shaken to its roots the *ancien régime* of Western Europe. Part and parcel of this *ancien régime*, in the main a régime of dynastic monarchies, were the temporal dominions of the papacy in Italy, which inevitably involved the Pope, as a monarch among monarchs, in the politics of Europe.

The French Revolution was temporarily defeated and the French monarchy restored. But the ferment of the revolution continued to work not only in France but in Europe at large, and not least in Italy. Pius IX was a young man when elected in 1846 to succeed Gregory XVI. His early 'liberalising' views were rudely disturbed by the events of 1848, when for a time he had had to take refuge from a revolutionary uprising. Thereafter his papacy developed on traditional, which in the circumstances were reactionary, lines. In 1854 he defined the doctrine of the immaculate conception of the Blessed Virgin Mary. In the sixties he issued the Syllabus of Errors, widely interpreted at the time as a rejection of the modern world. During that decade the Papal States in Italy came under increasing pressure from the Italian nationalist movement.

The first Vatican Council, which was also the first general council of the Church since the Counter-Reformation Council of Trent (1545 – 1563), opened in December 1869 and came to a premature close in July 1870 only just before the capture of Rome by the nationalist forces, which signalled the end of the 'temporal power' of the papacy. The Council, during the few months of its session, defined the universal primacy of the bishop of Rome and his role of infallible teaching in the realms of revealed truth. Politically, the Pope became the 'prisoner of the Vatican', retaining however the allegiance of the Catholic multitudes who made little distinction between the veneration due to his official role and a personality cult which was in due course transferred to his successors.

Leo XIII gave some indication of his approach to the problems of the modern Church when, soon after becoming Pope, he elevated to the cardinalate John Henry Newman, the famous convert from the Church of England and the champion of a theory of the development of doctrine which was pregnant of possibilities for the future. Leo also instigated a revival of the study of the philosophy and theology of Thomas Aquinas, and his 'social' encyclical, *Rerum Novarum*, was, for its period, a remarkable recognition of the justice of claims which were arising within the economic, as distinct from the political, framework of modern Europe. In politics he recommended an attempt at coming to terms with the new systems of government.

While Leo can be regarded as in some respects reacting against the 'conservatism' of Pius IX, the new Pope, St Pius X, swung the pendulum back in the conservative direction. Catholics, especially academic Catholics, cannot be completely untouched by movements of thought in the world to which they also belong. By the end of the nineteenth century the relatively new 'science' of historical scholarship and criticism had become an established feature of that world, which had also been rocked by Darwin's evolutionary hypothesis. Biblical studies, as well as the study of Church History, were bound to be affected by the new methods of scholarship and the new ideas to which they gave rise. Early in the new century the extreme (for its date) liberalism of the German Protestant scholar Harnack had called forth a brilliant riposte from the French Catholic scholar-priest Alfred Loisy, author of *L'Eglise et L'Evangile*. Harnack maintained that the core of the Christian gospel, when stripped of the superstitious accretions already present in the New Testament, was simply and solely a summons to love God and one's neighbour. But Loisy's reply to Harnack, so far from being a rejection of the modern critical method, was an *argumentum ad hominem*, utilising that method and conclusions based on it to refute Harnack's conclusions. Rome was not amused. Loisy, in fact, was only one leader of a whole 'school' of Catholic modernisers; and in France there was a parallel movement for social reform based on 'democratic' political principles. Within a few years Rome moved from detailed harassment to a general public condemnation of 'Modernism' (in the encyclical *Pascendi*, 1907). There ensued something like a reign of terror, stained by private 'delations' of alleged Modernists. My own predecessor, Abbot Cuthbert Butler of Downside, redirected his scholarly attentions into the safe backways of monastic and mystical history. The great French biblical scholar Lagrange turned (ironically, as it now seems) from Old Testament studies to the less hazardous task of commenting on the Gospels and the Epistles of St Paul. Friedrich Von Hügel himself, although as a well-connected layman he had been less vulnerable than priests like Loisy, surrendered nothing of his loyalty to critical method but in practice became more and more clearly a champion of the basic Christian and Catholic interpretation of human experience.

Benedict XV's short period as Pope is notable for his move away from the rigid 'party line' of his predecessor. He publicly disapproved of the habit of stigmatising good scholars as 'liberal' Catholics; we are all, he said, Catholics *tout court* and must not pillory one another with opprobrious designations. His efforts to shorten the disastrous 'World War' of 1914–18 were entirely admirable, though not very successful.

Pius XI brought to an end the long conflict between the Vatican and the new kingdom of Italy. By the Lateran Treaty of 1929 the 'prisoner of the Vatican' was left with a tiny enclave of autonomy in the heart of the capital city itself, along with a country residence, Castel Gandolfo, not far away. The extra-territorial status of the Vatican City was of course no defence against possible physical attack on the papacy, but enabled it to retain its position, for diplomatic purposes, of a sovereign power; its embassies (nunciatures, as they are called in the technical language of Roman politics) enjoy diplomatic immunity throughout the civilised world. Pius XI was also the Pope who took note of the growing ecumenical movement, but only to express reserves about its purposes and to warn Catholics against them. The second half of his pontificate witnessed the advent of National Socialism in Germany; and the Pope's condemnation of it in *Mit Brennende Sorge* was a brave act, in view of the difficulties threatening the Catholic population in Germany.

Pius XII's election coincided closely with the beginning of the Second World War. Politically, he was torn between the evils of Nazism and, in his eyes, the even greater eventual threat of Communism. He has been much criticised for his behaviour in this dilemma. More to the immediate purpose of the present study of the theology of Vatican II was his public though guarded approval of modern methods of biblical study. He also initiated some very fruitful reforms in the Church's liturgical life and matters connected therewith. His revision of the Easter liturgy was guided by the most scholarly re-examination of the history of this celebration; his reform of the rite or ordination to the priesthood was similarly authentic (and of great potential help in the ecumenical movement); and his radical relaxation of the law of the eucharistic fast was bold and helpful. In 1950 he defined the Assumption of the Blessed Virgin Mary, to the dismay of Christians outside the Catholic fold and also of some Catholics. The content of the dogma was a difficulty to some, and the methods of securing support for its definition seemed open to criticism. The theology of his encyclicals on the nature of the Church and on tendencies in modern theology (*Humani Generis*) was still backward looking. Great and loyal Catholic scholars like Karl Rahner, de Lubac and Congar (all still alive today) went through a difficult time in the latter years of Pius XII. Nevertheless, and certainly without knowing it, he did much to pave the way for his two successors.

John XXIII was in his late seventies when, after a long career as a papal diplomat abroad and then several years as Patriarch of Venice, he was elected to succeed Pius XII. He was not a great scholar, and in his personal piety he was an old-fashioned Catholic. But his humanity and his unselfconscious saintliness rapidly became proverbial; and it was, he used to maintain, by a special inspiration from God that he decided to call an 'ecumenical council' which, he hoped, would inaugurate a 'new Pentecost' for Christianity and the Catholic Church. Having successfully launched the council and intervened at one crucial point to extricate it from an impasse, he died between the first and second sessions and was succeeded by the Cardinal Archbishop of Milan, as he had expected (Popes cannot designate their successors).

The remaining sessions of the council took place in the pontificate of Paul VI. He was a genuine 'man of the council', but determined to avoid a split in the Church and, to judge by his actions and policies, was bent on maintaining the 'prerogatives of the Holy See' and the integrity of his inheritance as the successor of St Peter. To his credit, the decisions and acts of the council were all passed with overwhelming majorities and it was certainly not his fault, at least as regards his behaviour while the council was in session, that the Church was for so many years in a state of confusion and upheaval. Unrest was inevitable after the council; but it was powerfully intensified in 1968 on the publication of *Humanae Vitae*, the Pope's encyclical which condemned artificial birth control. We await a balanced evaluation of his pontificate; and this will require the lapse of some time for an appraisal that can distinguish the wood from the trees.

John Paul I was, like Paul VI's predecessor, Patriarch of Venice. He immediately captured the sympathy and interest of the Church and the world, and the shock of his sudden death is still with us. His successor, the present Pope, is the first non-Italian Pope for four and a half centuries. Coming from behind the Iron Curtain, he is uniquely qualified to view the world, and the Church in the world, in a light which is relatively free from the brilliances and shadows of a European age now gone beyond recall. It is too early to be sure how he will lead a Church which for over a century has oscillated between development and reaction.

In this enlarged edition, the eighth and ninth chapters are new. The first seven chapters are practically unchanged apart from one minor rearrangement of material and the addition, in square brackets, of some material in the notes.

1

Renewal and Adaptation

The pageantry of the opening day of the second Vatican Council, congenial as it was to the Roman sense of what befits a great occasion, gave little indication to those who took part in it of what lay ahead. The ceremony was protracted, though less so than that which inaugurated the first Vatican Council nearly a century before, when clerical stamina was greater; but the general sequence was similar. John XXIII, the aged Pope who had convoked the council, was carried to the entrance of St Peter's in the *sede gestatoria*, from which he descended to walk up the nave of the great basilica amid the applause of the assembled prelates – over two thousand of them, in ceremonial dress. Pontifical Mass was sung in Latin. Some additions in Greek, which might have given pleasure to the eastern Catholic bishops, had been prepared, but were, in the event, omitted. The Pope preached a sermon, and at last the council fathers made their ways back to convent, college, or hotel, to await further enlightenment when the council should meet, two days later, for the first day of ordinary business. Meanwhile, the weather had changed from rain to Roman sunshine.

Ecumenical councils are venerable, but theologically somewhat ambiguous, institutions in the Church.[1] From the so-

[1] Cf. H. Küng, *Structures of the Church*, pp. 1–25.

called Council of Jerusalem, described by St Luke in Acts, there were no such gatherings for nearly three hundred years. During that time the society which claimed as its origin the 'good news' of Jesus of Nazareth had found its way, geographically and culturally, to the heart of the Graeco-Roman world. It had braved the fires of persecution and had met and overcome the more insidious dangers of Gnosticism. It had found hierarchical expression in a network of bishops 'tending a single flock'[2] from Britain to beyond the eastern limits of the Roman Empire. Its baptismal creed and eucharistic liturgy had taken shape, basically homogeneous everywhere, though rich with local diversities. There had even been councils of bishops, but at a regional level. And there had been, it would seem, more than one occasion when the strong arm of the Church and bishop of Rome had intervened in crises of more than local significance.[3]

In the early years of the fourth century another such crisis resulted from measures taken by the bishop of Alexandria against his priest Arius for alleged heterodoxy. It happened to coincide with the accession to unshared supreme power of Constantine I, who – though not yet himself a Christian – had reversed the policy of the predecessors and accorded state patronage to the *corpus Christianorum.* Constantine was perturbed and annoyed by the publicity, the vehemence, and the dangers of the theological dispute consequent upon Arius' excommunication by his bishop. Roman emperors had no doubt about their rights and duties in regard to the religions of their subjects, and Constantine decided to take a step which might at once settle the dispute in the Church and proclaim to the world her place in imperial policy. He summoned a synod of bishops from the whole *ecumene*, to meet at Nicaea in Asia Minor – and to meet himself. The resulting council, traditionally numbering 318 prelates, was, in fact, mainly of eastern constitution; few bishops came from the western half of the Empire, and bishop Silvester of Rome was only represented by two priests as his legates. One might wonder whether an instinct of prudence prompted him to keep his person aloof from

[2] Cyprian, *Ep.* lxviii, 4: *unum tamen gregem pascimus.*

[3] E.g. St Victor and the question of the date of the Easter celebration; St Dionysius and the Christology of his namesake of Alexandria.

possible political pressure. Was the universal Church now to be led by the Roman emperor, and not rather, as in time past, by the bishop who sat, in Rome, 'in the chair' of Peter, the first of the apostles?

The Council of Nicaea (A.D. 325) is famous for its settlement of the theological issue raised by Arius' teaching. It defined that the son of Mary of Nazareth, whom Arius himself agreed to be far more than merely man, was consubstantial (*homoousion*) with God the Father; when Christians adored Jesus they were not performing an act of idolatry. It seemed to many regrettable that the dispute was settled by inserting into the Creed the unscriptural word 'consubstantial'. The trouble was that Arius and his friends would have been willing to accept any scriptural formula – retaining their right to interpret it according to their own theological system. The term 'consubstantial' was, with whatever reluctance, agreed to by nearly all the conciliar fathers as a necessary defence of scripture's true meaning. It became the first 'dogma' of an ecumenical council. The council also passed some legislation, a foretaste of the much-elaborated canon law of later times. Henceforth it would be taken for granted that an ecumenical council can both define articles of faith and take practical decisions binding on the whole Church.

The first Council of Nicaea has another significance. It set the stage for a new and perilous relationship between Church and state. Constantine's new attitude to Christianity was an unexpected, extraordinary and – so far as we can see – unnecessary reversal of policy. But it did not mean that the state had consciously changed its idea of its own omnicompetence. The Roman emperor, though not – for the moment – a persecutor of orthodoxy, was still *pontifex maximus*. He was, for the Church, an immensely powerful and politically uncontrollable patron. Might he kill by kindness a society which had thriven under the stern repression of his predecessors? When, after Constantine's death, Constans I sought to impose his will as supreme law upon a Church which he was seeking to wean from its exclusive loyalty to the 'consubstantial', a good Christian might have sighed for the days of Diocletian. However, at the time of Nicaea, Christians naturally preferred to look on the brighter side of things, and Eusebius of Caesarea, the great ecclesiastical historian who was not such a great theologian, was their spokesman in a panegyric of the emperor which delicately avoids actually deifying him.

Thus ecumenical councils entered the history of the Church not as a spontaneous development but in obedience to a secular statesman. Through the Byzantine centuries and on into the Middle Ages secular influence upon them was great. It was happily almost entirely absent from Vatican II.[4] It is, however, impossible to affirm that they are a necessary feature of her existence, like the episcopal college and the papacy. They are a way, originally indicated by an unbaptised Roman emperor, of discovering the mind of the Church or of the universal episcopate on doctrinal or disciplinary issues. Theology, walking in the footsteps of Athanasius and the Roman See, judges that the doctrinal definitions of ecumenical councils are guaranteed by the infallibility 'wherewith Christ willed to endow his Church in defining teaching on faith or morals.'[5] From the historian's point of view it might be said that such definitions are judged to be infallible because the Church has irrevocably committed herself to them.[6] They are milestones in the development of the Church's articulate mind. Like milestones, they do not merely assess the extent of a road already covered; they point forwards to a further journey to be pursued, and are themselves subject to the interpretations of subsequent theology, and to possible complementation by subsequent definitions.[7]

Before Vatican II there had been only two ecumenical councils since the Reformation. The counter-Reformation was ra-

[4] It appears, however, that strong near-eastern political pressure was enlisted against the Declaration on the Jews.

[5] Vatican I (Denz-Schönmetzer 3074), referring as it happens not to conciliar but to papal infallibility.

[6] The Church requires acceptance of these 'dogmas' from her members, and regards as heretics those who pertinaciously reject them. As it is a basic principle that *extra ecclesiam nulla salus*, it seems that the truth of these obligatory dogmas is guaranteed by the divine promise of the Church's indefectibility.

[7] Cf. K. Rahner, *Theological Investigations*, Vol. I, pp. 148f. H. Küng (*loc. cit.*) suggests that ecumenical councils are, formally, representative of the whole People of God, not only of the episcopate. In medieval and modern times they have included among their voting members some who were not bishops. This suggests that the theological distinction between *ecclesia docens* and *ecclesia discens* deserves further attention.

tified by the Council of Trent, and the last hesitations about the rôle of the papacy were laid to rest by Vatican I. To some it seemed that henceforth there would be no need for ecumenical councils. The Pope, now known to hold universal supreme authority over the Church and to be competent to issue infallible definitions without reference to their subsequent acceptance by the Church at large, could, it seemed, manage for himself. Why should resort ever again be had to the expensive, inconvenient and unnecessary device of an ecumenical council? It had become a fixed principle of Roman canon law that none but the Pope could convene such a council. Would any Pope wish to run the risk of inviting his fellow bishops to exercise – though subject to his final ratification – powers that might appear to be incompatible with his own? The Roman curia, or permanent civil service of the Holy See, found its own status enhanced and its position fortified by the decisions of Vatican I. For nearly a century after 1870 it directed the Church through crises both political and doctrinal, and during the latter half of that period it implemented a far-sighted papal strategy in the important field of the Asian and African missions. It could silence or outlaw criticism, and had behind it not only the formidable authority of the vicar of Christ but the national sentiment of Italian Catholicism. The Pope himself had for centuries always been an Italian; and the college of cardinals which elected him was, till quite recent years, predominantly Italian in its composition. It was easy for an Italian to feel that the true religion was in a special sense an Italian privilege, and that German or French theologians were provincial. Indeed, any western Catholic, as he walks the streets of Rome and passes by the Flavian amphitheatre and the forum, the basilica of San Clemente (with its subterranean Mithraeum and remains of pre-republican Roman walls) and the Pantheon to the superb church that marks the confession of St Peter, can hardly escape the sense that here, in this city, is the capital, the bastion and the criterion of all that he holds most dear.

It was therefore more than a little sensational when John XXIII, almost casually, announced that he would summon an ecumenical council; the more so since he seemed to link this project with the prospect of Christian, not merely Catholic, unity.

Joseph Roncalli became, before his death, so universally respected and loved that we have to remind ourselves that, when he was chosen to succeed his great predecessor Pius XII in November 1958, he seemed to many of us to represent the makeshift decision of a college of cardinals that, for the moment, found itself unable to agree on a candidate of an age and a quality that would make him a worthy successor of one who had steered the Church through the hazards of the Second World War and had opened up fresh horizons to Catholic scholarship and thought.[8] Roncalli was already in his late seventies, a former papal diplomat who had seen little of the workings of the Roman curia from within, though he had, as was natural, suffered somewhat at its hands from without. He was not a scholar, nor, so far as we knew, a fighter. An honourable career at Belgrade, Istanbul, and Paris had taken him to the dignity of the sacred purple and to the patriarchal see of Venice. We knew he was old and portly, and we soon discovered that he was a 'character' and a wit. We could be forgiven for not having suspected that he was a saint and a man prepared to trust and act on his grace-enlightened intuitions.

So there was to be a second Vatican Council. What would be its business? Nothing in particular, it would appear; or perhaps it would be truer to say: everything. The Pope soon found it necessary to explain that he did not suppose that one short Roman council could bring to an end the age-old divisions of Christendom. A fresh emphasis began to come into the forefront. Christian unity was the Pope's distant goal, no doubt, but his immediate aim was to 'let some fresh air into the Church' and to promote within her an *aggiornamento.* Meanwhile, let bishops and Catholic centres of higher studies send in their suggestions for the council's agenda. Preparatory commissions would work through these suggestions, and in due course there would appear draft documents for the council to approve and enact; in the end it was said that sixty-eight such documents had been prepared or were in preparation.

Aggiornamento means 'bringing up to date', something

[8] Archbishop Montini, who later succeeded John XXIII in the papacy, was not, when the conclave of 1958 met, yet a cardinal.

which any human institution may need from time to time. There is an inevitable lag in human affairs between the spirit and needs of the age and their clothing in institutional forms. Charters of political parties, even the foundation documents of national states or federations, cannot fail to reflect, in some measure, the special urgencies of the date of their composition; and a change of situation eventually presents the party or the nation with an option between archaism and *aggiornamento*. So, too, in the Church, diocesan and parochial organisation, general administration, canon law, liturgical forms, and theological and dogmatic expression all tend to reflect the needs and insights of an age that is always just previous, sometimes long previous, to that in which she is actually living.

In consequence, adaptation is always going on in the Church, and sometimes it advances fairly quickly. A good deal had already been effected before the council met, largely by Pius XII or with his sanction. John XXIII himself had made a gesture. The Pope is head of the Church because he 'sits in the chair of Peter', and that chair makes him, in particular, bishop of the local diocese of Rome. Pope John took his diocesan duties with some seriousness, and had held an *aggiornamento* diocesan synod in 1960. It enacted a whole host of instructions which, whether forgotten or not within the precincts of the city, have singularly failed to make an impression on the world outside.

If such was the kind of *aggiornamento* that was envisaged for the Church at large, curial circles might be forgiven for thinking that an ecumenical council was altogether too large and clumsy an instrument for effecting it. The curia itself seemed well placed to know the Church's current needs. If more information was required than their ordinary channels of communication could supply, then written suggestions from the bishops could have been examined at leisure by the appropriate Roman Congregations and a selection of proposals, suitably modified, could have been promulgated. Rome is eternal.

If, on the other hand, *aggiornamento* was to mean some really radical reappraisal of the whole bearing of the Church in the world of the twentieth century; if it meant raising fundamental questions; if, above all, it might seem to involve a threat to the curia itself or an, even implicit, criticism of its competence, then the Establishment could with some justice feel that this was a most alarming prospect, fraught with danger not only to curialists but to the Church as a whole. As the months passed by after the first announcement of the intention to hold a council a suspicion began to take shape in the minds of some observers that a determined effort was on foot to tailor John XXIII's rather vague plan down to a manageable size, and to 'contain' his intuitions within the framework of existing procedures and canon law. The Pope is in one western theory the very fount of ecclesiastical law, and the curia a pliant instrument for the expression and execution of his will. But in fact, of course, he rules normally within the limits of a long and crystallised tradition. The instrument which exists to serve him can, in fact, enmesh him in an almost unbreakable web. Even his power to change the personnel of the curia is hampered by the difficulty of finding replacements who can make the machine work. Despite his vast theoretical liberty of action, the Pope is in some ways more restricted even than many lesser rulers.

A case could, in fact, be made out for radical adaptations in the Church. If we accept the theory of the evolution of species, natural history has been the story of adaptations which have profoundly changed and in some respects enormously increased the capacities of living phyla. 'Here below', Newman observed, 'to live is to change, and to be perfect is to have changed often.'[9] A species which is incapable of such radical adaptation and transformation may perish altogether in an environment to which it is no longer adjusted. The Church is not a species. But she is a living entity composed of intelligent members, each of which is 'not just a higher system but a source of higher systems'.[10] Catholics believe that the Church cannot perish, not because of any inherent power of ultimate survival, but in virtue of the guaranteed assistance of God. However, besides evolution or extinction, there is a third possibility for a natural species: it may manage to survive in the backwaters of natural history, in some straitened milieu remote from the main currents of onward-moving life. And the question could have been asked, in the years before Vatican

[9] *The Development of Doctrine*, p. 40.
[10] B. Lonergan, *Insight*, p. 267.

II, whether the fate of the coelacanthus was not likely to become the fate of the Catholic Church.

There are those who hold that modern man's total environment is changing so rapidly and so fundamentally, above all through technological developments made possible by physical science, that man himself is responding to its challenge by what amounts to something analogous to a biological mutation. Not that his physical structure is being radically altered, but that his psychological pattern is becoming almost fundamentally different from that of earlier generations. It would be hazardous to attempt a brief description of this change. But it is characterised by two pervasive features: the horizon of each of us is tending to expand so as to embrace the whole of contemporary humanity, so that we are coming to share a common, socialised, human experience; and we are shifting from a static to a dynamic outlook – we are becoming more reflectively aware of the positive significance of duration both in human affairs and in our subhuman surroundings. If science and technology are largely responsible for the expansion of our horizons and for the sense that man himself carries the burden of creating his own future, it is evolutionary theory and scientific history that partly cause and partly express the new sense of the universality of orientated change. We are experiencing along our nerves and in our profound psychological reactions the truth of Heraclitus' great intuition: All things are in flux, and you cannot step twice into the same stream. This experience is reflected in a sceptical reaction to all propositions claiming to relate to an unchangeable reality. Metaphysics is at a discount; there is a reluctance to make any final self-commitment or to give, as some might say, a blank cheque to fate or chance – while, at the same time, there remains a despairing hunger for an absolute that seems to be contradicted by all the evidence of our exterior and interior senses.

The prelates who marched in procession into St Peter's on that autumn day in 1962 represented a society which, for all its acceptance of the aeroplane, television and internal communication systems, was still, it might be said, living on what survived of the great medieval synthesis. It was a society of status rather than of dynamic change, of fixed formulae rather than of flexible growing insights. It was above all, and knew that it must remain, a witness to the reality of the absolute – and to the absolute significance of a group of events enacted nearly two thousand years ago in Palestine. It had a built-in tendency, in other words, towards conservatism. And it was also a society which, though it made a universal claim, had come almost to the point of identifying itself with a west European tradition; this it was absent-mindedly seeking to impose both on the tiny groups of eastern Christians in communion with the See of Rome and on the new Asian and African churches growing up from the great, but far from sufficient, missionary efforts of the past hundred years, and facing, today, the new situation produced by political independence.

There was a particular contingent reason for the Church's conservative bias. The modern era had signalised its advent, in the ecclesiastical sphere, by the enormous upheaval of the Reformation, with its powerful protest against the state of the Catholic Church in the sixteenth century. The magnitude and gravity of the Reformation shook Catholicism to its core. The official response was the counter-Reformation Council of Trent, in which the Church acknowledged and met the need of some moral and organisational reform, but was less successful in accomplishing a theological renewal in any deep sense. The Council of Trent dominated the ensuing centuries of Catholic history and the Church assumed a fixed attitude of counter-protest. The idea of the Church tended to be restricted to her institutional and authoritarian aspects, seen by some of her ablest and most devoted sons as primarily a bulwark against change. Not only the sacred tradition of the gospel but the forms in which it was currently presented were endowed with an aura of absoluteness, and changes were presumed to be anti-Catholic, anti-Christian, even impious.[11]

Conservatism found its native home in the curia. The Roman See has recognised, at least since its baptismal controversy with St Cyprian, that it has an ultimate responsibility for the

[11] Soon after the use of vernacular languages in the western Liturgy had been approved in principle I was invited to sympathise with a lay person who had spent twenty years in defending the Latin Mass and now did not know how to face a mocking world.

safeguarding of the Sacred Tradition: *nihil innovetur nisi quod traditum est.*[12] And while individual Popes may be by temperament or conviction innovators, the curia exists to serve the papacy in its impersonal function of preservation and routine administration. Most of the members of the second Vatican Council had been nominated to their episcopal sees by the curia, which could naturally expect that they would follow its lead. Moreover, in the nature of the case, most of the council fathers were of an age more given to circumspection than to experiment.

If, however, the council contented itself with an *aggiornamento* touching only the surface of ecclesiastical administration and affairs, was there not a grave danger that, by the end of another century, the Church would appear to have contracted out of the whole current of modern history? She claims to have a mission to all mankind and a relevance to every stratum of human experience. But in order to convey a message, you must take the trouble to learn the language and study the needs and the mentality of those to whom you propose to address it. Even at the most down-to-earth level, it could be argued that the intellectual formation imposed by the curial Congregation for Seminaries and Universities as suitable for candidates for the priesthood might have been calculated to render them incapable of dialogue with the people to whom they would have to minister. Whatever the merits of scholastic philosophy and theology, and they are great, they are given body in a conceptual and linguistic system which is alien even to the educated modern man. And if the Church refused to understand the world and to make herself understood by it, would not the world pass her by and seek, in vain, a settlement of its problems without reference to the Church's message?

There were already ominous signs of such indifference, and historical causes for it. In the century following the Council of Trent there had been the unfortunate episode of Galileo. Nothing is quite simple in such affairs; it can be argued that Galileo's case was, even scientifically, a poor one, and his claim to certainty one that no modern scientist would make. But to the world, rough and ready in its judgments, it seemed that,

[12] Cf. Cyprian, *Ep.* lxxiv, 1, quoting St Stephen of Rome.

at a crucial turning-point, the Church had canonised the geocentric hypothesis, which St Thomas Aquinas himself had accepted only as the best available in his day. In the following century Rome's abasement before the outmoded *ancien régime* had culminated in the dissolution of the Society of Jesus, formerly the spearhead of counter-reform. Yet a little later came the revolution, inadequately described as French, the proscription of Catholicism in France itself and the seizure by Napoleon of the Pope's person. A moment of liberalism in the papal policy of Pius IX was overtaken by the troubles of 1848 and that pontiff eventually became the reactionary 'prisoner of the Vatican', notorious (in the eyes of the world) as the declared enemy of the nineteenth-century secular creed and programme of progress. By 1870 it could seem that Rome had lost the great campaign for the soul of Europe, and the first Vatican Council's proclamation of the Pope's universal jurisdiction and dogmatic infallibility sounded like the defiant 'no surrender' of a great institution that had out-lived its relevance.

Meanwhile, in the intellectual field, new problems had arisen with the advent of modern evolutionary theory and the advances in scientific historical scholarship. The Church of the early nineteenth century was ill equipped to face such challenges. Rome's political disarray was matched by her theological and philosophical decadence. When Newman, shortly after his reception into the Catholic Church, visited Rome, he found that even St Thomas Aquinas was regarded there as doubtless a saint but by no means a guide for the modern theologian; yet there was none to replace him. The modern revival of Thomism dates from the pontificate of Leo XIII. In default of a Thomas, who might have found the theory of evolution no less acceptable than Aquinas had found Aristotelianism in his day, and in an age when Disraeli, asking whether men were of heavenly or of simian origin, replied that he was on the side of the angels, it is perhaps not surprising that a local Council of Cologne condemned the hypothesis of man's evolution from a subhuman form of life. But it must be considered unfortunate that the theory was still, in my own lifetime, struggling for its right to exist within the Catholic fold. As for the new science of history, it was soon applied, sometimes, of course, in what we should judge to be a very unscientific fashion, to the lives of the saints, the early history of Christianity, and to both Old and New Testaments. This was a field in which the Church was bound to be peculiarly sensitive; the native field of her own Sacred Tradition. In the years just before the first world war Rome reacted with a blanket condemnation of so-called Modernism and with an imposition of controls on biblical scholarship which gravely hampered Catholic scholars till the issue, in the course of the second world war, of Pius XII's great encyclical, *Divino afflante Spiritu.*

The mention of this encyclical may remind us that not everything was black in the record of Rome, still less of the Church as a whole, between 1870 and 1962. As already observed, Leo XIII, undoubtedly a great Pope, had begun a revival of speculative theology by his advocacy of St Thomas's work as the basis of the formation of the clergy. He had also sketched out the lines for a positive relation of the Church to the constitutional and democratic states of the new age. His celebrated encyclical, *Rerum Novarum*, was the beginning of a new epoch in the public attitude of Rome to modern economic and social problems, though its somewhat paternalistic tone is unfortunate. It was followed in due course by similar and more progressive encyclicals from Pius XI (*Quadragesimo Anno*) and John XXIII (*Mater et Magistra*). In the nineteenth century Rome had seemed to frown on the idea of liberty of conscience, but the reaction of Pius XI to German National Socialism adumbrated a new attitude in this matter, provoked by dangers precisely opposite to those that had alarmed Pius IX. As for Pius XII, history will probably accord to him an important rôle in preparing the way for Vatican II.[13] Not only did he evince a lively interest in modern natural science, but he had a personal taste for biblical scholarship, and the fruits of his encyclical, *Divino afflante Spiritu*, have been seen in a wonderful renaissance of Catholic biblical studies and publications.

There were, in fact, two sides to Catholicism in 1960. While the curia gave little evidence of realising the need for far-

[13] Cf. W. A. Purdy, *The Church on the Move; the Characters and Policies of Pius XII and John XXIII*; which needs to be balanced by E. E. Y. Hales, *Pope John and his Revolution.*

reaching changes, the Church as a whole, and particularly in western Europe north of the Alps, had for some time been experiencing a second spring. Early signs of this had been the revival of the religious orders in the nineteenth century, the stimulus to philosophy and theology given by Leo XIII, and the gradual renewal of interest in mystical theology. A liturgical movement (foreshadowed by the French Benedictine Guéranger in the nineteenth century), pastoral in its intention but heavily indebted to erudition and theology, had advanced so far by 1962 that the draft of the Constitution of the Liturgy was one of the best documents presented to the Council. The liturgical movement was a natural ally of the new biblical scholarship and theology, as also, from a different point of view, of a fresh concern for the place and rôle of the laity in the Church. Interest in the apostolate of the laity took, indeed, two rather different forms. The papacy, under Pius XI and Pius XII, was a promoter of what was called Catholic Action, which sought to make an organised laity into an instrument of hierarchical policy and the subject of a hierarchical mandate. But movements like that of the Young Christian Workers sprang up from the grass roots of the Church's local pastoral anxieties, and were far more suitable, in most countries, than Catholic Action could ever be as a stimulus of genuine lay initiative. In the wake of the second world war, and especially in France and Germany, where the effects of that war had been peculiarly devastating, there began to take shape, under the suspicious eyes of Roman authority, what was called, by those who disliked it, 'the new theology'. It is not easy to characterise this movement of thought. Enough, for the moment, to say that while neo-Thomism aimed at carrying forward the intellectual achievement of the high Middle Ages, the new theology sought to go back behind scholastic systematisations and to find a richer inspiration in patristic theology and a foundation in biblical scholarship and theology. Its promoters were often the victims of official discouragement or repression, but its inherent vitality and adaptation to the age enabled it to survive and to develop, so that when the council met in 1962 there were at hand to advise its members and to collaborate with its commissions not only the canon lawyers and strict Thomists who enjoyed the favour of the curia, but a host of others of a very different type, including men like de Lubac, Karl Rahner, and Congar, who had all suffered for their convictions, but who became, in fact, in large measure the artificers of the theology of Vatican II.

Three other factors tending to threaten the conservatism of the curia and its allies deserve mention here. The years since the end of the second world war had seen the gradual, difficult development of a small Catholic ecumenical 'movement'. John XXIII took a decisive step when, in June 1960, he announced the establishment of a Secretariat for Unity; and this new formation, under the presidency of the biblical scholar Cardinal Bea, was able to draw its membership in large measure from a previously existing Catholic International Conference for Ecumenical Questions (founded in 1952).[14] The Secretariat rapidly became a powerful force in the council, and it was inevitably committed to a non-scholastic, patristic and biblical approach to theological issues. Secondly, the prelates from the eastern Churches of the Catholic communion provided a standing critique of narrow western concepts of Catholic truth and polity, with a constant reference back to the tradition of the first Christian millennium. Thirdly, there were many bishops from Asia and Africa who needed freedom from western European trammels in order to proclaim, in recently 'decolonialised' countries, a gospel which was authentically universal.

There were thus various possibilities confronting the council when it met in St Peter's, on 11 October 1962, round the latest of the successors of the first of the apostles. What were the probabilities? It must be confessed that to some, who wished for profound changes, it seemed that they favoured the conservatives. There were many seedlings of hope in the Church. But were they not, as yet, too weak to stand before the scrutiny of a body of elderly bishops, most of whom must be out of touch with the most recent theological developments, though well aware of the disapproval which these had met at Rome? There is, in any great human institution with a long history behind it, a *vis inertiae* that must present formidable opposition to advocates of new thinking. The Church, while claiming divine

[14] When the council opened, the Secretariat for Unity was given the standing of a conciliar commission. Cf. C. J. Dumont, 'La Génèse du Décret sur l'Écuménisme', in *Istina*, 1964, no. 4.

foundation and the assistance of the Holy Spirit, is also a very human, and very ancient, institution. Yet John XXIII had invited us to look forward to a second Pentecost.

The first indication that the conciliar fathers were not prepared to see their function as a rather passive acceptance of prefabricated curial decisions came on 13 October 1962, the first working day of Vatican II. In a brief encounter with the Presidency of the council it was settled that time should be allowed for the council fathers to consult and exchange information before voting the panels of the conciliar commissions which were due to replace the preparatory commissions with their strong curial colouring.

It was about half-way through the first session that a major clash occurred. A draft document, On the Sources of Revelation, was presented for 'first reading' by the council.[15] This document came at once under heavy fire. Its treatment of the historical character of the four Gospels seemed to be more conservative than dogmatic certainty required and to pay too little attention to the actual state of biblical scholarship. But the brunt of the criticism tended to concentrate itself on the very idea latent in the draft's title. If you spoke of sources of revelation, meaning thereby scripture and tradition, you placed yourself at the standpoint of a Church far removed from its origins and asking herself how she knew about these origins and the content of her essential patrimony. In other words, you were not contemplating primarily revelation itself and its rôle in the economy of our salvation. And it further became clear that the draft document wished to commit the council to the theological opinion (held by some to be guar-

[15] By normal council procedure, such drafts, prepared either by preparatory commissions (as in this case) or by conciliar commissions (as in the case of the draft On Divine Revelation which eventually replaced the Two Sources) were circulated to the council fathers and then debated in general. After such debate, if a favourable vote was given, they would be debated section by section, in detail, and emendations would be proposed. The conciliar commission would then revise the draft in the light of the debate and the proposed emendations, and the revised draft would be explained to the council by a spokesman (or spokesmen) of the commission, and its sections voted on in detail. This process of voting gave a further opportunity for proposals of emendation, which, however, if the document on 'second reading' had received a two-thirds majority in its favour, could only be accepted if they did not involve a contradiction of the approved text.

anteed already by the Church's magisterium) that tradition provided a substantial supplement to the elements of faith contained, explicitly or implicitly, in scripture. This tendency of the document aroused considerable anxiety not only in the minds of some whose main interest was pure theological speculation, but also among those who, like Cardinal Bea and his Secretariat for Unity, were anxious to close no doors to future dialogue with the Protestants, whose inherited devotion to the idea of *sola scriptura* is well known.

The opposition conducted its attack with such ability and fire that, after a few days, the Presidency decided to test the attitude of the council fathers as a whole – most of whom, of course, had had no opportunity to speak in the debate. The result of the secret ballot showed a large majority against the draft, and on the next morning the council was informed that the Pope was withdrawing it. The Pope, in fact, appointed a special commission, on which not only Cardinal Ottaviani, the president of the doctrinal commission (to whose sphere the draft, as a 'dogmatic' one, naturally belonged), but Cardinal Bea also sat, as joint presidents. The Secretariat for Unity had won a great victory and had immensely enhanced its power to influence the council.

The importance of this dramatic episode, taken in conjunction with the story of the second half of the first session, may be said to lie in the fact that, in it, the council fathers opted for an *aggiornamento* not of the surface but in depth, and even in the fields of biblical scholarship and dogmatic theology. There were many vicissitudes in the subsequent history of the council, but it never looked back from this fundamental option, though, of course, its realisation of its own intentions was only partial.

This option, however, raised, implicitly, some important questions. It meant that the council would not take, as its uncriticised starting-point, the Catholic Church and religion as they actually existed in 1962, merely seeking to find ways of further advance in an already determined direction. It meant accepting a distinction between the Church as she ought to be or ideally is, and the Church as she actually exists. And it meant, in consequence, some at least implicit attempt to discover the right basis or standpoint from which to pursue a critique of the Church as she exists.

The nearest the council ever came to defining *aggiornamento* was perhaps its acceptance of the title of the decree of the Religious Life: On the Accommodated Renewal of Religious Life. This decree was, in its present form, emended and approved in the last session of the council; and although, so far as I am aware, the fact has never been publicly stated, I take it that the term 'accommodated renewal' is here offered as a Latin translation of *aggiornamento*. The decree states (n. 2) that accommodated renewal (of Religious Life) involves two simultaneous processes: 1. 'a continuous return to the sources of all Christian life' (i.e. the gospel) 'and to the original inspiration of the religious institutes'; 2. 'the adjustment of these institutes to the changed conditions of the times'. The former process is covered by the word 'renewal' (which therefore does not mean 'changing' but 'recovering' one's origins), and the latter by the word 'accommodated'.

Religious institutes, of course, have a double source. Their remoter source is the gospel, and their more immediate source is the 'spirit and purposes of their founders' (*ibid*). The Church has only one source: the gospel;[16] so that *aggiornamento* for the Church as a whole will mean: a recovery of the original gospel, its spirit and purposes, and an adaptation of it which will be at once faithful to the same gospel as originally given, and suited to 'the changed conditions of the times'. It is obvious that the primary condition of such adaptation must be that it remains within limits laid down by the objective essence of the Christian faith and Church; while the – sole – secondary condition will be its appropriateness to the needs of the Church and her mission in history.

Thus the council was, in fact, committed to taking Christ, who is 'at once the mediator and the fullness' of divine revelation,[17] as the basis of its critique of the existing Church and as the basic norm of its teaching and enactments. And here

[16] Throughout I use the word 'gospel' (without a capital initial) to mean the content of the Christian revelation, which includes, subsumes, and at the same time transcends, all previous 'public revelation', and in particular the revelation of the Old Covenant. Cf. *De Divina Revelatione*, n. 7.

[17] *De Divina Revelatione*, n. 2.

precisely arises the question: how do we know what Christ taught, what he was, what his work for mankind was? We are back at the question raised by the draft document on 'the sources of revelation' – or, to use the preferable language of the Constitution on Divine Revelation – the question of the mode of transmission of the gospel. The council, as we shall see, did not answer the disputed question whether Tradition contains substantially *more* 'information' than is at least implicit in the Bible. But it had no doubt that the Bible is a privileged, inasmuch as inspired, medium of gospel transmission.

However, no one who surveys either the diversity of confessional systems claiming to interpret the Bible, or the condition of biblical scholarship today, would be sanguine about an uncontrolled 'appeal to the Bible'. The Church and the council find a guide to the meaning of the Bible in the Christian tradition. But that tradition is again very various, and itself subject to varying interpretation. It is expressed – inadequately – in the total history of Christianity and especially of the Church. But history is a teacher *sui generis*:

> History is not a creed or a catechism, it gives lessons rather than rules; still no one can mistake its general teaching in this matter [Catholicism *v.* Protestantism], whether he accepts it or stumbles at it. Bold outlines and broad masses of colour rise out of the records of the past. They may be dim, they may be incomplete; but they are definite.[18]

The council, however, was not concerned simply with a broad comparison between Protestantism and Catholicism. It needed answers to questions rather more detailed than that. And we may quote Newman again:

> For myself, I would simply confess that no doctrine of the Church can be rigorously proved by historical evidence. . . . Historical evidence reaches a certain way, more or less, towards a proof of the Catholic doctrines . . .; in all cases, there is a margin left for the exercise of faith in the word of the Church.[19]

The council was, of course, not intended to 'prove' doctrine to the satisfaction of the non-Catholic. But it needed a criterion valid within the terms of its own faith. And the criterion was

[18] Newman, *Development of Christian Doctrine*, p. 7.
[19] 'Letter to the Duke of Norfolk', in *Difficulties of Anglicans*, ii, p. 312.

to hand. The council fathers worked within a context settled in principle by the first ecumenical council of Nicaea, A.D. 325. The basic issue faced and answered in that council was whether or not the Church could pronounce upon the compatibility of monotheism with the rendering of divine honours, in her cultus, to Jesus. Its answers to the question was the practical one of defining and imposing the dogma of consubstantiality. In the imposition of this dogma as a condition of communion there was a latent implication, subsequently drawn out into the light of day: the Church has the power to articulate elements or implications of her own faith, and when she exercises this power she can rely on divine assistance to preserve her from irreparable mistakes. The conviction that this is so is an aspect of belief in what is called the Church's 'infallibility' – a word which is in some respects unfortunate, and not specially ancient in this context. This is not the place to argue the merits of the Church's understanding of her own infallibility. It is, however, perhaps relevant to observe that the alternative position means, in the end, thoroughgoing liberalism, or the abandonment of the supposition that the gospel has an objective content accessible to our conceptualising intellect. In any case, it was in the dogmas, or doctrines defined and imposed by the Church's supreme authority, that Vatican II in practice found the firm ground needed for its enterprise of 'accommodated renewal' of the Christian and Catholic religion.

Two accessory observations are here in place. 1. A dogma is the statement of a proposition, in human language. Like all statements, it is subject to interpretation, and interpretation has to take account of the historical, and especially linguistic, context in which the statements were made. In the measure in which speech moves from the sphere of abstract mathematics to that of metaphysics and religious mystery, the impossibility of a 'rule of thumb' interpretation increases. Language, in fact, creates itself according to the exigencies of the truth to be communicated. The word 'consubstantial' had to meet the difficulty that it could suggest a Sabellian doctrine of the godhead. The Catholic position as regards dogmas steers a middle course between liberalism and 'magic'. 2. There is no need to suppose that a mere list of dogmas will give one a complete and balanced picture of the Christian faith. Definitions of faith are the outcome of contingent circumstances, needs and interests. Any list of them is a record of the vicissitudes of Christian history rather than a systematic exposition of the gospel. All dogmas are true, but all are not equally important; some of them are doubtless less important than truths of faith which have never been defined.[20] They serve, nevertheless, as points of reference and control, and their authority has only been reaffirmed by Vatican II – which, however, has not added to their list.

It may be asked whether the infallibility of the Church's teaching is confined within the narrow range of its exercise in what theologians call the 'extraordinary' circumstances of a definition by her supreme teaching authority. Is there not an infallibility of her 'ordinary magisterium', discernible when the worldwide episcopate, within the complete communion of the Catholic Church, is found to propound some truth, as involved in the gospel, with 'moral unanimity'? That some such infallibility exists seems to have been an abiding conviction, already expressed by St Irenaeus in his appeal to the teaching of the universal episcopate as refuting Gnosticism; this at a time when, so far as we know, there were no 'dogmas'. The appeal to the ordinary magisterium was strongly pressed in Vatican II by those who wished for a clear statement of the 'material insufficiency' of scripture. That this appeal was successfully resisted does not mean that the council rejected the idea of an infallible ordinary magisterium. On the contrary, it affirmed it, together with a third 'locus' of infallibility: the *sensus fidelium*. But the episode does illustrate the fact that, as a criterion, the infallibility of the ordinary magisterium is difficult in use. How does one ascertain the existence of a moral unanimity; and how determine its precise objective? One may perhaps take, as an illustration of the latter difficulty, the doctrine that 'there is no salvation outside the Church' (*extra ecclesiam nulla salus*). Few doctrines rest upon a more complete unanimity of the ordinary magisterium; and this one has the support, it is thought, of the extraordinary magisterium, at least in a statement of Boniface VIII. Yet few

[20] Cf. the Decree on Ecumenism n. 11: (Catholic theologians) 'should remember that there is an order or "hierarchy" of the truths of Catholic doctrine; their links with the basis of the Christian faith are various'.

statements have suffered so startling a transformation through the development of doctrine. It would have been very difficult, in the early Church, to determine the precise objective and bearing of this indubitable truth. We may add that, if the infallibility of the ordinary magisterium were, in itself, an adequate criterion, it is not easy to see either why an extraordinary magisterium exists or why, when – as in Vatican I with regard to papal infallibility – it proposes to act, the determination of an exact definition is so laborious, difficult, and often controversial a procedure. Such considerations suggest the reflection that it is a mistake to construct one's idea of infallibility merely from the special circumstances of its exercise in definitions by the extraordinary magisterium, and then to apply this idea, without further refinement, criticism, or qualification, to the more general notion of the infallibility of the Church, or to the notion of the ordinary magisterium or the *sensus fidelium*. A definition by the extraordinary magisterium is an act of final judgment delivered by the teaching Church upon a given statement alleged to expound or to appertain to the gospel. The situation after such a final judgment is not the same as before it – and I venture to suggest that the difference is not merely a canonical one (no one can be adjudged a 'heretic' unless he rejects a defined dogma) but is theological.

At least for practical purposes, the infallibility of the ordinary magisterium and of the *sensus fidelium* means that the Church conducts her doctrinal and theological reflections within a collective or collaborative climate of opinion which so far from being agnostic, is controlled by the pervading presence of a total truth revealed by God, a truth which is always carried and in some measure expressed in the 'mind of the Church' and in the teaching of her magisterium, and which is capable, when circumstances require it, of partial formulation in definitions of faith.

We may conclude this discussion by asking what is the authority to be attached by a believing Catholic to the teaching of Vatican II. The answer to this question involves certain distinctions. The council, in the first place, reiterated some past definitions of faith; such teaching, of course, remains as infallible as it always was – it can hardly be said to benefit by the accident of its reiteration. Secondly, as already observed, the council made no new definition of faith. Thirdly, it made various assertions, of differing quality, on doctrinal issues. Of these perhaps the most impressive is its statement about episcopal consecration: The council teaches that by episcopal consecration there is conferred the fullness of the sacrament of Order (*De Ecclesia*, n. 21). The weight of this statement can be determined by two contrasting considerations. 1. The council was, in this chapter of the Constitution on the Church, deliberately undertaking to throw light on two issues (*a*) the question whether episcopal consecration is or is not strictly a sacrament, and, if so, whether it is the fullness of the sacrament of Order; (*b*) the position of the episcopate *vis-à-vis* Vatican I's teaching on the position of the bishop of Rome in particular; and that bishops by their consecration, have the fullness of the ministerial priesthood is an essential step in its argument in this matter. 2. The council eschews here the word 'define', which was manifestly available if definition had been its intention; it also omits, in using the milder word 'teaches', any such qualification as 'solemnly'. It seems prudent to conclude that this conciliar statement carries almost the highest authority short of that which would belong to a definition of faith; but that the precision of the language employed in it is subject to scrutiny, as also – of course – the exact bearing of its teaching in the totality of Christian truth. There is a great deal of teaching scattered through the Acts of the council which, while it lacks the deliberate application of the impressive phrase: 'The council teaches', is plainly carefully considered and intentionally didactic. All such teaching is bound to be normative for future theological developments. Elsewhere, the council merely repeats, or assumes, without special emphasis, current or traditional opinions. Broadly speaking, one may assume that teaching in exposition of a main theme in a dogmatic constitution has *per se* a greater authority than doctrinal statements in pastoral constitutions, decrees, or declarations.[21]

[21] Once or twice in the course of the council an attempt was made to obtain an explicit statement of the degree of authority to be claimed for the council's teachings. The doctrinal commission, in substance, evaded the question by reference to 'approved authors'. There is a conciliar note to the *proëm* of the

(pastoral) Constitution on the Church in the World of Today: '... In the second part (of this constitution) the Church concentrates her attention on various aspects of modern life and human society, and in particular on questions and problems which, in this field, seem of more urgent importance at the present time. Hence the material which is in this part doctrinally evaluated is not wholly permanent, but sometimes contingent, in its nature. The constitution, then, is to be interpreted, according to the general norms of theological interpretation and with due regard, especially in its second part, to the changeable circumstances of the matters therein treated.'

2

Revelation and Inspiration

The draft document On the Sources of Revelation was withdrawn from the council after a preliminary debate and hostile vote in November 1962. It was eventually replaced by the document On Divine Revelation, passed and promulgated three years later, in November 1965. The subject of revelation thus spanned practically the whole course of the council, and there is a respectable theological view that, outstanding as is the importance of the much larger dogmatic Constitution on the Church, the Constitution on Divine Revelation may prove to be the supreme achievement of this council. It deals with an issue which is at the heart of the Christian religion, and does so in a way which makes possible dialogue on this basic subject between the Catholic and the other Churches.

The constitution consists of a *proëm* and six short chapters, the whole covering, without notes, only about ten pages. The chapters deal in order with: Revelation itself; its transmission; the Inspiration and Interpretation of Holy Scripture; the Old Testament; the New Testament; and Holy Scripture in the Life of the Church. Of the subjects thus treated, the most important theologically are: Revelation and its transmission; the Inspiration and Truth of the Bible; and the historicity of the four Gospels.

I

We may perhaps assume that the title of this constitution is due to its having replaced the draft on the sources of revelation. The real theme of the conciliar document is the word of God, which, in fact, it mentions in its opening words: *Dei verbum religiose audiens et fidenter proclamans. . . .* 'Hearing the word of God with religious deference and boldly proclaiming the same, the holy Synod takes its cue from the words of St John when he says: "We announce to you the eternal life which was with the Father and was made manifest to us – that which we have seen and heard we proclaim also to you, so that you may have fellowship with us; and our fellowship is with the Father and with his Son Jesus Christ" (1 Jn 1:2–3).'

There is a latent ambiguity in the word 'revelation': it may mean either the act of revealing or the truths revealed. The constitution employs it in both senses. It speaks of 'divine revelation and its transmission' (n. 1), but elsewhere says: 'It has pleased God, in his goodness and wisdom, to reveal himself and to make known the mystery of his will. . . . By this revelation God who is invisible addresses, in the abundance of his love, men as his friends and holds converse with them, that he may invite and take them into fellowship with himself' (n. 2).

The passage just quoted is impregnated with biblical language. We remark that the constitution does not begin, as a manual of dogmatic theology might, with a scholastic definition of the meaning of 'divine revelation' considered as a term of general connotation. I take, for example, the definition given in one such manual:[1] (Divine revelation is) 'the manifestation of some truth made to us by God through a supernatural illumination of our mind'; the learned author proceeds to give a discourse on scholastic cognitive psychology. What is missing here is any reference to the personal, Thou-and-I relationship which may be set up between him who receives a divine revelation and God who reveals. God only comes into the manualist's account in so far as he is recognised or inferred to guarantee the truth of what is revealed. The content of the

[1] Tanquerey, *Brevior Synopsis Theologiae Dogmaticae*, ed. 6, pp. 22f.

revelation might be the logarithmic tables, or it might be the trinity of persons in the divine unity; but in either case, one has the feeling that it could be a third-personal enrichment of the intellect rather than a second-personal self-disclosure to the heart.

It is precisely this personal element that is brought into the foreground in the constitution: God does not simply increase men's store of speculative knowledge; he addresses them as his friends and 'holds converse with them'; his immediate purpose is both to make known the mystery of his will and to disclose himself, and his ulterior purpose is not only to invite but to take them into fellowship with himself. We are not in the schoolroom where a divine philosopher, himself unseen, dictates abstract ideas to pupils of high intelligence. We seem rather to be in the original paradise, where an infinitely loving God calls to us, accosts us as his friends, woos us to his friendship. It is the 'heart speaketh to heart' of John Henry Newman's motto. It is the divine side of the lovers' dialogue in the Song of Solomon: 'I sleep, and my heart watcheth: the voice of my beloved knocking: Open to me, my sister, my love, my dove, my undefiled: for my head is full of dew, and my locks of the drops of the nights' (Song of Songs 5:2). If it suggests anything to me in the history of Greek philosophy, it reminds me not of Plato's brilliant dialectic, but of his refusal to write down the heart of his message, 'because it is not a thing that can be taught in words' (*Ep.* VII).

In communication between friends or lovers the personal element is always present, and it is often preponderant. Often the truth that my friend imparts to me, like the gift he gives me, is less valuable for its intrinsic content than for its source; and it brings me into an act of communion with this source, my friend. An act of communion is an act of love, an act therefore, of knowledge, since knowledge and will are alike involved in an act of love. Our knowledge of God is indeed at the core of Christianity, that knowledge of him that we can only have if he discloses himself to us in 'revelation'. But we have to bear in mind that the word 'knowledge' in Old Testament scripture has its own resonance. In the Old Testament, if God knows his chosen, and if they know him, the knowledge in question is better compared to the mutual knowledge of husband and wife than to the science and speculation of the Greeks, or the 'clear and distinct ideas' of Descartes. Already, then, we see that it is inadequate to think of the Christian revelation as the enlargement of our speculative intelligence by the divine bestowal of a set of true propositions. That true propositions may be involved is not excluded, but revelation will transcend them much as, when a young lover says, 'I love you', the disclosure made far transcends the scientific meaning of those banal words.

God then has disclosed himself and his will. And the constitution goes on to say how: 'This plan (*oeconomia*) of revelation takes place by deeds and words intrinsically interconnected, so that the works wrought by God in the history of salvation manifest the teaching and the realities signified by the words and corroborate them; while the words proclaim the works and illuminate the mystery contained in them' (n. 2).

Thus we see that, according to our constitution, the notion of divine revelation, as it concerns the Christian gospel, is part of a larger notion of divine action in history: it is not by 'words' alone but by 'deeds and words' that the revelation is given. Our modern western idea of revelation has been too much influenced by the very necessary Hellenisation of the gospel, whereby Christianity was made communicable to the men of the Graeco-Roman culture. Greek philosophy was familiar with the idea of revelation. At the heart of Socrates' life work, it was said, was an oracular piece of information; being oracular, it was, of course, ambiguous; it proposed a question to Socrates' intelligence. At a poignant point in Plato's *Phaedo* we are reminded that the question of the immortality of the soul is of such, even practical, importance that one must either find the answer or, at least, the best answer one can – unless one were able to make the journey through life in a surer, less perilous, way upon the raft of some word from the gods (85, c.d.). The Christians, moving into the world of Graeco-Roman culture, were confident that they had the divine word which Socrates, or Plato, would so thankfully have accepted. This very confidence, I suggest, led them unconsciously to accept the uncriticised presuppositions of Greek philosophy: what man needs is a firm basis of truth that can be articulated in propositions. There is a continuity in Christian thinking from the Greek apologists on through St Thomas Aquinas to the nineteenth century, and it has led us to envisage the first treatise in a course of theology as being *De Divina Revelatione* and to understand this revelation as primarily an intellectual enrichment of the kind that Descartes would have wanted.

Yet the Greek noun for 'revelation' (*apocalypsis*) occurs only once in the four Gospels (Lk 2:32, very suitably: 'a light for the revelation of the gentiles'). It occurs only four times in the Septuagint, and only once there in a religious context (of the uncovering of a man's misdeeds at his death). The foundation insights of Old Testament religion look back to, and spring from, the exodus from Egypt, interpreted as a marvellous act of divine redemption. Obviously, not only the act but its interpretation is vital; and so the constitution speaks of God's deeds and words, intrinsically interconnected. Yet it remains true that the first treatise of a course of Old Testament theology would better be entitled *De Divina Actione* than *De Divina Revelatione.*[2]

Our constitution views the Old Testament phase of the history of salvation as a preparation for the fullness of the gospel. It proceeds: 'The innermost truth[3] conveyed through this revelation both about God and about man's salvation shines forth for us in Christ, who is at once the mediator and the fullness of the whole revelation.' 'Jesus Christ,' it proceeds a little lower down, 'the Word made flesh, "a man sent to men", "speaks the words of God", and consummates the work of salvation which his Father had given him to do. Hence he himself, to see whom is to see the Father (cf. Jn 14:9), by his whole presence and manifestation, by words and works, signs and miracles, and especially by his death and glorious resurrection from the dead, and finally by the sending of the Spirit of truth, completes and perfects revelation and confirms it with a divine testimony: the revelation namely that God is with us to free us from the darkness of sin and death and to raise us up to eternal life' (nn. 2, 4).

[2] The prehistory of ancient Israel as the People of God may be said to begin with Abraham, and with the divine call which he received. Here, God's word is indeed primary. But it is a word not of information but of command and promise; the revelation it gives of God's character is incidental.

[3] On the constitution's notion of truth, *vide infra*, p. 35.

It will be observed that, in full consonance with what has preceded them, these passages do not limit the New Testament revelation to the teaching of Christ. They extend the notion to his deeds and sufferings, to his resurrection and to the mission of the Holy Spirit. But further: it is not by an external addition of these elements that we can designate the totality of revelation. This totality is Christ himself, its mediator and its fullness. Christ, in fact, *was* the divine word which he conveyed. It goes, of course, without saying that this divine revelation, being identical with a particular human life, was given in personal intercourse – and it is manifest that it is incapable of being fully expressed in a set of propositions; even a poet like Browning could never have expressed all that his wife was to him in words.

We must not allow ourselves to be led astray by the fact that the constitution here considers the incarnation in the perspective of revelation. This was a necessary consequence of its theme: Divine Revelation. We have to bear steadily in mind that the aspect of the incarnation as revelation is, in a real sense, consequential upon its basic nature as act. Christianity is committed to the view that the human history of Jesus of Nazareth, a history which forms part of the total web of our human history, from which it takes and to which it gives significance and orientation, is, at a deeper level of our understanding of it, a divine intervention into our human history, and, in fact, an assumption of our history at a key point, *the* key point, by a redeemer God. This redemptive act of God was not a supersession of our human spontaneity and responsibility; man cannot be redeemed simply *ab extra*, because redemption is precisely a restoration of a human dignity which wells up from within man; and, in fact, the divine act of our redemption was the act of one who became a member and the representative head of the human family.

There is an important corollary to this chapter's main theme, and it is broached in n. 5. A revelation is not fully given until it is received. It exists, in other words, in a revelational situation which is an interpersonal situation. How is the revelation, which is Christ, received? The constitution says that to God as he reveals there is owing, on our part, 'the obedience of faith' (Rm 16:26). Faith is one of those Christian keywords that have had a long history, in which their meaning has been, it may be, more deeply penetrated and enriched – though sometimes their current meaning, at least in theological jargon, has been impoverished and superficialised. The biblical meaning of 'faith' is aptly summed up by the words immediately following this citation of the Epistle to the Romans: (the obedience of faith) 'by which a man freely submits his whole self to God'. Faith thus understood is an act of the whole man, springing from the depths of his person, and involving in its totality everything that is interiorly his. We could perhaps say that it is the response called for by the object of ultimate concern.

But this Pauline concept of faith has been investigated in depth by theology, and it is concluded that the *locus* of the act of faith precisely as an act of faith is the intellect (aided, of course, by divine illumination, and determined in its assent by the will). Thus located, faith is at the same time distinguished from hope and charity, both of which are regarded as having their seat in the will, and as presupposing faith. Thus scholastic theology has been able to envisage the existence of faith continuing after the loss of charity and even of hope; and it reminds us that the Epistle of St James speaks of 'dead faith'. Unfortunately, this has sometimes led to a treatment of faith in separation from charity, and even to the omission of any reference to charity or holiness in defining the Church.

The Constitution, at this point, reflects the active influence in conciliar circles of those who were anxious not to discard the treasures of scholastic theology. Hence, after describing faith as an act in which 'man commits his whole self to God', it proceeds: 'by giving "full homage of intellect and will to God revealing" and by voluntarily assenting to the revelation given by him'. It goes on to observe that such faith is impossible without the preventing and helping grace of God; and that faith, once given, can be perfected by the gifts of the Holy Spirit, so that our understanding of the revelation may grow ever deeper (*ibid.*).

The interpersonal situation in which revelation is given and received is therefore one in which a completely gratuitous divine act in history, pregnant with a disclosure of God and his saving will, is met by a grace-enabled response of the human person in which he completely surrenders himself to God known in and through this act.

The chapter is completed by a section which affords a link with Vatican I and sets the act and virtue of faith in their human context. The council here acknowledges that 'God, the beginning and end of all things, can be certainly known by the natural light of human reason from created things'. Catholic theology, in fact, steadily maintains that faith is not an alien meteorite in our human experience, but finds, in our metaphysical situation and its cognitive implications, a point of insertion which makes it not only a grace-enabled but a 'reasonable' homage of God. It is, however, worth observing that our section is here speaking of the capacity of human reason considered in abstraction from our existential situation. This situation is one that has been profoundly modified by sin and its obfuscating influence. Hence the section continues: 'It is to God's revelation that we owe it "that truths relating to God (*ea quae in rebus divinis* . . .) which are not in themselves impenetrable by human reason can, even in the present condition of the human race, be known by everyone, with firm certitude and without admixture of any error" ' (n. 6). Redemptive grace is traditionally viewed as not only 'elevating' our natural capacities to a level above the natural but as 'healing' them. The council here teaches that divine revelation, received in faith, can exert this healing influence even on our human reason in its metaphysical quest.[4]

II

Christ, in his incarnation, is not only the mediator but the fullness of redemptive revelation. All down the ages the Christian Church has echoed the words of Acts 4:12; except in

[4] Aquinas (*Summa c. Gentiles* I.4), too, held that basic theism, as distinct from the Christian knowledge of the triune God, was a truth in itself within the compass of reason. But, he argued, its attainment would normally be so retarded by the fact that human knowledge begins with the senses and loiters on its journey of exploration that those few who attained to theism, apart from revelation, would usually only do so late in life; whereas man needs a knowledge of God to guide his daily practice throughout. The council points to the further disability caused by human sin. It may be a point of some ecumenical significance that the Church thus authorises the view that, in existential fact, divine faith does not suppose a chronologically prior philosophic theism.

Christ, there is no salvation; 'for there is no other name under heaven given among men by which we must be saved'. And we have seen that this saving revelation is not really given unless it is received in an interpersonal act of faith.

But Jesus of Nazareth suffered in Palestine under Pontius Pilate, and we men have lived dispersed over the face of the earth and down the irreversible centuries. How, then, does he who is the fullness of revelation communicate himself to us? If it were merely a matter of communicating truth about him, that could be done by oral tradition or written documents or both – as we know about Plato by his own writings and those of others, and as, no doubt, in the Academy they knew about him by an oral tradition. But the saving disclosure which God has given us is not merely truth about Christ; it is Christ himself in his person and his history. The problem of transmission is nothing less than the problem of the actual presence of one who was born about 6 B.C. and died about A.D. 30 just outside Jerusalem; his actual presence in the fullness of his historicity to and in every human 'present' throughout the centuries and in all the world. This is something unique in human affairs. No one but Christ has this universalised actual presence. It is not a question of the ubiquity of the second person of the Holy Trinity as God. It is a question of Christ in his past, completed and now glorified, historical life being present, to evoke and make possible the living response which is faith.

We may call this unique presence a 'sacramental' presence, if we take the word 'sacrament' as a rendering of the Greek word *mysterion*, and if we bear in mind that Catholics speak of a presence of Christ, at once real and sacramental, in the eucharistic food and drink.

Christ is not only the fullness of the revelation; he is its mediator. How, then, does the historical Christ *mediate* his own presence to us? To answer this question we turn back to the constitution: 'The Lord Christ, in whom the whole revelation of God the highest is consummated, gave a mandate to the apostles that they should proclaim, to all, the gospel, which has been promised beforehand through the prophets and which he himself fulfilled and promulgated with his own voice, as the source of all saving truth and moral discipline; and he communicated to them divine gifts' (n. 7).

A word of explanation is needed here. The term gospel is here used in an inclusive sense to mean the whole revelation as anticipated under the Old Covenant and as realised under the New. And it is to be observed that the council is here silent about a vital step in the argument. Not only did Christ give his mandate to the apostles; he had himself received a mandate from his heavenly Father. The argument seems to require that it was this heavenly mandate that Christ conveyed to the apostles; so that, in speaking as his envoys they would be speaking as God's envoys: 'As my Father hath sent me, even so send I you'.

This mandate, the council continues, was faithfully executed, by the apostles who by their oral preaching (*kerygma*), examples and institutions handed on what they had received from the lips, personal converse and works of Christ or had learnt from the suggestion of the Holy Spirit; and also by those apostles and apostolic men who, under the inspiration of the same Holy Spirit, committed the message of salvation to writing. And in order that the gospel might be preserved, in its wholeness and living character in the Church continuously, the apostles have left the bishops as their successors, handing on to them 'their own teaching position'. 'Hence this Sacred Tradition and Holy Writ in both testaments are as it were a mirror in which the Church in her earthly pilgrimage contemplates God, from whom she receives everything, till she be brought to see him face to face as he is' (*ibid.*).

There appears to be some conflated thinking here. The basic insight of Chapter 1, according to which Christ is the revelation not simply in virtue of his teaching but in his own historical person, life, sufferings and resurrection, seems to have receded temporarily into the background, yielding place to the notion of tradition (or transmission) as the handing-on of speculative truth conveyed in words. Two attempts are made to escape from this confusion: Christ is described as 'communicating divine gifts' to the apostles – and we may charitably suppose that these gifts were given for further transmission; and the reference to apostolic 'institutions' may include the notion of the sacramental system.[5]

The constitution recovers itself partially in n. 8, where we are told that 'What has been handed on by the apostles includes all that contributes to the holy conduct of the life of her People and to the increase of faith; and so the Church, in teaching life and worship, perpetuates and transmits to all generations all that she herself is, all that she believes'. Here, then, the Church's own intrinsic being – rather than her existential complexity – is identified with tradition; and, as we have seen, the significance of tradition in Christianity is that it renders Christ sacramentally present to mankind. This most important sentence of our chapter should be understood in the light of *Lumen Gentium*'s reference to the Church as being 'as it were a sacrament or sign and instrument of intimate union with God' (n. 1), bearing in mind that union with God is in and through Christ, in the fullness of his self-disclosure. We presuppose, of course, that the Church is not just a visible society ruled, like an empire, by absolute power from the centre, but that she is that mysterious reality of grace presented to us in the teaching of this council. The word of God implanted in, entrusted to, and conveyed to men by this mystery of the Church is the Word incarnate.

The next paragraph of the Constitution on Divine Revelation teaches that 'This tradition from the apostles makes progress in the Church under the assistance of the Holy Spirit', and it is explained that insight into the realities and words transmitted grows, 'both by the contemplation and study of believers, who compare these things in their heart (cf. Lk 2:19 and 51), and from their inner understanding of the spiritual realities which they experience, as well as by the preaching (*praeconio*, cf. the Greek *kerygma*) of those who along with succession to the episcopal office have received a certain charism of truth.'

The sentence just quoted is practically a précis of Newman's theory of the development of doctrine. It shows us the Chris-

[5] (a) The 'inspiration' of scripture is considered directly at a later point in the constitution. (b) That the apostles 'have left the bishops as their successors' must be understood in the light of *De Ecclesia* n. 20, which is careful not to state that the episcopate, *as we know it today*, goes back to explicit apostolic institution.

tian revelation actively living, in a vital interaction with the life of the Church herself and her children; and while, in the reference to 'study', it makes room for theology, both professional and amateur, it seems to emphasise particularly the spiritual life and 'experience' of the faithful as a major source of development – always under the implied normative influence of the Church's official teaching body. The council was, of course, quite clear that there is no new public revelation given since the age of the apostles (cf. nn. 4, 10). But the truth and reality once given is not perpetuated as a lifeless object, but as a living reality within the life of the body of Christ. The Church can progress ever further in her vital appropriation of revelation, tending as the ages pass (to quote once again from this paragraph) 'always towards the fullness of divine truth, till the words of God are accomplished in her'. The 'life-giving presence of this tradition' makes itself felt in the practice and life of 'the believing and praying Church'. 'Thus God, who spoke of old, converses uninterruptedly with the bride of his beloved Son; and the Holy Spirit, through whom the living voice of the gospel echoes in the Church and through her in the world, leads believers into all truth, and makes the word of Christ indwell them abundantly' (n. 8).

Christianity is an historical religion, in the special sense that it holds that 'grace and truth' were given once for all at a given point of time and space. The temptation for such a religion is to become historicist – to be fettered by its own past. This tendency is part of the reason for modern scholarship's long preoccupation with the 'quest of the historical Jesus'; as though the Church could not know the certainty of what she stood for until historical scholarship had reached its own conclusions about Christian origins. The constitution has a different understanding of our predicament. God, who spoke in Palestine nineteen hundred years ago 'by a Son' (Heb 1:2), speaks still today, through his Church, by the 'living voice' of that same Son, interpreted to us by the Holy Spirit whom he has sent. He speaks in the voice of the Church, as he spoke to the converts of Thessalonica: 'When you received the word of God which you heard from us, you accepted it not as the word of men, but as what it really is, the word of God, which is at work in you believers' (I Th 2:13). And that word of God is not just information for the human intellect; it is the Word made flesh, alive and operative, life-giving and educative, self-communicative and assimilative – the gift and word of divine love more truly given and spoken as it is more completely received.

It will be remembered that the debate on the draft document of the Sources of Revelation had highlighted the question whether the council was to give its support to the view that the contents of divine revelation are only partially enshrined in the Bible, the defects of this 'source' having to be supplied from 'tradition'. This whole question is tied up into a Counter-Reformation problematic. Protestantism had appealed from alleged 'traditions' to the Bible, and this appeal was pushed to the final point of reliance on 'scripture alone'. In reply, the Council of Trent had affirmed that the gospel is conveyed to us by 'scripture and traditions' – it did not clearly say whether 'traditions' were a source supplementary to scripture, or only confirmatory and explicative. But the former inference was commonly drawn in subsequent centuries. Such a view was, of course, highly convenient – and, at a time when scriptural exegesis was rudimentary, almost inevitable – for a Church which wished to proclaim, for example, that our Lady was immaculately conceived and corporally assumed into heaven. However, it was questioned in the nineteenth century, alike in Germany and, by Newman, in England; and in the twentieth century its inconvenience with regard to ecumenical dialogue was obvious. Its defenders at the council, however, pressed for its adoption as entailed by the measure of official support which it had gathered over the years since Trent. The struggle went on till the last moments before the council's final acceptance of our constitution, and it has left its mark on the text. We have already seen that Sacred Tradition (note the change from Trent's plural word 'traditions') and Holy Writ are described not as 'mirrors' but as 'a sort of mirror' in which God may be contemplated. This unity of tradition and scripture is further emphasised in n. 9: 'Sacred Tradition and Holy Writ are closely interconnected and communicate each with the other. Both flow from the same divine source and in a certain way they coalesce, and they tend to the same end. Holy Writ is the utterance of God as consigned to writing under the inspiration of the Holy Spirit; Sacred Tradition transmits the word of God, entrusted to the apostles by Christ the Lord and the Holy Spirit, completely to their successors, that, illuminated by the Spirit of truth, they may by their preaching faithfully preserve, expound and propagate it. . . . Each is to be received and venerated with a like[6] piety and reverence.' Again in n. 10 we are told: 'Sacred Tradition and Holy Writ are a single holy deposit of the word of God entrusted to the Church.'

In all this the scales are impartially held between the contending parties in the debate. There is one concession to the post-Tridentines in n. 8: 'Through tradition the complete canon of the sacred books becomes known to the Church'; but this is a point often conceded by the heirs of the Reformation. One other statement deserves mention here, partly because it owes its place in the text to the last effort of the post-Tridentines. After speaking of the virtual 'coalescence' of tradition and scripture (n. 9), it states that 'the Church does not derive through scripture alone her certitude about all that has been revealed'. This statement does not affirm that scripture has a defective content, but that the cognitive process whereby the Church becomes certain of the full range of her faith is not a mere scrutiny of scripture but is a process to which tradition contributes. This is almost exactly the position adopted by Newman in his reply to the *Irenicon* of Pusey; Catholics do not say, he claims, that scripture is defective, but that tradition is needed for a discovery of the full contents and implications of scripture.[7]

The chapter ends by pointing out that the 'sacred deposit of the word of God' is entrusted to the (whole) Church, while its authoritative interpretation is the prerogative of the Church's teaching authority. But this 'teaching authority is not above the word of God but is in its service, teaching only what has been handed down, listening with religious reverence to this

[6] The word is *pari*, perhaps less definite than *aequa* would have been; the distinction can hardly be conveyed in English.

[7] It is unfortunate that the constitution uses the Protestant watchword *sola scriptura* in this negative context, but it was not easy to find an acceptable formula which would avoid it. However, the Doctrinal Commission avoided the phrase *ex sola scriptura* and chose instead *per solam scripturam*; in this way it avoided the impression that it was considering scripture as a defective *source*.

word, guarding it and faithfully expounding it'. Thus, it concludes, Holy Writ, Sacred Tradition and the Church's teaching authority are so interconnected and combined that one does not stand firm without the others, and that all taken together, and each in its own way, they efficaciously contribute to the salvation of souls under the action of the one Holy Spirit (n. 10).

Just as the first chapter of *De Divina Revelatione* shows signs of a conflict between a conceptualist and a more biblical notion of revelation, so the chapter on the transmission of the revelation shows signs both of this conflict and of the old controversial problematic of *scriptura sola* or *scriptura et traditiones.* As we have seen, the attempt to affirm the 'material insufficiency' of scripture has, in the main, been successfully resisted. But the chapter continues to speak, as a rule, of Sacred Tradition as one thing and Holy Writ as another. It is my opinion that such language is not faithful to the deepest insight of the chapter itself – which manages to find expression in the sentence already cited: 'What has been handed on by (or from) the apostles embraces all those things that contribute to the holy conduct of the life of the People of God and to the increase of faith; and so the Church transmits . . . all that she is, all that she believes.' Scripture must obviously be included in the things that contribute to a holy life and to the increase of faith. In fact, then, Sacred Tradition should not be distinguished from scripture as though they were two distinct realities, but only as a whole is distinguishable from one of its constituents. The relevant theological question is not: 'What does tradition give us that scripture does not contain?' but: 'What is the function of scripture within the total fact of tradition?' The word 'tradition' needs to be cleansed of its associations with an anti-Protestant polemic. It will then be seen to pose an issue which, as already suggested, is vital to Christianity: how is the unique history of Jesus Christ which, together with his person informing that history, is the fullness of divine revelation, is, in fact, the word of God made actual in historical event, made available to every man in every place and age; how is the particular 'universalised'? This is the question of sacramental actual presence – or rather of sacramental real action in human history. Scripture by itself can tell us about Jesus Christ; as inspired by the Holy Ghost, it can even, in its own appropriate way, put us into personal contact with Jesus Christ. But the witness alike of the Bible itself and of post-biblical Christian history seems to show that the Bible is not our only means of contact with the historical Christ. We find him also, or rather he finds us, in the mystery of the body of Christ, that body which is at once the inner reality of the Church and her eucharistic focus and vital source. Within this total context of tradition, scripture has an important role. In all our personal relationships, while at the heart of them there is the fact that we 'know' the other, this personal knowledge does not exist without an element of 'knowing about' the other. Inspired scripture enables us to 'know about' Christ – about him whom we offer and who comes to us in the Eucharist, and who is the mystery at once indwelling, in some sense constituting, and transcending his body which is the Church.

When tradition is seen in this light it becomes obvious that the vehicle of tradition is not the Pope (Pius IX is alleged to have said: '*La tradizione son' io*') nor the episcopal college, but the whole People of God. This fact, as we shall see later, is recognised in the Constitution on the Church in its teaching on the *sensus fidei*, the believing mind, which belongs to the faithful as a whole. The early Gnostics appealed from the common teaching of the Church to private traditions, which – they alleged – had been handed down from man to man and so passed into their own possession. The sacred tradition of the Church is something very different from this. It is not stored up in the Vatican or in the curias of residential bishops. It is carried in the mind and heart of believers everywhere, and is the source of their Christian reflection. The rôle of the Church's Teaching Body is to preserve in its integrity, and if occasion requires to give authentic articulation to, this common Christian possession.

After its first two chapters, the Constitution on Divine Revelation is concerned almost exclusively with the Bible. Let it be said at once that, while the subject of the Bible is of immense importance for the renewal of the Church and her theology, for the ecumenical dialogue, and for the credibility of the Church's message, it is one of extreme difficulty in an age of alert and expert historical criticism. The notion of an inspired or sacred, and therefore authoritative, literature is not peculiar to Christianity; it was inherited from Judaism and has been taken up in Islam and Mormonism. But for an age as conscious as our own of the extremely human and contingent character of literary records, an age so suspicious of miraculous claims and so sensitive to the approximative character of human evidence, the notion of inspiration, especially when it is spelt out in terms of 'inerrancy', is hardly marketable at all. Of this difficulty some, but not all, the council fathers were anxiously aware. It remains to be seen how far they were able to meet it. The question is, whether the Catholic Church is committed to a kind of biblical fundamentalism.[8]

That the Bible is true is a fundamental conviction of the patristic age and has been bequeathed to all subsequent ages of the Church. At the same time, it did not entirely escape the notice of antiquity that the assertion raises certain problems. Both St Gregory of Nyssa and St Augustine interpret the creation story of Genesis and the 'six days' of creation in ways which the modern mind would not easily regard as conveying the 'literal sense'. St Augustine thought it worth while to write a whole treatise in order to iron out apparent contradictions between the Gospels. On the whole, however, the problem of the Bible's veracity was made easier for the ancients especially by the Alexandrian principle of the allegorical interpretation of scripture. If you can believe, with Origen, that the wars of Joshua are to be taken as prefiguring our redemption in Christ, you need not, they seem to have felt, worry too much about the sun standing still upon Gibeon (Jos 10:12). In any case, it seemed obvious to them that the story of God's providence over his people should be replete with marvels. The Middle Ages inherited the patristic attitude to the Bible and

[8] Here I would say that I have a great respect for the motives of the fundamentalists. They are actuated by a profound faith in divine revelation; and they have realised, as some others appear not to have done, that the notion of a public historical revelation is bound up with that of doctrinal authority. They are aware that without authority, Christianity dissolves into mere subjectivism. The trouble is that fundamentalism is simply not viable today, and can never be made viable unless humanity is willing to renounce its own intellectual inheritance. The problem of authority, by no means an easy one, requires solution on different lines.

passed it on to both Catholics and Protestants of more modern times. Meanwhile, eastern Orthodoxy seemed to continue to live in the very atmosphere of the great Fathers of the Church.

The Reformers' protest against supposed accretions and corruptions in medieval Catholicism may have been a factor in awakening a more general interest in the study of historical origins. It would hardly be an exaggeration to say that the science of history, as we know it, was founded by the French Maurist Benedictines (and, in Germany, by Ranke). The application of this science and of its daughter, the scientific criticism of historical documents, to the Old and then the New Testament has produced an acute crisis for western Christianity, and not least for Protestantism, in view of its traditional insistence on the Bible as the sole ultimate criterion of Christian truth. It was above all Protestant German historians and scholars who, in the nineteenth century, advocated extreme liberal solutions of the problem of the Bible, involving, for some, a complete rejection first of the received opinion of biblical inerrancy and then of scriptural inspiration as it had been commonly understood. The attempt of the Catholic scholar, Loisy, to answer Harnack's *Wesen des Christentums* by an *argumentum ad hominem*, accepting his radical New Testament criticism but denying the conclusions he drew from it, was a major factor in the Catholic Modernist crisis of the early years of the present century, which in turn provoked the strongly repressive measures taken against biblical scholarship under Pius X.

Since 1914 the situation has changed in various ways. The very radical position taken up by the Protestant Tübingen school had already been successfully challenged in the previous century by J. B. Lightfoot. But radicalism had always been fertile in ideas, and the modern period saw the emergence of the school of Form Criticism, of which Bultmann became the leader. Bultmann appeared to commit himself to a twofold radicalism: the recovery of the 'historical Jesus' was, in fact, impossible; and it was in principle unnecessary – indeed, the 'quest' was a virtual treason against the supremacy of faith in a Christian *kerygma* which – as presented by Bultmann – seemed rather jejune, but must be accepted without dependence on any external support from 'reason'. Outside the Bultmann school, however, there began to take shape a tendency to combine a full acceptance of critical method and of the principle of critical autonomy with a more or less orthodox theology.

The Roman reaction to the Modernist crisis and the heavy hand of the Biblical Commission in its early days made it almost impossible for Catholic scholars to co-operate in an international biblical scholarship which recognised no authority outside itself. The orthodox campaign against rationalistic radicalism had, for thirty years, to be waged almost solely by non-Catholic scholars. It is hardly an exaggeration to say that in the field of gospel studies the only Catholic scholar of that period whose voice was heard by his non-Catholic compeers was the heroic J.-M. Lagrange. The situation has been immensely improved since the publication of Pius XII's encyclical, *Divino afflante Spiritu*, and a large number of Catholic scholars are now respected members of the important international Society of New Testament Studies. But the struggle for legitimate scientific autonomy for Catholic biblical scholarship was still being waged when the second Vatican Council opened, and was far from having been won within the curia itself. In conciliar debate there was a regrettable tendency to identify the method of Form Criticism with the radical presuppositions and negative results of Bultmann, its greatest exponent.

Opposition to modern biblical criticism in Catholic circles is not to be explained as due merely to the innate conservative prejudices of an authoritarian 'government' in a society whose members were, for the most part, destitute of critical education. It appeals also to doctrinal considerations. The patristic teaching, that 'the Holy Spirit spoke by the prophets' and that the Bible is God's word, has taken shape in a doctrine of biblical inspiration epitomised in the first Vatican Council's teaching that, beyond the human authors of the books of scripture, these books have God as their divine 'author'. Since God cannot be accused of mendacity, the inference is drawn that what the Bible tells us is true. If this is so, it has seemed obvious to some minds that, if the Bible affirms that sunset was delayed in order to let Joshua reap the fruits of a famous victory, then the sunset was in literal fact delayed. This might seem rather awkward for the solar system, but after all God is Lord of his creation.

I have chosen a rather extreme Old Testament illustration; and it was on the Old Testament front that the reactionary conservative position was first broken. It is easy to imagine the weight of the combined attack on it from geology, astronomy, ancient history and literary analysis. Almost the first sign of official surrender was a letter from the secretary of the Biblical Commission to Cardinal Suhard of Paris in 1940, conceding that the first eleven chapters of Genesis need not be taken as historically true in precisely the same sense as, for instance, Thucydides would claim truth for his account of the plague of Athens.

Meanwhile the real implications of the doctrine of biblical inspiration had been closely examined, above all by Lagrange. Lagrange drew attention to the fact that veracity is a matter of intention, and that an author's intentions are not always to be crudely identified with the verbal expression in which he clothes his thought. I can refer to 'sunrise' and 'sunset' without thereby committing myself to the geocentric hypothesis. The Bible, therefore, asserts only what its human authors intended to assert, and in the measure that they intended it. This principle of interpretation is developed in *Divino afflante Spiritu* when it directs our attention to the 'literary types' (*genera litteraria*) used by the inspired authors. If an author is using a literary type other than that of scientific history, his veracity is not to be judged by the criteria which we should apply to a Napier, or even a Livy. As Samuel Johnson said, a composer of epitaphs is not to be supposed to be giving evidence under oath.[9]

The problems of 'scriptural inerrancy' can be very considerably lessened by such considerations. As regards the Old Testament, it is probable that relatively little controversy would have been aroused by their applications. The New Testament, however, particularly the Gospels, remained as a field of lively

[9] The question arises how far even a scientific historian intends to commit his personal veracity in his writings. It may often be the fact that he speaks categorically for convenience, by convention, or by inadvertence, when he would admit, and would wish it to be supposed, that he is merely repeating a received opinion or hazarding a reasonable conjecture.

discussion and anxiety. Orthodox Christianity is committed to the claim that God's final covenant with mankind was sealed in the actual historical existence of the Word made flesh. And for the record of that supreme intervention of God in history it has looked especially to the four canonical Gospels. But modern biblical scholars have seemed to some to be dissolving the historical figure of Jesus of Nazareth. What were once held to be trustworthy records of his acts, words, sufferings and resurrection have been explained as elements in the self-expression of the primitive Church and credited to the creative myth-making of a collectivity of low culture. They tell us more, it is alleged, of the apologetic, controversial and liturgical needs of the early Christian communities than they do of the carpenter of Galilee. This dissolving criticism was specially at work among German Protestant scholars. But notable Catholic scholars in the last few years have been applying Form Criticism to the Gospels, and it was only to be expected that some of them would apply it rashly and with alarmingly negative results. Then what was to become of the 'traditional' apologetics, which had been accustomed first to establish the existence, the transcendent claims, the miracles and the miraculous resurrection of Jesus, to infer the authority of the Church he could (it was thought) be shown to have founded, and thence to proceed happily to the infallibility of the Pope and the corporal assumption of the Blessed Virgin Mary? The council seemed to some of those alarmed by the perils of criticism to be a heaven-sent opportunity to strengthen the repressive control of authority over the vagaries of scholars, inseparable as such vagaries are from scholarly freedom.

There was, however, an inner contradiction in the conservative position. It held that the historical accuracy of the Gospels was a necessary ingredient in the complex of arguments which constitute the credibility of the Christian and Catholic religion; and that therefore the historical truth of the Gospels must be protected by ecclesiastical authority. But what is the value of alleged historical evidence, if this value has not been allowed to emerge by the free operation of historical science but has been imposed on historians by an external authority? A witness in a court of law who is only allowed to say what the judge dictates is a witness discredited *ab initio*. If Christianity is sure of its historical foundation, it has every reason to give ample liberty to its scholars in the scientific investigation of its origins.

As in so many other issues of the *aggiornamento*, the council's statement on the Gospels shows the interplay of conflicting tendencies:

> The Church holds, as it has always everywhere held, that the four Gospels have an apostolic origin. What the Apostles preached by command of Christ, was later handed on to us by divine inspiration of the (Holy) Spirit in writings by them and by apostolic men, that is to say the fourfold gospel, according to Matthew, Mark, Luke and John. Holy Mother Church has held and does hold firmly and most constantly that these four Gospels, the historicity of which she unhesitatingly affirms, faithfully transmit what Jesus the Son of God, living his life among men, really did and taught for their salvation, till the day when he was taken up (cf. Acts 1:1, 2). The Apostles after his Ascension passed on to their hearers what he had said and done, with that fuller understanding which they enjoyed through being instructed by Christ's glorious experiences and taught by the light of the Spirit of truth. And the sacred authors wrote the four Gospels, selecting material from the mass of oral (or written) tradition, some of which they synthesised, or expanded with reference to the state of the churches, while retaining the form of preaching (*praeconium*, i.e. *kerygma*), but so as always to convey to us what was true and sincere concerning Jesus. Their intention in writing was, whether from their own memory and recollection, or from the testimony of those 'who from the beginning had themselves seen and been servants of the word,' that we might know the 'truth' of those words in which we have been instructed (cf. Luke 1:2–4).

This extract from the constitution requires rather careful attention. The words 'apostolic origin' do not mean that the evangelists were apostles (obviously, St Mark and St Luke were not). And (at least if we may take 'by them and apostolic men' as designating a single group) it is not asserted that any of the Gospels had an apostle as immediate author. The affirmation of the Gospels' 'historicity' was due to a last-minute intervention. The word 'historicity' is not altogether a happy one, and could be misinterpreted, in Germany for example. It is in any case somewhat vague, and should be compared with the statement of 'literary types' in n. 12: 'Truth is expressed in different ways in texts which may be historical in one way or another, prophetical, poetical, or of other literary types.'

The word 'historicity' is therefore susceptible of a wide diversity of interpretation: what it certainly excludes is any suggestion that the Gospels are merely mythological. Its meaning is, in fact, explained by the ensuing statement that they 'faithfully transmit what Jesus . . . living among men, really did and taught for their salvation'; Christianity is based on actual facts, and the Gospels put us in contact with these facts. The danger that this affirmation might be taken in a 'fundamentalist' or unscientific sense is obviated by the further observation that the apostles conveyed the message of Christ's words and works as interpreted in the light of his resurrection and ascension and of the Holy Spirit enlightening their understanding, and that the evangelists relayed to us the message thus interpreted, which they have further edited and applied to the *Sitz im Leben* of the early Christian communities. The Gospels are thus not just bare factual history (if that were ever a realisable object) but are *kerygma*, or at least kerygmatic history. And here again, the danger at the opposite extreme to fundamentalism is averted by the statement that nevertheless they always tell us 'what is true and sincere' about Jesus. In the last sentence St Luke's own declaration of intention (that we might know the 'truth' of what is conveyed in Christian catechesis, as it comes down through eyewitnesses and official preachers of the message) is generalised and applied to all four evangelists.

While it may legitimately be asked whether the constitution, in seeking to steer a course between the Scylla of radicalism and the Charybdis of fundamentalism, has succeeded in being fully coherent with itself, I think its intention is fairly clear: it means to say that (*a*) the Gospels are, by and large, valuable documents for the knowledge of Christ's historical life, (*b*) they are to be treated with reverent but scientific scholarship.

The conservative anxieties about biblical criticism operated also at a second level. The teaching of the Catholic Church is that the books of the Bible were inspired by the Holy Spirit. As already stated, it is inferred that what these books tell us is 'true', and this is usually stated as involving 'the inerrancy of the Bible'. We have seen, however, that the encyclical *Divino afflante Spiritu* accepted the exegetical principle of 'literary types', and this principle was taken into the teaching of the constitution's chapter on The Inspiration and Interpretation of Holy Writ. This chapter eschews any idea of a divine dictation of inspired words to passive human subjects, affirming that the inspired writers used their own faculties and powers, but in such a way that, God acting in and through them, they conveyed to writing all and only what he willed them to. Both the human authorship and the divine 'authorship' of the Bible are thus affirmed. It is not here stated, but is, of course, the fact that when God is described as the 'author' of these books the word 'author' is used in an analogical sense; when this point is forgotten, the notion of a divine dictation, destructive of the reality of the human authorship, almost inevitably creeps in.

The next sentence of the constitution (n. 11) needs to be carefully considered: 'Since, then, all that the inspired authors or hagiographers assert must be held to be asserted by the Holy Spirit, it follows that the books of scripture are to be professed to teach faithfully and without error the truth which God, for the sake of our salvation, willed to be consigned to sacred literature.' This sentence incorporates a last-minute change, and its understanding depends on the meaning of the word 'truth' as here used, with reference to the passages of St Augustine and St Thomas Aquinas cited in the notes.

It has been well said that, face to face with modern science, Catholic exegesis before the council had been in an impasse.[10] Efforts had been made, by Newman and others, to impose a material limit on inspiration (and therefore on inerrancy) by exempting certain categories of scriptural statements from its operation. Such efforts had already been officially discountenanced before Vatican II. The Bible as a whole is 'religious'; its inspiration must not be regarded as intermittent. And if it were said that inspiration is confined to 'matters of faith or morals', where were you to draw the line? Moreover, the underlying notion of inspiration, implied by such efforts, was of

[10] P. Grelot, 'Études sur la Théologie du Livre Saint', in *Nouvelle Revue Théologique*, 1963; quoted in I. de la Potterie, 'La Vérité de la Sainte Écriture et l'Histoire du Salut d'après la Constitution dogmatique "Dei Verbum"', *ibid.*, 1966. In what follows in the text I am deeply indebted to this article of Père Potterie.

a conveyance of 'truths'. But, as we have already seen, divine revelation (with which inspiration must be closely linked) is not just a disclosure of intellectual truths; it is the divine meaning of a supernatural intervention in history by 'deeds and words'. And if inspiration means that the inspired books have (at different levels, and analogically speaking) a double authorship, human and divine, is it not reasonable to make the notion of divine authorship as wide in its scope as that of human authorship? We know, in fact, that human authors are not always making assertions claimed to be 'true'. They do not only affirm; they exhort, they exult or lament, they express, in other words, not only truths but emotions, they 'edify' not only their readers' intellect but his sensibility and his spirit. P. Benoit[11] has helpfully placed the notion of scriptural inspiration within the wider biblical notion of inspiration. In the Bible scriptural inspiration is mentioned rarely, and in rather late strata; heroes and kings and others are inspired to *actions* for the upbuilding of the People of God. It seems proper to see scriptural inspiration as directed to the same end: the 'upbuilding' rather than – more narrowly – the intellectual information, of God's people. Similarly, Grelot has emphasised that the divine purpose of inspired scripture is that of the word of God: to communicate the mystery of our salvation, a mystery that only reaches its climax in Christ.

The constitution does not use the word 'inerrance' of scripture, though it does speak of 'teaching without error'; what we take the term 'without error' to mean will depend on our view of 'the truth' which scripture is here said to 'teach': 'The inspired authors . . . teach without error the truth which for the sake of our salvation God willed to be consigned to sacred literature'. Here the word 'truth' is qualified by a statement of the finality or purpose of inspiration; it is a question of truth relevant to God's saving purpose summed up in Christ. It can at once be appreciated that material truth in details of profane history or science has no necessary connection with this purpose. Thus St Augustine, in a passage cited in a note to this sentence of the constitution, warns us against seeking in scripture a scientific cosmogony, and says that the Holy Spirit has

[11] Cf. *Inspiration and the Bible*, 1965.

not willed to teach us these things, which are of no profit for salvation.[12] And Aquinas, after referring to this passage of Augustine, adds (citing Jn 16:13): 'When that Spirit of truth comes he will teach you all truth needful for salvation'. In other words, the criterion of the truth of scripture is not one of material accuracy but of formal relevance. For instance, the date of the appearance of the human species in natural history is not formally relevant to our salvation; the reality of Christ's death and resurrection is formally relevant.

Underlying this distinction there is a distinction between two concepts of truth. Truth for the Greeks is that which gives legitimate satisfaction to our intellectual curiosity; this is the notion of truth which was dominant in nineteenth-century aspirations towards a science of history. For the Bible and for Christianity truth is above all the genuineness of the manifestation of God's saving purposes. The Epistle to the Ephesians, for instance, identifies 'the word of truth' with 'the gospel of your salvation' (1:13); and in the Gospel of St John 'the truth' is identified with Christ himself (the Word made flesh) (14:6). We may say, then, that the 'truth' which scripture 'teaches without error' is the truth of salvation history, a truth which, even in its Old Testament stage, is oriented towards Christ and which in the end *is* Christ, the mediator and fullness of divine revelation.[13]

The position with regard to the truth of scripture reached by the council in this important section of the constitution was not achieved without resistance and difficulty. Its merit is twofold. It rescues exegesis from the impasse created by the apparent contrast between the 'inerrancy' which theologians

[12] *De Genesi ad litteram*, 2:9:20.

[13] It will be observed that, in n. 19, the council similarly speaks of the Gospels as conveying faithfully what Jesus Christ really did and suffered for our salvation. The present writer, in a little book entitled *The Church and the Bible* and published in 1960, wrote: 'The books of the Bible, then, are each a word of God addressed to humanity as incorporated in the divinely founded universal fellowship which is called the Catholic Church. Each book has something to tell us. But if we want to sum up the message of the whole collection of books, this can be done in the single word: Christ. . . . It is obvious that Christ is the focal point and the meaning of the New Testament books. And if Christ, his gospel, and the Church his body, are the divinely intended consummation of the revelation, and promises to ancient Israel . . . then it follows that Christ is also the goal and meaning of the Old Testament books' (pp. 85, 92f.).

have inferred from the inspiration of scripture and the findings of modern scientific scholarship. And it takes us back behind the Hellenised theology of the Middle Ages and the Church fathers to the biblical insights of the actual period of 'salvation history'. *Non in dialectica placuit Deo salvare populum suum.* This recovery of biblical insights is also pregnant with the possibility of recovering the positive significance of inspiration and the inexhaustible creative potentialities of a revelation which is not confined to verbal propositions but is alive with the life of the historical and risen Christ.

Scripture, in short, its inspiration and its truth, are to be seen within the context of the notion of divine revelation which is the subject of the opening chapters of this constitution. As we have seen, this notion itself refers us back to the still more basic notion of God's redeeming intervention in the very texture of human history, and this intervention reaches its all-inclusive climax in Christ. Revelation is not just a divine satisfaction offered to our intellectual curiosity. It is an answer to the need and grace-inspired desire of the human person to know and to enter into the meaning of human existence. The Bible is a pointer to the history of salvation and to Christ, its consummation. Its purpose is not directly to enlighten us with regard to profane history, whether natural or human. But in Christ the whole of nature and history find a focus point. Thus the doctrine of biblical inspiration guarantees for us the religious truth of the scriptures in their supreme task of bringing us face to face with the life and person of Jesus Christ. To talk about 'the inerrancy of scripture' is to adopt a negative attitude to the Bible. What inspiration really guarantees is the Bible's religious truth, and its historical truth in so far as that is relevant to our redemption.

3

The Church a Mystery

From the first it was emphasised in the council that its task was pre-eminently 'pastoral', and therefore practical. The council was to aim at promoting the effective preaching of the gospel and the improvement of the Christian quality of the life of the Church's members; and to bring the influence of Christ to bear on the whole collection of human activities.[1] This pastoral emphasis seemed to disconcert those who thought of ecumenical councils as concerned primarily with doctrine and dogmatic formulations. They reminded the pragmatists that the Church's first pastoral task is to safeguard the integral wholeness of the deposit of faith. Out of this dialectic were born the council's dogmatic constitutions, the *De Divina Revelatione* and the *De Ecclesia*. Of these, the former has, of course, the more exalted theme, which it treats with creative freshness. But the central document of the whole council, and the one which exerted the most pervasive influence on those subsequently debated, was *Lumen Gentium*, the dogmatic Constitution on the Church.

No previous ecumenical council had succeeded in presenting to the world anything like a comprehensive ecclesiology. Vatican I had had ambitions in that direction, but broke off its work after dealing, directly, only with papal supremacy and

[1] John XXIII, *Humanae Salutis*, Christmas 1961, convoking the council.

infallibility. It is only in comparatively modern times that the Church has become the object even of a separate theological treatise; St Cyprian's *De Catholicae Ecclesiae Unitate* was, as the title indicates, an exploration of only one aspect of the subject. If you wish to discover what St Thomas Aquinas thought about the Church, you have to search for it under quite different headings in his *Summa Theologica*. Modern interest in ecclesiology, owing something to the late medieval theorising about Church and state and the controversy, at that period, between conciliarism, and papalism, is largely a result of the Reformation and the Protestant attack on the Church as she existed in the age of the great upheaval. In consequence, Catholic theological writing on the Church has tended to be controversial or polemical, and has concentrated on the visible, authoritarian, juridical and legal aspects of the subject, these being the aspects more often criticised by Protestants. Extreme Protestantism on the other side, while not rejecting the Church as an item in the Christian creed, has at times gone so far as to affirm that the real Church is not 'visible' at all, or at least not visible in any way that permitted her identification as a distinct entity in the historical order. Catholic theologians spent much time in refuting this negation; but, in so doing, they were tempted to say too little about the 'invisible', or 'mystical' or 'mysterious' aspects of the Church; this subject was often relegated to treatises on grace and on ascetico-mystical theology.

Ecclesiology is one of the departments of theology that have profited most by modern biblical and historical research and interest, and in the last decades also by ecumenism.[2] A great deal of work had been done on it before Vatican II opened, though evidence of progress was less abundant in circles more closely connected with Rome.[3]

The last major official pronouncement on ecclesiology before Vatican II was Pius XII's encyclical *Mystici Corporis*. We may

[2] For an outline, cf. O. Rousseau, 'La Constitution Lumen Gentium dans le cadre des mouvements rénovateurs de théologie et de pastorale des dernières décades', in *L'Église de Vatican II*, ed. G. Baraúna, Tome II, pp. 35ff.

[3] The work of S. Tromp, *Corpus Christi quod est Ecclesia: I, Introductio Generalis, II, De Spiritu Christi Anima*, comes from a professor of the Gregorian University, Rome. Its author was secretary to the Preparatory Theological Commission and the conciliar Doctrinal Commission.

at once remark that to treat the Church under the dominant aspect of the mystical body of Christ was an advance on a certain treatise *de Ecclesia* 'which devoted only two pages to the Church's relations with Christ'.[4] We shall find, however, that this particular image, the body of Christ, is not made the unique key to the doctrine of the Church in our constitution. In *Mystici Corporis* the image is treated not merely as an image but as a concept; and it is applied without qualification to the Church on earth, although it is recognised that the image denotes primarily the whole Church, including the saints in heaven. More important still, the Church as the mystical body of Christ is simply and materially identified with the Roman Catholic communion: Jesus Christ willed to bestow his graces 'by means of a visible Church in which men would be united. . . . And so, to describe this true Church of Christ – which is the holy, catholic, apostolic Roman Church – there is no title more noble, none more excellent, none more divine, than "the mystical body of Christ".'

From this material identification of the Church as Christ's body with the institutional Church visibly united under the vicar of Christ, the encyclical infers that 'only those are to be accounted really (*reapse*) members of the Church' who have been baptised, profess the true faith, and 'have not cut themselves off from the structure of the body by their unhappy act or been severed therefrom, for very grave crimes, by the legitimate authority'. (Note the perilous suggestion that the structures of the visible Church are, univocally, the structures of the mystical body.) 'It follows that those who are divided from one another in faith or government cannot be living in the one body so described (sc. by Eph 4:4, and by its one divine spirit.' On the other hand, sinners, provided that they have not apostatised or been cut off, remain members of the Church if they have once been such.[5]

Thus the encyclical's trend seems to be to establish a simple

[4] Mentioned by C. Moeller, 'Le Ferment des Idées dans l'élaboration de la Constitution', in *L'Église de Vatican II,* ed. G. Baraúna, Tome II, pp. 85ff.

[5] It will be observed that, whereas the former quotation could be so interpreted as to allow membership of the body to baptised non-Catholics who had not 'cut themselves off by their own unhappy act or been severed therefrom by legitimate authority', the second quotation seems to exclude all who are 'divided in faith or government'.

dichotomy between those who belong visibly to the Roman Catholic communion, and everyone else, be he Christian or non-Christian, religious or irreligious, man of good will or man of bad will. All the former are 'really' members of the Church, the body of Christ; none of the latter classes is. In taking this line, Pius XII was faithful to one set of convictions which are traditional in the Catholic Church, though there were other considerations which, taken together, could suggest that a fully nuanced view of the Church as a reality existing in actual history had not yet been reached. No one can fail to see what difficult problems *Mystici Corporis* posed for the Catholic theologians who wished to co-operate with the ecumenical movement.

Thus, among the council's problems was that of doing justice to what was positive and genuinely traditional in the ecclesiology of *Mystici Corporis*, while at the same time giving a more rounded view of the various aspects that must be held together in a complete ecclesiology. It could leave theological synthesis to the theologians; but it must try not to exclude any of the data with which ecclesiology is called upon to deal. A basic consideration here is that 'outside the Church there is no salvation' – a patristic dictum which Roman Catholic theology cannot overlook. On the other hand, it is a firm Christian conviction that, for all who have reached moral adulthood, there is no destiny other than achieved salvation or final condemnation; and it is also certain that God condemns no man unless he is not merely 'juridically' in the wrong but really guilty. Thirdly, it seems to be an empirical fact that very many, whom we have no right to accuse of basic wickedness, in fact die outside the visible communion of the Catholic Church, and we have at least no evidence that such people, by and large, make even an interior act of adhesion to what they recognise as that communion – of which indeed they may never have heard.

From a slightly different point of view, account is required to be taken of those who have been baptised but have never been visibly incorporated into the full communion of the Catholic Church. Baptism, of its nature, incorporates its recipient into the Church, and Catholic theology teaches that the sacramental 'character' of baptism is indelible in this life.

Unity given through baptism is a recurring theme in ecumenical theology, and was a favourite one with Cardinal Bea, the president of the Secretariat for Unity.[6] It seems short-sighted, to say the least, to classify all non-Roman-Catholic baptised Christians along with unbaptised pagans.

I

A decisive step was taken when it was decided that the first chapter of the Constitution on the Church should be entitled not (as was the first chapter of the rejected draft) 'The Nature of the Church militant', but 'The Mystery of the Church'. It is true that, in New Testament and most patristic usage, the word 'church' refers either to a local community of baptised Christians, or to the totality of the Church actually living at a given time in history. Only by degrees did the thought of the multitude of past Christians who had departed to heaven, or to purification after death, lead to a clear verbal distinction between the Church 'militant', the Church 'triumphant', and the Church 'suffering', and so to a vision of the one Church in three differing phases of her existence. The question arises, how far all that is said about the Church in the Bible is, in fact, predicable, without qualification, of the Church militant. Even after the first draft of a document on the Church had been criticised in the first session of the council, and then quietly discarded, the new document in its first presentation was still almost wholly concerned, in fact, with the Church on earth. A decisive enlargement of view was necessitated by the decision, during the second session, to include a treatment of our Lady in the constitution; and this was followed by a decision to add a chapter on 'the eschatological character of the pilgrim Church and her union with the Church in heaven'. The implications of the chapter title, 'The Mystery of the Church', thus had justice done to them.

This first chapter, after an introductory paragraph, opens with a group of three paragraphs in which the Church is set forth as sprung from the purpose of God the Father 'to call together those who believe in Christ in the holy Church'; as the reign of Christ, God's Son, a reign or kingdom already

[6] Cf. A. Bea, *The Unity of Christians*, pp. 32f.

present in the Church in mystery; and as indwelt and sanctified by the Holy Spirit. 'Thus the whole Church is seen as a people whose unity has its source in that of the Father, the Son and the Holy Spirit' (n. 4).

Continuing, the constitution considers the Church in the light of Christ's preaching of the reign of God, which reign was manifested in the very person of Christ, Son of God and Son of man, who 'came to serve and to give his life as a ransom for many', and was shown to be present by Christ's miracles. Those who believe Christ's preaching 'receive the Kingdom' and they become, through the sending of the Holy Spirit by the risen Christ, the Church, which 'is given the mission of announcing the reign of Christ and God and of restoring it in all nations, and constitutes the germ and beginning of this reign on earth, while still aspiring to the perfected reign' (n. 5).

The charge has often been made against Catholic theology that it crudely identifies the kingdom of God with the visible Church. The constitution may be said to take a middle line in this matter. It sees the 'perfect kingdom' as the object of the Church's eschatological hope, and makes the kingdom the content of the Church's preaching, and its inauguration the purpose of her work. On the other hand, it affirms that the Church herself is 'the germ and beginning' of the reign of Christ and God on earth. Scripture scholars will observe that there is a blurring of ideas here. The New Testament distinguishes from the reign of God that kingship of Christ which, at the end of all things, Christ will 'hand over' to his Father; the constitution fails to make this distinction. There is probably another equivocation in our text, having its roots in the New Testament itself. The Greek phrase which we have translated sometimes as 'kingdom', sometimes as 'reign', of God is, in fact, susceptible of both these meanings. It can refer to God's supreme rule over his creatures; and it can refer to his 'realm', or the sphere or population over which this rule is exercised. In the former sense, the reign of God 'is not an organisation, an institution; it knows no development, it does not include both the just and sinners; it does not depend on earthly and human factors'; and in this sense the Church is not the reign of God. In the sense, however, of God's 'realm' the biblical term can be applied, with due qualifications, to the Church – especially if, as in this passage of the constitution, distinctions have not yet been drawn between the visible-institutional and interior-spiritual aspects of the Church.[7]

The constitution next mentions a number of biblical 'images' of the Church: sheepfold, flock, God's field, his vineyard, his building (of which Christ is the foundation), the house of God's family, his temple, the 'Jerusalem which is above', 'our mother', the bride of the immaculate lamb. This rather discursive passage is not unimportant. The accumulation of figures helps us to realise that we are reflecting upon a mystery and approaching it from several standpoints – not analysing an object of scientific enquiry with the help of concepts that must be fully consistent each with all the others. We are not defining the Church,[8] but groping towards some insight into its unfathomable and mysterious depths.

Only now does the constitution concentrate its attention on the view of the Church as the body of Christ:

> The Son of God, in the human nature united to himself, by his death and by overcoming death by his resurrection, redeemed man and transformed him into a new creature (cf. Ga 6:15; 2 Co 5:17). For by communicating his Spirit, he mystically constituted his brethren, called together from all peoples, as his body. In that body the life of Christ is poured into believers. . . . By baptism we are conformed to Christ: 'in one Spirit we have all been baptised into one body'. . . . In the breaking of the eucharistic bread we really share in the Lord's body, and are raised to communion with him and with one another. . . . Thus are we all made members of his body, 'and each of us members of one another'. . . . The head of this body is Christ. . . . That we might be constantly renewed in him, he has given us of his Spirit, who being one and the same in the head (i.e. Christ) and in the members, so enlivens the whole body, unifies it and gives it (vital) movement, that his rôle could be likened by the holy fathers to that which the life-principle or soul

[7] B. Rigaux, 'Le Mystère de l'Église à la Lumière de la Bible', in *L'Église de Vatican II*, ed. G. Baraúna, Tome II, pp. 223ff.

[8] Contrast Tanquerey, *Brevior Synposis Theologiae Dogmaticae*, p. 154: 'The Church of Christ can be defined as "a society of men in their earthly condition under the teaching and ruling authority of legitimate pastors, and especially of the Roman Pontiff, men united by profession of the same Christian faith and communion in the same sacraments, with a view to the attainment of eternal salvation".' Note that this definition relates solely to the Church on earth, and that it identifies it without qualifications with the Roman Catholic communion in its visible structure. The sixth edition of this excellent manual carries the date 1925.

fulfils in a human body. Christ loves the Church as his spouse . . . and the Church for her part, is subject to her head' (n. 7).

It is important here to notice two points. First, the metaphor of the 'body' is often so interpreted as if that term could be used univocally both of a single human organism and of a 'body politic'. The constitution on the whole avoids this confusion, keeping to the former understanding of the term. Secondly, the body of Christ as here described is given its substance and reality not by juridical links but by sacramental ones. It is to be observed that, in the first paragraph of the constitution, the Church herself is described as being 'in Christ as it were a sacrament or sign and instrument of inward union with God and of the unity of the whole human race' (n. 1). Such a notion of the Church, more profound and more genuinely religious than the notion (true within its limits of reference) of her as a quasi-political society in relations, sometimes amicable and sometimes hostile, with civil governments, finds its complement in the teaching of this paragraph, that the Church is founded in, and built up out of the sacraments and the sacramental life. When it is borne in mind that, in Catholic theology, not the Church but Christ himself is the real agent in the sacraments, it begins to become clear that the Church herself is totally 'referred to' and dependent on Christ.

The first chapter of the constitution concludes with a section relating this teaching to the doctrine, more familiar to our modern manuals of theology, of the Church as a visible institution. It tells us that Christ established his holy Church, a fellowship of faith, hope and charity as, on earth, a visible structure (*compaginem*), and continually supports her (as such); by her means, thus visibly structured, he pours forth grace and truth to all men. What, then, is the relation between this institutional notion and the sacramental, 'mystical' notion of the Church?

Christian reflection has come to see sacraments as signs of spiritual realities; these spiritual realities they not only signify but convey. Already St Paul, who knew of baptism as an act of immersion in water, saw it as a sign of the Christian 'dying' and 'being buried' with Christ, in order that he might 'rise' out of it to a new life in Christ. That the physical act of immersion should carry such a Christian signification, it needs, of course, to be marked off from ordinary immersions – e.g. an athlete's plunge into a bathing pool – by some further determination, normally a form of words. Similarly, the Eucharist is distinguished from an ordinary meal by the prayer of thanksgiving which links it up with Christ's redemptive work. The complete sacramental sign is the complex of act and explanation: the immersion, together with the form of words. It is, of course, a highly 'conventional' sign; it is to be ranged not with the smoke which is a 'sign' of fire, but with language.

As a conventional sign, a sacrament has its natural milieu – as all such conventional signs have – in a human fellowship with its own traditions and common life. Seen outside that milieu, it becomes either ambiguous or non-significant. Herodotus tells of an Egyptian monarch who discovered that the first articulate sound made by children who had been kept separate from all educative influences was *brekos*. He assumed that this curious noise might be a word in some existing language; and when he found that it existed in the vocabulary of the Scythians, for whom it meant 'bread', he concluded that the Scythian language was the original one. The noise, assumed by him to carry a signification, was yet meaningless until related to a particular human context, that of the Scythians and their conventions of intercommunication. For an example of ambiguity, we may take the written word 'Fund' which means something different in a German context from what it means in English; or the spoken word 'succour' which conveys a quite different meaning from its English one to an American listener.

Sacraments therefore presuppose a fellowship of men living on earth who have to communicate by physical signs. If the Church has sacraments at its core and as the source and sustenance of its life, the Church is a concrete human fellowship. As fellowship tending to community, it needs a structure; only through social structure does a number of human individuals become a community. There is thus no incoherence between the council's vision of the Church as basically sacramental and its presentation of the same Church, on earth, as a visible structured human community.

The constitution's originality, however, emerges in the most carefully chosen language in which it combines its 'mystical' and 'institutional' views of the Church: 'The society equipped with hierarchical organs, the visible group, the earthly Church, is not to be viewed as a different entity from the mystical body of Christ, the spiritual fellowship, the Church endowed with heavenly blessings; they constitute one complex reality, made up of a human and a divine element. It is no trivial analogy which likens the Church to the mystery of the Word incarnate. The (human) nature assumed by the divine Word serves him, to whom it is indissolubly united, as a living organ of salvation; in like fashion the social structure of the Church serves Christ's Spirit, who vivifies it, for the increase of the body (sc. of Christ).' If we may add a gloss to this passage: the divine Word, in becoming incarnate, did not lose his divine ubiquity. There was, during his incarnate life, a special truth in saying that the word of God was there where his human nature was; but it would have been grossly untrue to say that the same word of God was not everywhere else in the universe.

Having thus passed from the Church's mystical to her visible aspect, our chapter proceeds to an identification of her. There is a story in St John's Gospel that certain Greeks told Philip 'we would see Jesus' – who would not wish thus to identify the Word made flesh? So, too, granted that the one Church has a visible aspect, we want to know where she can be found.[9] And – again using a most carefully selected form of words – the council states: 'This Church, established and arranged in this world as a society, subsists in the Catholic Church, governed by Peter's successor and the bishops in his communion.' There is a deliberate preference of the phrase 'subsists in' instead of the simple 'is'. We have here the measure of the constitution's advance upon *Mystici Corporis*, and a foundation for the Decree on Ecumenism and for other elements of the council's teaching and proposals. An exclusive material identification of the Church and the Roman Catholic communion is carefully avoided.

[9] Cf. J. M. Cameron, *Images of Authority*, pp. 70ff., e.g. 'It is only within the linguistic community of the Church that the sacraments have their authentic meaning'.

It is doubtless appropriate that after this restatement of a doctrine and an identification that are fundamental for Catholicism, the chapter ends with what amounts to a renunciation of the 'triumphalism' charged against the Catholic Church not only by non-Catholics but by some of her own sons. The Church, we are now told, is called to follow Christ's own path, in poverty and persecution. She is set up not to seek earthly glory but to give a practical lesson of humility and abnegation, concerned with every human affliction, and seeing Christ in the poor. But while Christ 'knew no sin', the Church embraces in her fold men who are sinners; she is both (in one aspect) holy and (in another) in need of constant purification and ever aims at both penitence and renewal. It is on this path that, strengthened by the power of her risen Lord, she manifests, though 'in shadows', the mystery of Christ till the day when that mystery will be shown forth in full light. Thus we are reminded of the paradoxes in which the 'mystery' of the Church finds expression: a lofty claim that impels to humility, suffering and compassion; a holiness that does not dispense from penitence; a sacramental actualisation of Christ which transcends itself in an eschatological hope; a divine origin and a lowly human visage.

II

The constitution, having moved on in the course of its first chapter from reflection upon the total mystery of the Church to her earthly existence as a structured community, might have been expected to turn next to a delineation of her hierarchical structure. In fact, however, it first devotes a whole chapter to a consideration of the Church on earth as the 'People of God'. The order of exposition thus adopted is in line with the council's vision of hierarchy, government, and teaching authority as all constituting a form of 'ministry' or service of the Christian community and indeed of all mankind. In the order of means to the Christian end, there is a genuine subordination of ordinary Christians to the hierarchy; but in the order of ends, the hierarchy itself is subordinate to the whole People of God. As we shall see, the council's vision of the hierarchy is essentially sacramental rather than jurisdictional; and it is a constant Catholic principle that, like the Jewish sabbath, the sacraments are 'for the sake of men', not *vice versa*.

The chapter on the People of God begins with a fundamental assertion: 'At every time and in every nation, whoever fears God and works righteousness is acceptable to God' – a reference to St Peter's observation in the house of the Gentile centurion at Caesarea. The council does not here explain what is meant by this 'fear of God and working of righteousness'. Later on, however (n. 16), it remarks that 'divine providence does not deny help needful for salvation to those who, without their own fault, have not yet reached an express recognition of God and who strive to attain to a life of rectitude – in which striving they are (in fact) helped by God's grace'. We shall hardly be going beyond the intention of the constitution if we identify the fear of God with a genuine docility towards the reality of 'ultimate concern', and the working of righteousness with a basic obedience to conscience even though conscience is inculpably misinformed.

The breadth of view thus shown by the council might cause surprise to some who are aware of the Church's constant teaching, already referred to above, that 'outside the Church there is no salvation'. But the constitution at once goes on, after thus describing the subjective conditions of salvation, to affirm the opposite pole of our human paradox: 'It was God's good pleasure to sanctify and save men, not individually and without any interrelationship among themselves, but to establish them as a people that should acknowledge him in truth and give him holy service' (n. 9). This states, in a preliminary broad generality, the objective aspect of man's salvation, which, on the Christian view, is something we cannot achieve for ourselves, but is a gift from God, with qualities therefore deriving not from our own nature or self-determination but from God's will. While every genuinely conscientious man will be saved, salvation itself is not a private possession but a participation in a common, communal, social salvation.

God's dealings with Israel in the period of the Old Covenant were a figure of the 'new covenant' in Christ, whereby those who believe in him are constituted, through baptism, 'an elect race, a royal priesthood, a people of choice . . . who were once not a people but are now the People of God' (1 P 2:9f). This, the Church of Christ, his messianic people, has Christ as its head, and the Holy Spirit dwells in its members' hearts 'as in a temple'. Its law is the 'new commandment' of Christ's own charity; and its end is the Kingdom of God, inaugurated on earth by God himself, and to be expanded until he consummates it at the end of history. Though it may not actually comprise all men, it is yet the germ of unity, salvation and hope for the whole human race, is used by Christ as an instrument for the redemption of all, and is sent into all the world by him. Thus it enters into human history, but transcends all limits of space and time. It is itself a priestly people, and all its baptised members share in this priesthood, itself a participation of the one priesthood of Christ.[10] But it is important that the priesthood of the whole People of God is not regarded as a purely metaphorical thing, but as really founded in the sacraments of baptism and confirmation. And by a truly priestly act the Church's members are said to offer – not merely assist at the offering of – the eucharistic sacrifice.

The Church participates not only in Christ's priesthood but in his prophetic rôle. Christians are a prophetic as well as a priestly people. A prophet is a mediator of God's word of salvation, a spokesman of God. The Church as a whole bears witness to the gospel, a witness derived from the 'unction of the Holy Spirit' (cf. 1 Jn 2:20 and 27). And here the council repeats a common Catholic teaching that 'the whole body of the believers cannot be deceived in believing'. It is in virtue of the resulting 'sense of faith ' (*sensus fidei*) that God's people, guided by the teaching authority, adheres indefectibly to the faith once delivered, penetrates its meaning ever more deeply, and applies it in practice with growing fullness (n. 12).

This doctrine, of which Rousseau's theory of the General Will may be regarded as a somewhat degenerate, and of course de-supernaturalised, offspring, is important because it enrich-

[10] To this important statement of 'the priesthood of all' baptised believers, there is added an explanation that the 'ministerial or hierarchical priesthood' is essentially different from it, since the ministerial priesthood has its own powers of forming and ruling the priestly people, of consecrating the eucharistic sacrifice 'in the person of Christ' and offering it in the name of the whole People of God. This explanation anticipates what will be said in the third chapter of the constitution, where the ministerial priesthood is considered in its own right.

es the meaning of the doctrine of the infallibility of the Church. Too often the Church's infallibility has been seen as a peculiar prerogative of the hierarchy, not to say of the Pope in person. Such infallibility, seen in isolation, while the body of the faithful is viewed as the passive recipients of its utterances, takes on an oracular colouring, as if the Pope were in receipt of private messages from on high; or else the idea is suggested that the hierarchy, or the Pope, is in possession of a sort of secret tradition of truth, like the *Acta* of Julius Caesar which Mark Antony claimed to have secreted in his own house. But, in fact, if we follow the thought of Vatican I's definition of papal infallibility, infallibility is a gift of Christ to the Church primarily, of which the hierarchy or the Pope is the organ. The Sacred Tradition is expounded by the 'teaching Church'; but it lives in the People of God as a whole, with a life derived from the Holy Spirit, who 'animates' the Church (*De Ecclesia*, n. 7), and guaranteed by a divine promise of the Church's indefectibility. The duty of the Pope or the hierarchy, before expounding Christian doctrine, is to listen with docility to 'what the Spirit saith to the churches'.

It may be suggested that the constitution could have developed a little further what it has to say about the *sensus fidei*. This 'understanding enlightened by faith' is described as the means by which the infallibility of the whole believing Church is brought into action. We shall see, however, that the Church's organ of infallible definition, the magisterium or teaching authority of the episcopal college and its papal head, claims respect, in varying degrees, for its pronouncements even when they are less than infallible. It would have been helpful if, in this present section of the constitution, it had been made clear that, similarly, the 'mind of the faithful' deserves respect even when its opinions fall short of moral unanimity. The point is recognised in practice elsewhere, when the clergy are urged to listen to and take account of the views of the faithful, and when the place of 'public opinion' in the Church is recognised.[11]

So far, the prophetic function of the People of God has been presented as an 'unction of the Holy Spirit' enabling that

[11] On public opinion, cf. the Secretary of State's letter to the Nice *Semaine Sociale*, 1968, quoted in *The Tablet*, 23 July 1966, pp. 852f.

People to bear witness to the unchanging truths of the gospel. Now a further paragraph draws attention to the 'special graces' poured out by the same Spirit on Christians of every rank in the Church and enabling them to work for her renewal and edification. Such graces are here given the New Testament name: *charismata*. These may be ordinary or extraordinary; and a warning is interposed that extraordinary *charismata* are not to be rashly sought and are subject to authentication by the Church's leaders – whose task, however, is not 'to quench the Spirit' but to 'prove all things and hold fast to that which is good' (cf. 1 Th 5:12 and 19–21). This paragraph, so pregnant and so carefully balanced, is characteristic of the second Vatican Council. The image of the Church which the modern pre-conciliar Roman Catholic Church had succeeded in conveying to the public was of a guardian of tradition and a bulwark against revolutionary change; an image of conservatism. Conservatism, however, can degenerate into resistance to even legitimate change; it can too easily become reactionary obstructiveness. Yet conservation is a major duty of the teaching and governing authority of a religious society which must ever look back to its ancient charter of foundation and to the first proclamation of its saving message. We cannot look to the episcopal college as such, still less to the Roman See as such, for the dynamic, creative, ingredient of Christianity, for the perennial sources of its unpredictable novelty. These sources spring from the action of the life-giving Spirit of God, an action that is applied to the very roots of human personality and that is no respecter either of persons or of office. A humble nun, a country curé, a young Belgian city pastor, a French layman holding a university chair of philosophy, an industrialist or a trade union official, may be the recipient of such 'special graces'. Sometimes these graces may be so unusual and at first questionable as to merit the epithet 'extraordinary'; and especially in such cases it has to be borne in mind that while all such inspirational graces are given for the good of the Church as a whole and of mankind as a whole, there is no automatic guarantee of the genuineness of an alleged inspiration which threatens the settled order. It is in such circumstances that ecclesiastical authority has to fulfil its delicate rôle of judgment and control, yet without stifling genuine inspiration. One may be allowed to think that the second Vatican Council itself set a magnificent example of such prudent yet welcoming judgment on a great mass of theoretical and practical experimentation clamouring for recognition in the early decades of the present century. Indeed, it may be said to have substituted for an image of the Church in which its static element was predominant the image of a dynamic Church whose potentialities, under the wise guidance of the episcopal college, are immeasurable. The Church's life does not flow down from Pope through bishops and clergy to a passive laity; it springs up from the grass-roots of the People of God, and the function of authority is co-ordination, authentication and, in exceptional cases, control. The council's Decree on the Lay Apostolate may be said to find in this paragraph of *Lumen Gentium* the theological justification of its best and most creative instructions.[12]

III

In their distinct and complementary ways, both the sacraments (including that of Holy Orders) and *charismata* are directed to the renewal and edification of the Church. And it is steadily emphasised by the council that the Church has a mission to all mankind and exists to promote our common human welfare. She is, in fact, 'as it were a sign and instrument of the unity of the whole human race' (n. 1) and she 'both prays and labours that the fullness of the whole world may pass into God's people, the Lord's body and the temple of the Holy Spirit' (n. 17); she is, in fact, 'a germ of salvation for the whole human race' (n. 9).

The question arises: What is the content of the notion of salvation; or, for that matter, of 'our common human welfare'? Over a large field the Christian can and does accept the values recognised by well-intentioned non-Christians. The Pastoral

[12] It would be a mistake to suppose that the 'charismatic' gifts of God are always directed to immediately 'religious' or 'ecclesiastical' action. The People of God is mankind as a whole, in so far as mankind responds to the gift of redemption. This response is a total response in a total situation, and will find expression – more often perhaps than in the sphere of the 'sacred' – in secular activities of every kind. The word 'ecclesiastical' has unfortunately taken on such a sacristy complexion that modern theologians, in search of a word better able to suggest the realities of the redeemed life, have taken to using the neologism 'ecclesial' when they wish to break free from clericalism.

Constitution on the Church in the World of Today has much to say about the dignity and freedom of the human person and the harmony and stability of a social life that recognises the rights of the person. It by no means disapproves of modern interest in natural science or of technological advance. It has special chapters on marriage and the family, on culture, on economic and political life, and on the urgent, permanent and ever-changing problem of peace between peoples. But it would be a mistake to think that the Church's only rôle is to recognise such commonly accepted values and to offer her services in promoting them. She is something more than an international friendly society. And if she were not something more, it is doubtful whether she would have a valid message of hope for man, who has never found in the wisdom of statesmen or of philosophers the means to achieve his recognised ends.

The Church's message is of a transcendent value and of the existence of means for its attainment; and as this value is inclusive of all values, it is implicit in her message that she has the clue also to man's attainment of the finite values of this life.[13]

The Church's message, in fact, concerns holiness, and a chapter of *Lumen Gentium* is devoted to the subject of 'The Universal Call to Holiness in the Church'. The chapter begins with a reminder that the Church herself is 'indefectibly holy'. Such an assertion is liable to provoke questioning when we contemplate the actually existing Church, the People of God in its actual dusty pilgrimage on earth, 'always in need of purification', as the constitution itself has told us. But we are aware, when we thus speak of purification, that the existing Church on earth is a field of tension between what we may

[13] After giving a talk, to a group concerned to forward the cause of world government, on the teaching of John XXIII's last encyclical, *Pacem in Terris*, I was faced with the question: Granted that John's vision of a universal commonwealth based on accepted moral principles of justice and charity is attractive and looks like being the answer to our problem, how can we hope to attain it, experienced as we are in the failure of human will to match human insight? A partial answer to this question could be that man has unplumbed resources, and the urgency of our present world need is such as to call these hidden powers into action. But the full Christian answer is surely that the Church, in offering more than man needs for any earthly end, does actually offer him strength and grace for the achieving also of his earthly ends.

call an ontological presupposition and its actual embodiment. The Church is founded in the holy sacraments, in the sacramental reality of divine grace flowing from our redemption. A baptised person is one who, as St Paul says, has died with Christ and risen again with the risen Christ to a life of Christian holiness. We may say, then, that the God-given purpose of the Church is that in her we should 'become' what through her sacraments we already 'are': you have died with Christ, mortify therefore your members which are upon the earth. As the constitution puts it: Christ died in order to sanctify his spouse the Church; *therefore* all in the Church are called to holiness. Or again: 'Christ's followers . . . have in the baptism of faith been made truly sons of God and sharers in the divine nature; hence they have really been made holy. Their task is to preserve in their life and to perfect the holiness which they have received by the gift of God' (n. 40). And again: 'All Christ's faithful are called to the fullness of Christian life and the perfection of charity', and this means holiness.

The programme of the quest of holiness is not something separate from the ordinary conditions of life of the faithful. On the contrary, it is by faith in God's providence in these conditions and by co-operation with his will in them that they will both practise charity and bear witness to it. And although charity is something which we realistically practise, it is at the same time 'the first and most necessary of God's gifts to us' (n. 42). It is not mere love of our fellow human beings, but a love of God above all things and of our neighbour for God's sake (*ibid.*). The greatest of all witness to it is borne by the suffering of martyrdom, which is a grace given to few, though all are bound to bear witness to the gospel and endure consequent persecution.

This is solid, practical teaching; and what is most striking is the forthright statement that holiness – sanctity – is not a special divine call issued to a privileged Christian *élite* but a universal invitation implied in baptism, the sacrament of Christian initiation. There are factors in Catholic history that have tended to convey the impression that the Church recognised two (or more) classes or castes of Christians, according as believers were given a divine call to ordinary or to extraordinary goodness. The canonisation of saints has had the effect of putting a small group of past heroes of the faith upon a pedestal that seemed to remove them from the common lot of Christians. And a theology of 'states of perfection' (members of religious orders and congregations being in a state of 'perfection to be acquired', while bishops are in a state of 'perfection acquired') has introduced a similar, and perhaps more dangerous, notion of class distinction among Christians even in this life. An aspect of modern moral theology has worked in the same direction. The textbooks of moral theology studied in seminaries by prospective priests have usually been composed with a particular eye for the ministry of the sacrament of penance, and have tended to concentrate on the minimal conditions required for giving absolution and hence authorising approach to Holy Communion. It is easy to slip over from the laudable principle that one must not demand more than is strictly necessary to the dangerous notion that one may not expect and need not seek to elicit more than this minimum. Needless to say, actual pastoral practice has frequently been admirable; but an effect of the moral theology books may have been, in the end, to encourage in the minds of some Christians the idea that 'holiness is not for me', indeed that it would be somewhat presumptuous to aspire to it. Similarly, it is possible that some members of religious orders or congregations have been tempted to a sort of spiritual pride or vanity by the thought that they are in a 'state of perfection'. All such misconceptions are swept away by the constitution. While there is no suggestion that holiness admits of no gradations or that a general call to holiness may not become the basis of a more specific and even more urgent divine invitation, it is clearly laid down that a horizon of infinite holiness is opened up for everyone by his incorporation through baptism in the body of Christ, who is the archetype of all creaturely holiness.

Nevertheless, the constitution does devote a separate chapter to the subject of 'Religious', which is the somewhat unfortunate generic name given in western tradition to those who dedicate themselves by a special act, usually in the form of a public 'profession', to a lifelong deliberate quest of closer union with God through prayer and asceticism. Monasticism, both eremitical and cenobite, has been a feature of the Church from the fourth century onwards. The Fathers of the Desert were, in fact, already foreshadowed in the order of dedicated virgins existing in the pre-Constantinian Church, and perhaps in the New Testament class of 'widows who are widows indeed'. In the Middle Ages the west saw a fresh development of the 'religious life' in the establishment of the great orders of friars, and more recent centuries have seen a prodigious growth of religious congregations, usually devoted to some specific service or services to the needs of the Church and the world. Amongst these, the missionary congregations deserve a particular mention.

It must be confessed that this chapter is not among the best of the constitution. This is probably because the theological presuppositions of the religious life have not yet received adequate attention. It will suffice here to draw attention to two points in the chapter.

First, it is clearly stated that membership of a religious order or congregation does not constitute a 'third state' in the Church alongside those of the laity and the sacramental ministry. Baptism, by which one becomes a member of the Church, and Holy Orders, by which one becomes a member of the clergy, are divinely instituted sacraments imparting a divinely given status. But religious profession, while grounded in 'the words and example of the Lord', is not a sacrament, and is, in fact, open to both lay people and clergy. It gives rise, to use a convenient modern distinction, not to a structure or institution *of* the Church, but to a structure or institution *in* the Church.

Secondly, to speak of a structure in the Church is to invite the question of the structure's ecclesial rôle. Religious are 'specially related to the Church and the mystery of the Church, and so their spiritual life must be devoted to the good of the whole Church' (n. 44). And, in fact, 'the profession of the gospel counsels'[14] is said by the constitution to stand forth as a 'sign'

[14] Religious are said to 'profess the evangelical counsels' as publicly committing themselves, usually in the western Church by vows, to practise our Lord's counsels, especially celibate chastity, poverty, and obedience. One may think that the theology behind this phrase requires examination. It suggests, *prima facie*, that Christ both promulgated a law for everyone and counselled a minority to add to obedience to this law conformity with certain optional recommendations. And this, in turn, suggests that Christianity is a kind of higher legalism (the 'law of charity' replacing the Mosaic Law) for a Church in which there would be two classes of members, those who contented themselves with legal conformity, and those who chose – or were called – to

of eschatological significance. God's people has 'no abiding city' on earth, but seeks a future home; and the religious state, freeing as it does its adherents from the earthly cares of family, property and career, bears witness thereby to our general Christian inheritance of a 'new and eternal life' and to our future resurrection and the glory of the heavenly Kingdom (n. 44). We may compare some words written before the promulgation of our constitution: 'The state of life according to the counsels . . . develops to the maximum, and realises in one's mode of being, the hope of glory which was given in baptism: virgins anticipate that completeness which, like every Christian, they have already received in substance. The idea of virginity as an anticipation of eschatology . . . is fully traditional. It implies the mortification in man of what still bears the character of this world, even though it is good in itself; and it implies, more positively, an exclusive concern for prayer and life in the Holy Spirit. . . . If such (dedicated persons) return to the haunts of men . . . they do so as witnesses of the Kingdom, to pass on the word of the gospel and to disclose to the world the meaning of the mysterious movement by which it lives.'[15] Such a view of the theology of the religious

graduate into a higher, but voluntary, class. Obviously scripture texts can be found in support of this opinion (though it might be hard to discover a 'counsel' of obedience). The question is, whether these texts demand this theological explanation, and whether the deeper view of St Paul, that Christians are 'not under law but under grace', is not basic to the gospel. It must be borne in mind that when Christ offered the two precepts of charity as the two greatest commandments of the Law, he was answering a Jewish question and presumably accepting Jewish presuppositions. An adequate theology of the religious state would need to take account of such considerations and to consult scriptural exegetes. It is quite true that St Paul appears to give a standing to religious virginity above that of Christian marriage. Our Lord, however, suggests that such virginity is not so much a free option as a particular vocation; it may be asked whether, for a man or woman who has such a vocation, fidelity to it is any more a matter of 'counsel' than, for the married man, is fidelity to his wife. The second Vatican Council did not face these difficulties. It did, however, steer clear of any suggestion that the so-called gospel counsels have relevance only for those who, by religious profession, assume an obligation to fulfil them literally. The spirit of the counsels must surely inspire all fully Christian living.

[15] G. Lafont, 'Les Voies de la Sainteté dans le Peuple de Dieu', in Guillou et Lafont, *L'Église en Marche*, pp. 200f. The imprimatur of this book carries the date 16 May 1964. *Lumen Gentium* was promulgated in November of the same year.

life, deeply biblical in its approach, holds promise for the future. The council has but sketched out the idea; it will be for theologians to take it further.

IV

Among the movements of thought and interest in the Church of the half-century culminating in Vatican II, one of the most vigorous was concerned with the Blessed Virgin Mary.[16] It has been both devotional or practical and literary or theological. Two and a half million pilgrims visit the shrine of our Lady at Lourdes annually. There were forty-three Marian congresses in the year 1954. Written works (books, brochures, pamphlets, periodicals, omitting 'the more popular non-scientific periodicals') were appearing at the rate of about a thousand a year.[17] Real or alleged apparitions of Mary (without her divine Son) have been frequent for a century and a half. Recent Popes, up to and including Pius XII, had given their support to this movement, and a culminating moment was reached when, in 1950, the Pope defined the doctrine of our Lady's assumption into heaven. Meanwhile, there was a strong demand for a further definition of Mary as mediatrix of all graces.

On the other hand, this great movement stood somewhat apart from most of those which were preparing the 'renewal' of Catholic theology, piety and practice. These movements were on the whole seeking their inspiration on the one hand from a return to patristic and, still more, to biblical Christianity; and on the other hand were reaching out towards cooperation with similar movements in non-Catholic Christian bodies – this is obviously true of the ecumenical movement; but most of the others had an 'ecumenical' dimension. The Marian movement, however, could hardly claim to be ecumenical at all. For Protestantism, the place of Mary in Catholic belief and devotion was a chronic stumbling-block. Much the same was true of Anglicanism; Newman's long hesitation,

[16] Cf. R. Laurentin, *Mary's Place in the Church* (the French original is entitled *La Question Mariale*). The author of this book is an outstanding authority, and had great influence in conciliar circles, above all from the moment when it was decided to treat of our Lady within the limits of the constitution *De Ecclesia*. Reference may be made also to his earlier *Court Traité de théologie mariale*.

[17] For the figures, cf. Laurentin, *Mary's Place in the Church*, pp. 9–11.

as in other respects he drew nearer to Roman Catholicism, will be remembered. Anglican theologians were especially disconcerted by the definitions of the immaculate conception (1854) and of the assumption. As regards eastern Orthodoxy, while it was true that its devotion to the Mother of God was most impressive and deeply embedded in its tradition, its theological approach was very different from that of the Latin Church, and it had no love for the two modern definitions. And if the Marian movement was not ecumenical, it was also not strongly marked by a desire to 'return to the sources'. On the contrary, it was ever looking forwards, seeking to build on its most recent triumphs as uncriticisable bases for some still loftier exaltation of Mary, uncontrolled by serious regard for earlier tradition.

The Marian movement presented the second Vatican Council with a serious, indeed an agonising, problem and dilemma, and it threatened to split the council along a different line of demarcation from the usual one between 'conservatives' and 'progressives'. On the one hand, if there is any meaning in the notions of *charismata* as a dynamic element in the Church, and of the *sensus fidei* as a guide to the real content of the Sacred Tradition, the movement was a phenomenon which could not be overlooked by theology or by practical prudence. On the other hand, many theologians and most ecumenists were gravely anxious about a development which seemed to be heading off at a tangent and endangering the very possibility of fruitful dialogue with non-Catholics.

An abortive attempt to submit a draft document on our Lady 'Mother of God and Mother of men' took place in the council near the end of the first session. In the course of the second session (1963) an idea, already mooted before the council opened, began to exert its influence: Why not include the subject of our Lady in the constitution on the Church? The proposal was submitted to a vote, and was passed by the narrowest of all conciliar majorities (forty votes out of 2,188). This very closely contested decision was of the greatest importance. It ensured that Marian theology would not be viewed in isolation from the general corpus of renewed Catholic theology, but would take its place within the wider and controlling perspectives of a theology of the Church as the 'sacrament of salvation'. It also meant that the document prepared on this subject before the council opened would be revised to make it a coherent and organic part of the great Constitution on the Church. Such revision would mean, incidentally, that the resultant chapter would benefit by the theological insights that were becoming more and more dominant as the council progressed. This is not the place to recount the painful process of gestation of this chapter, but a few words about the theology of the chapter itself will be relevant to our theme.

The chapter is entitled: the Blessed Virgin Mary Mother of God in the Mystery of Christ and of the Church. 'Mother of God' here renders the late Latin word *deipara*, a translation of the Greek *theotokos*. The title *theotokos* was already in use to designate our Lady in the early years of the fifth century, when it was challenged by Nestorius. It was sanctioned by the ensuing ecumenical Council of Ephesus (A.D. 431), one of the four ecumenical councils appealed to in early Anglican documents, and one of the seven recognised by eastern Orthodoxy. The title was viewed by the Council of Ephesus primarily in its Christological implication: the son of Mary was not just a man uniquely indwelt by God the Son; he *was* God the Son incarnate. The Marian repercussions of the title, however, were and are obvious. It became a powerful influence in the growth of Christian devotion to our Lady, and has always remained at the heart of eastern Orthodox piety. Similarly in the Constitution on the Church it controls the development of the chapter on our Lady and ensures that its Mariology will be deeply rooted alike in tradition and in the basic themes of general theology.

In the *proëm* of this chapter the council states its theme: Mary is 'a supereminent and most unique member of the Church and the Church's type and exemplar; the Church, taught by the Holy Spirit, honours her with a sense of filial piety as a most loving mother' (n. 53). The description here of Mary as a member, though unique, of the Church is deliberate and important. It has been observed that there are two alternative emphases in the Christian attitude to our Lady, as in the Catholic attitude to the Pope. The Pope can be seen either as 'in' the Church (on earth) or as 'above' her. Similarly, our Lady can be seen either as 'in' the whole Church or as 'above' it. There is truth in both attitudes. The danger of the 'transcendent' emphasis is that its object will become, for theology, as it were detached from the total corpus of *le fait chrétien*. The constitution lays its emphasis on our Lady's inherence in the Church. It was partly for this reason that it avoided a direct designation of her as 'the Mother of the Church',[18] preferring to reverse the turn of phrase and say that the Catholic Church, taught by the Holy Spirit, 'pays homage to her with filial affection, as to a most loving Mother'. The *proëm* adds that the council does not intend to set forth 'a complete doctrine concerning Mary', nor to settle theological questions not yet fully elucidated. 'Hence nothing here puts out of court opinions which are freely propounded in the Catholic schools of theology about her who holds in the holy Church a position which is at once the highest after Christ and the closest to us' (n. 54). Among the disputed questions thus referred to must be reckoned the theological explanation of our Lady's mediatorial position and of her share in her Son's redemptive work. It must be admitted that, while both these truths have the support of venerable tradition (already St Irenaeus viewed Mary as her Son's co-operator in his redemptive work), modern Mariologists have entered into subtleties of explanation of them which many find rather unhelpful to their devotional life.

The council avoids the term 'co-redemptrix', but states that Mary in conceiving, bearing and nourishing Christ, in presenting him to the Father in the temple, and in her compassion with him as he was dying on the cross, co-operated uniquely with the Saviour's work, by obedience, faith, hope and ardent charity, for the restoration of the supernatural life of souls. This statement should be evaluated along with that of the preceding paragraph, which affirms that our only mediator is Christ, and that all the Blessed Virgin's influence on men arises not from any necessity but from the divine good pleasure, and flows from the superabundance of the merits of

[18] Subsequently the Pope, in a public session of the council, himself, *motu proprio*, assigned this title to our Lady. He immediately gave his own exegesis of it: she is the Mother of God's People, that is of all the faithful – a subtle substitution of a numerical aggregate for an organic unity, of which unity Mary, of course, is a *member*.

Christ. It depends utterly on that mediation and draws from it all its power. We infer that her co-operation with him in his passion was itself not a complementary but a dependent factor in our redemption.

The modern title of our Lady, Mediatrix, is mentioned in the constitution, though without the addition 'of all graces': 'The Blessed Virgin is invoked in the Church under the titles of Advocate, Help, Adiutrix, Mediatrix' (n. 62). But at once an explanation is appended: 'Such invocation is understood in no way to subtract from or add to the dignity and efficaciousness of Christ the one mediator. No creature can be reckoned alongside the incarnate Word, the redeemer; but as Christ's priesthood is in various ways shared in by both ministers and the believing people, and as the one goodness of God is really diffused in various ways among creatures, so also the redeemer's unique mediation does not exclude but gives rise to a varied co-operation among creatures, all springing from that one source' (n. 62).

There was strong opposition in the council to any mention of the Marian title of Mediatrix. Ecumenists held that it would constitute a difficulty for the ecumenical dialogue. It was also feared that the simple faithful, less accustomed than theologians to reflect upon and understand the notion of participated values, might be led to think of the Mediatrix as in some sense on the same level as Christ the mediator. On the other side it was felt that the doctrine had become so traditional, and had received such official approbation from recent Popes, that to omit or obscure it would amount to a treason. The constitution steers a middle course which was not entirely to the liking of either group in the council. It mentions, as we have seen, the *title* Mediatrix but mentions it alongside other less controversial titles, and at once seeks to avoid any interpretation which would derogate from the unicity of Christ. The explanation offered is indeed, from the Catholic point of view, unexceptionable. As the first Epistle to Timothy says that there is one mediator, so – and in the same sentence – it says that there is one God. And the Gospels tell us that 'none is good save God'. Yet we do, in fact, admit that by creation and again by grace there is in creatures a participated goodness, limited, derived, and entirely dependent on God's goodness, just as we admit that creatures have a being which is participated from the unique being of God. More particularly, Catholic doctrine teaches that the goodness of acts of virtue (e.g. of faith) is a real, creaturely, but derived goodness. And we believe that we can really help one another on our road to God, and thus, dependently on God and his grace, co-operate with our redeemer towards one another's salvation. Fundamental objection to this teaching of the constitution about our Lady can only come from those who hold that man's justification is *only* imputed and not really participated; and discussion between holders of this view and Catholics must obviously range over a far wider field than any particular title accorded by the latter to our Lady.

The constitution is careful to mention explicitly the chief points of defined Marian doctrine: not only the *theotokos* but the immaculate conception and the assumption. But it chooses to present her to the faithful mainly in her biblical rôle, within the context of the history of salvation. Her unique contribution to this history, as 'the daughter of Sion' whose consent to Gabriel's message gave us our redeemer, is continued by her intercession for us in heaven. Both in her life on earth, where her humble and obedient faith gave birth to Christ, and in her heavenly glory, she is the type and example of the Church as our spiritual mother and as predestined to a like glory in the world to come. She is the model of Christian holiness in her own devotion to her Son and his work, and is an object of the devotion of the Church and its members, which, however, is essentially different from the worship which can only be paid to God. The tendency of all genuinely Christian devotion to her is to lead us on to know, love, glorify and obey her Son (n. 66). She has indeed a mediatorial rôle; it in no way hinders but rather promotes 'the immediate union of believers with Christ' (n. 60).[19] The council ratifies in principle such devotion to Mary, while warning preachers and theologians against both excess and defects in this sphere, and

[19] This point needed to be made. A common criticism, whether justified or not, of some 'Marian piety' is that it tends to interpose Mary between the Christian and his Saviour. A similar charge has been made against the Catholic priesthood, despite the Church's full acceptance of St Augustine's doctrine that, whoever may serve as the human instrument of the sacraments, the real agent is always Christ himself.

against anything that could convey a false impression of the Church's real doctrine concerning the Mother of God. True devotion is such as leads the believer to an imitation of Mary's virtues.

4

The Church's Ministry

The first chapter of the Constitution on the Church affirmed that the Church was a mystery to which actuality on earth was given in a visible entity, a society endowed with hierarchical organs. The Church is neither merely a mystery, nor merely an earthly institution. She is a single complex reality in which both these aspects can be discerned; and she 'subsists in the Catholic Church, governed by the successor of Peter and the bishops in communion with him' (n. 8).

The third chapter takes as its principle subject 'the hierarchical constitution of the Church', and treats of it in the light of the first Vatican Council's findings on the primacy of the Roman Pontiff and his infallible teaching authority.

Towards the end of the Middle Ages the Great Western Schism and the mode of its termination gravely injured the papacy's prestige and raised issues which, while not altogether new, had slept for centuries. What, in fact, was the relationship between papal authority and the authority of the whole body of the bishops, especially when they found themselves in ecumenical council? Faced with the claims of rival pretenders to the See of Rome, the Church had turned to conciliar action for the solution of its difficulties, and it became for many a disputable question whether the ultimate seat of authority was the papacy or an ecumenical council. The ecumenical Council of Constance (A.D. 1415) claimed to have 'immediate power from Christ, which every state and dignity, even if it be the papal dignity, must obey in what concerns faith, the eradication of the schism and the reformation of the Church'.[1] The implied claim of a certain superiority of council over Pope is thus expounded by Hans Küng: 'What was *defined* was a distinct kind of superiority of the council . . . according to which an ecumenical council has the function of a "control authority", not only in connection with the emergency situation of that time but also for the future, on the premise that a possible future Pope might again lapse into heresy, schism, or the like'.

The papacy, of course, survived the troubles of the Schism, but despite attempts by its apologists to deny the authority of the Council of Constance so far as it related to the above pronouncement, the question of the seat of ultimate authority in the Church was kept alive by Gallicanism till, in the years preceding Vatican I, a neo-Ultramontane movement began to press for a final – and extreme – settlement of the issue in favour of the papacy. In 1870, after intense debate in which a substantial minority remained unconvinced of the opportuneness of such a settlement, the council reached its famous decisions on both the primacy and the infallibility of the Pope. The council, at least as regards papal infallibility, did not go all the way with the neo-Ultramontane extremists, but its findings are determinative for Catholic faith and theology. They were achieved in the mental atmosphere of an age when jurisdiction was in the ascendant. And it is of the greatest historical importance that this victory of papalism was not accompanied by any correspondingly full and authoritative statement of the powers and inherent functions of the universal episcopate. For almost a century the Roman curia found itself in a position, by appeal to this settlement, to consolidate and intensify the centralising tendencies which are an almost inevitable expression of the papal primacy, but which need – as many theologians were aware – the balancing influence of an articulate theory of the episcopate. Among the fruits of Vatican I we may count the fact that the Modernist crisis of the first decade of the present century was overcome by Rome

[1] H. Küng, *Structures of the Church*, p. 241. The quotation that follows in our text is from the same book, p. 255.

almost single-handed; and again that the issue of contraception was dealt with by Pius XI in an encyclical (*Casti Connubii*, 1931) which was received without protest by the body of the bishops – who exercised their own *magisterium*, if at all, in this matter by relaying the papal decisions.

The practical advantages of such centralisation are obvious, as is its accordance with a general tendency of the age in both politics and economies. But even in the practical field it involved some dangers. The central administration of a vast international body can become overburdened, with a consequent lack of efficiency. And the life of the Church at large can lose vigour through the discouragement of local and personal initiative and through limitations on freedom of question, criticism, and experiment. There was further a tendency to treat all that issued from the curia as if it came immediately from the Pope, and to overlook the gradations of authority in papal pronouncements.[2] Theologically, it was always possible to attempt to explain the contrast between a virtually monarchical modern Catholicism and the records of the Christian past by appeal to the principle of the development of doctrine and practice. But too little attention may be paid to the fact that a development, even when true and prudent in itself might be utilised to drive from view other elements of tradition, even of the Sacred Tradition. It has been pointed out[3] that 'it often happens that deeply traditional attitudes remain for a long period consigned to the common Christian conscience of the Church without becoming the objects of particular study' – and this can occur, not only 'just because of their traditional character and universal acceptance' but because of the disfavour of a dominant theological or governmental group. 'Ecclesiology has often developed according to the pressure of circumstances rather than according to a substantial hierarchy of absolute values.'

By 1962 there was a growing sense among theologians that some complementation of Vatican I's papalism was overdue.

[2] Cf. R. Laurentin, *Mary's Place in the Church*, pp. 94–100, e.g. 'The authority of the magisterium is not so monolithic and does not speak with so single a voice as our desire for simplification and clean lines would lead some into thinking' (p. 95).

[3] These quotations are from G. Alberigo, *Lo Sviluppo della Dottrina sui Poteri nella Chiesa Universale*, p. 8.

Its ecumenical importance and even urgency needs no proof, but may be illustrated by some words of Dr Michael Ramsey, who was then Archbishop of Canterbury; they are taken from the second edition of his work *The Gospel and the Catholic Church* (1950), p. 172, and refer to the papal teaching of Vatican I: 'The climax of papal supremacy marks the climax of the distortion of genuine Catholic order. For the unity of the one race there has been substituted the governmental unity of the Roman See with the unchurching of those who do not submit to it. For the authority of the one body there has been substituted the external authority of the ruler "ex cathedra". The institutional has triumphed over the organic, and the institution represents something narrower than the body of Christ.' The same scholar writes, in an appendix to this book: 'It was stated in Chapter V that a papacy which acted as an organ of the Church's general consciousness and authority in doctrine, and which focussed the unity of the one Episcopate might claim to fulfil the tests of a true development. . . . A primacy should depend upon and express the organic authority of the body; and the discovery of its precise functions will come not by discussion of the Petrine claims in isolation but by the recovery everywhere of the body's organic life, with its bishops, presbyters and people.' In this body Peter will find his true place.[4]

Ecumenical considerations, however, were not alone in prompting a re-examination of the divinely established hierarchical structure of the Church. Some Catholics of the eastern rites, though not all of them, were alienated in sentiment from the practical papalism of the Roman curia. Historians of Church and of doctrine were aware that Vatican I had not fully expressed the tradition. And as the council drew near there was a widespread hope, if not expectation, that its works might include an attempt to restore doctrinal balance, rather

[4] He also quotes B. J. Kidd's conclusion that, without communion with the bishop of Rome, 'there is no prospect of a reunited Christendom' (*ibid.*, p. 228). Professor E. L. Mascall, an eminent Anglo-Catholic theologian, agrees with Dr Ramsey's criticism of the papacy as it existed from 1870 till 1962, and adds that under these conditions 'the Pope is in effect not a member of the Church at all, but an external authority to which the Church is subjected' (*The Recovery of Unity*, p. 210).

as the Council of Chalcedon had counterbalanced the results of the Council of Ephesus.

It may be pointed out that one of the arguments used at Vatican I to recommend the doctrine of the papal primacy was that it rested on the same foundation (Christ's words in the Gospels) as did the 'full power' of the bishops 'gathered together along with their head'. In other words: we all admit the full authority of the episcopal college, finding authority for this belief in the words of Christ. We cannot withhold acceptance of a similar belief in the supreme authority of the successor of Peter, which has the same warranty.[5] But once the primacy had been defined, it was easy, if not to 'despise the base rungs' by which it had climbed to recognition, at least to let them fall away from attention and to concentrate on the theological, canonical and administrative conclusions that could be drawn from the definition. Meanwhile, there must have been more than one professor in the world of the seminaries, as there began to be a growing number of writers, who had not forgotten that the papal primacy needs to be seen within a wider context of ecclesiology and who felt that neo-Ultramontanism, deprived of its victory in the Vatican Council, was being translated nevertheless into the Church's practical life and into the systematisations of the lawyers.[6] It was one of Vatican II's little ironies that those who opposed the doctrine of a genuine collegiality were regarded as conservatives and champions of tradition, and their adversaries as progressives, not to say radicals.

Chapter III of *Lumen Gentium*, presupposing the teaching of Chapter I that the Church of God has a real concrete embodiment on earth and that, thus embodied, she 'subsists in the Catholic Church', begins by laying it down that 'for the direction and increase of God's people, Christ has instituted

[5] Cf. Alberigo, *op. cit.*, pp. 438f., expounding and quoting Zinelli, the 'relator' for the crucial third chapter of the constitution *Pastor aeternus*, in which the doctrine of the papal primacy is expounded.

[6] Cf. Alberigo, *op. cit.*, p. 448, quoting Palmieri's theory of the powers of the bishops in ecumenical council: 'the power of legislating for the universal Church comes to the bishops neither from themselves nor immediately from God; it can only be theirs immediately as given by the Roman pontiff in summoning the council'. This opinion Alberigo stigmatises as 'wholly strange to tradition'.

various ministries in his Church, which tend to the good of the whole Body' (n. 18).[7] The constitution then reiterates Vatican I's teaching on the primacy and infallible teaching-office of the Pope and states its intention to 'profess and declare' the doctrine about the bishops, the successors of the apostles, 'who along with Peter's successor, Christ's vicar and the visible head of the whole Church, rule the house of the living God'. Two points may be mentioned here. The Pope is here described as the *visible* head of the Church; this safeguards the constitution's own doctrine that the Church's head, in an unqualified sense, is none other than Christ himself. Secondly, it may be observed once for all that the constitution sometimes finds difficulty in expressing simultaneously the facts that the Pope is himself a bishop and that he has a unique rôle among the bishops – as Peter was an apostle yet had a unique rôle among the apostles. So in our passage its mention of 'the bishops along with Christ's vicar' does not imply that the latter is not a bishop, or that 'the bishops' as a college can be conceived as a unit excluding him.

The constitution now passes in review the accepted Catholic belief about Christ's institution of the apostles with Peter at their head, the apostles' institution of assistants in their ministry, and their concern for the perpetuation of the ministry after their own death. For the last point, it utilises words of Clement of Rome: 'They established such men and thereafter instructed them that, when they should have died, other approved men should take over their ministry.' Thus from the first the Church was provided with a continuing ministry whose origin was Christ's own institution of the apostles, and this ministry, exercised from earliest times in the Church, included especially those who held the episcopate. 'Thus, as St Irenaeus testifies, through those who were established bishops by the apostles, and through their successors, the apostolic

[7] The reason for such 'ministries' is not here more explicitly probed, but a little lower down the constitution quotes from Vatican I that council's reason for the institution of a head of the episcopal ministry itself: '*In order that the Episcopate might be one and undivided*' Christ instituted in Peter 'a perpetual principle of unity' (Denz. 3051). In other words, a universal episcopate with no structural principle of coherence would be irremediably centrifugal. We may, by analogy, say that a universal Church without a ministry of hierarchy would not cohere as a body but be a mere sum of individuals.

tradition is manifested and guarded' (n. 20). The bishops have presbyters and deacons to help them in their task. They are teachers of doctrine, priests of sacred worship, and ministers of government; and, in fact, they inherit the pastoral rôle of the apostles.

In this brief review of accepted doctrine, the salient points are three. 1. The apostles are said to have been instituted 'in the fashion of a college or a stable group'; they are not seen as just twelve individuals, but as a social unity made up of the twelve. This is an important element in the argument of this part of our chapter. It is based on such scriptural considerations as, that the original apostles are entitled, in the gospels, not only 'the twelve apostles' but 'the Twelve'; that the number seems to have had a reference to the twelve tribes of the one People of God or their twelve patriarchs; and that in the opening of Acts there is shown a concern for replenishing this number after the defection of Judas Iscariot. 2. The council expresses itself very cautiously about the immediate sub-apostolic period of Church history. It is well known that the early history of the episcopate is shrouded in a good deal of obscurity, although by the end of the second Christian century it seems to have taken almost universally the non-episcopal form with which we are familiar. The council only affirms an historical and theological continuity between New Testament times and that later, clearer period and its belief that this continuity is due to an apostolic intention. 3. It would seem consistent with the Council's presentation of its view of Christian history to say that 'apostolic succession', to use a well-worn term, is a matter of the bishops in general succeeding to the apostles considered as a body, rather than of twelve individual apostles being succeeded, through individual transmission of powers, by three thousand individual bishops.[8]

Against this fairly familiar background the constitution now proceeds to make two affirmations which at first sight may seem to have little connection with each other, but which,

[8] It may be useful to remark that the council had no wish to deny that the apostles had one or more functions which were not transmissible. They were, for instance, accredited 'eyewitnesses' of Christ. The Church today depends not on the eyewitness of the contemporary bishops but on that of the original twelve.

taken together, can be said to present a single core of teaching of immense importance.

Traditionally, bishops have been viewed as at once priests, teachers and rulers. It is commonly accepted that their priestly powers derive immediately from the sacrament of order. But there has been a long-continuing view in the Western Church that their powers of teaching and especially of ruling are derived from the Pope, although their episcopal consecration was sometimes regarded as giving them an 'aptitude' or passive potentiality to receive such powers. Along with this view went a theory that the sacrament of order is seen in, so to speak, its typical state in the ordination of presbyters; episcopal consecration being variously explained as a sort of addition to what was already present in the presbyteral priesthood. This western tradition stems, it would seem, from St Jerome and could boast of the support of St Thomas Aquinas. It was contradicted by early liturgical evidence and by the constant tradition of the East, and had come under heavy fire before the opening of Vatican II. The council excludes it formally: 'The Sacred Synod teaches that episcopal consecration confers the fullness of the sacrament of Order, which fullness is called by liturgical tradition and by the holy Fathers the high priesthood, the sum-total of sacred ministry. Episcopal consecration confers, along with the task of sanctifying, also the tasks of teaching and ruling; but these by their nature can be exercised only in hierarchical communion with the head and members of the College.' It can hardly be doubted that by this clear affirmation, the council linked itself with the profound tradition of the Church and took its stand firmly against an aberrant western theology of Holy Orders.[9]

This immensely important paragraph ends with the brief statement, appended without connecting particle, that 'It is the task of bishops to adopt by the sacrament of Order new chosen men into the episcopal college'. This sentence is a mere

[9] There were probably those in the council who would have held that this teaching on episcopal consecration was apt for formal definition. It should, however, be observed that the constitution avoids here the word 'defines'; that no anathema is attached to a contradiction of the doctrine propounded; and that a proposal to say not simply 'teaches' but 'solemnly teaches' was discarded. Nevertheless the council's language is deliberate and categoric, and relates to a matter which was of central concern to its members.

statement of fact, and especially of current practice. Among the obscurer points in the early history of the episcopate is a story relayed by St Jerome, that in early days the presbyters of Alexandria used to choose and appoint from among themselves when a vacancy occurred in the local episcopal chair.

The next section (n. 22) of the constitution proceeds to state that as, by Christ's ordinance, Peter and the other apostles make up a single apostolic college,[10] similarly (*pari ratione*) Peter's successor and the bishops, the successors of the apostles, are connected. Historical evidence is then adduced for the ancient Church's conviction that the episcopate forms an *ordo* and has a collegial structure (*rationem*). And it is affirmed that a man is constituted a member of the episcopal college 'in virtue of his sacramental consecration and by hierarchical communion with the head and members of the College'.

Thus there exists in the Church a body, order, or college which is at least analogous[11] to the apostolic college instituted by Christ himself. Has this body as such, of men, each of whom has received in his episcopal consecration the tasks of teaching and ruling, a corporate authority in the Church? The question

[10] Objection was made against this word on the grounds that in legal usage a college consists of a group of persons with strictly equal powers; but the bishops include in their ranks one (the bishop of Rome) who, as successor of Peter, has powers exceeding those of his fellows. The doctrinal commission took account of this objection by varying its terminology, sometimes speaking of 'college', sometimes of *ordo* or group (*coetus*). By using the word 'college' the council intends to signify that the bishops are more than a mere number of individuals; they constitute a moral unity, a body, of which each bishop taken singly, can be described as a representative. St Cyprian (Ep. xlviii, 3) speaks of the other bishops (in writing to Cornelius of Rome) as *universi collegae nostri*. He declares that all the bishops 'feed one flock' – not several flocks; and urges that they must insist on the oneness of the Church so as to demonstrate that the episcopal power is one and undivided, too. 'The authority of the bishops forms a unity, of which each holds his part in its totality' (*De Unitate Catholicae Ecclesiae*, 4, transl. Bévenot; the Latin is: *episcopatus unus est cuius a singulis in solidum pars tenetur*. The exact meaning is disputed; but there is no doubt that Cyprian held that the 'concord' and communicating unity of the bishops was basic to the unity of the Church).

[11] This analogy is expressed in the text of the constitution by the phrase *pari ratione*. The phrase *eadem ratione* or its equivalent was avoided. As already pointed out, the scope of the rôle of the apostles exceeded that of the rôle of their successors, and this may be considered to give rise to a difference between the apostolic college and the episcopal college. But there is certainly a real continuity between the two; see below.

is answered in the next paragraph, after a possible misconception has been excluded. It is first stated that no question of such authority for the episcopal college can arise unless it is borne in mind that the college includes within it 'the Roman pontiff, Peter's successor, the head of the college, whose power of primacy in regard to all, both faithful and pastors, remains intact' (n. 22). The framers of this paragraph were very conscious that the doctrine which was about to be propounded, however genuinely traditional, would strike many Catholics as novel and might be taken as in some way contradicting the decisions of Vatican I. Hence the rather wearisome reiterations of the truth of the papal primacy. Nevertheless, the paragraph now goes on to take that primacy as a paradigm for the authority of the apostolic college:

> The Roman pontiff has, in relation to the Church, by virtue of his rôle as vicar of Christ and pastor of the whole Church, full supreme and universal power, which he can[12] always freely exert. But the order of bishops, which succeeds to the college of the apostles in teaching authority and pastoral rule, in which in fact the apostolic body continually exists, is – along with its head the Roman pontiff and never without this head – also a subject[13] of supreme and full power in relation to[14] the universal Church, though this power can never be exercised save with the consent of the Roman pontiff.

The constitution goes on to remark that the apostolic-episcopal college as composed of many members, expresses 'the variety and universality of God's people', while the same college, as concentrated under one head, expresses 'the oneness of Christ's flock'. The college's supreme authority is exerted in ecumenical

[12] The word translated 'can' is *valet*. It appears to mean that when the Pope so acts his action is 'valid'. It does not, in that case, imply that the Pope is morally justified in acting without due consultation.

[13] To be a 'subject' of power, in Latin usage, is to be the agent in possession of such power. Those whom we in English call 'subjects' are, in Latin usage, the 'objects' of the exercise of power or authority.

[14] The words here (and above) translated 'in relation to the (universal) Church' are *in (universam) ecclesiam*. A proposal was made that, in the former case, this phrase should be rewritten *in universa ecclesia*. The reason for the suggestion was a fear that, by using the accusative case, the council might seem to be viewing the Pope as above and outside the Church, and his authority therefore as something external, to which the Church is subjected. The difficulty loses much of its weight when it is observed that the accusative case is also used when the authority of the episcopal college is being affirmed. It may also be pointed out that *in ecclesiam* is less objectionable than *supra ecclesiam* would have been.

councils, but can also be exercised 'by the bishops living throughout the world' – that is without the convocation of an ecumenical council – provided the Pope either invites, or at least approves or freely accepts, their collegial action.

The first point calling for comment in this important paragraph is that here we are not only told that the episcopal college is analogous to the apostolic college, nor only that it succeeds to it: it is affirmed that the apostolic college survives in it. We are here taught that the college is substantially identical in both its original apostolic and its subsequent episcopal phases. The structural character of the Church, as established by Christ, has been one throughout.

Secondly, a word should be said about the rôle of the Pope in the college. It is unique, inasmuch as the college cannot be 'conceived' as existing apart from its head, the Pope; and inasmuch as no collegial act can exist unless it includes within its motivation the Pope's free consent – this is not true as regards the consent of any other member of the college, which has to seek not literal, but at the most 'moral', unanimity.[15]

[15] A question of considerable theoretical interest may here be raised: What is the condition of the Church between the abdication, or death, of one Pope and the election of his successor? If the college is 'inconceivable' without its head, where is authority in the Church when there is no head of the college? I think it may be true to say that the council did not mean to settle this question, and that, when it denies that the college has any reality apart from its head, it is considering only a normal situation in which there is a living, functioning, and sane Pope. It is concerned to exclude the possibility of a conflict of authority between Pope and college. This danger does not arise if there is no Pope. *Sede vacante*, the authority of the defunct Pope presumably lapses, and along with it the authority of those who have enjoyed delegated authority from him. Where else, except in the – now temporarily headless – episcopal college can a living authority covering the universal Church be found? It seems possible to hold, despite the superficial tenor of the council's words, that the college and its authority survives the *demise* of the Pope, though in an abnormal form which calls urgently for normalisation by the lawful election of a new bishop of Rome.

It seems theologically obvious that, *sede vacante*, the college of cardinals, which is not of divine but human foundation, has no intrinsic authority *per se*. I would suggest that its surviving authority in fact derives from the implicit assent, and indeed delegation, of the episcopal college.

[This note requires correction. When the college of cardinals is examined in theological depth interesting ecclesiological principles are brought into evidence. Reference may be made to *Romano Pontifici Eligendo*, 1 October 1975, in which Paul VI reformed the process of the election of Popes (*Acta Apostolicae Sedis*, November 1975). The Pope here points out that there has been development in the process of papal elections, though 'the chief originally

There is no hint in the constitution that the powers of the college are derived from the Pope. On the contrary, there is reason to think that they derive from the sacrament of Order. As we have seen, the council, in the immediately previous section of this chapter, has already stated that the individual bishop's rôle of teaching and governance is so given. The present section, in turn, states that it is in virtue of his consecration and by hierarchical communion with the college's head and members that a man becomes a member of the col-

---

established elements of episcopal election have been preserved'. The implication is that the election of a Pope is fundamentally the election of a bishop of the local diocese (the *local* church) of the city of Rome. It is inasmuch as a man is the legitimate bishop of the diocese of Rome that he is also the centre of Catholic unity and the supreme pastor of the Church.

In early Christian times there was a tendency to see a bishop as intrinsically related to his diocese, his local church: *episcopus in ecclesia, ecclesia in episcopo*. A bishop without the local church of which he was the pastor was hardly conceivable (though the eastern practice of appointing *chorepiscopi*, rural bishops, who seem to have had functions similar to that of auxiliary area bishops in some English dioceses at the present time, was a step away from the primitive idea). Today the Eastern churches have preserved the ancient conception in practice to a very large extent, while in the Latin Rite a profusion of titular and auxiliary bishops (not to speak of John XXIII's innovation by which all Cardinals are consecrated bishops) has made the old idea seem old-fashioned and obsolete.

When in the early times a bishop died it fell to his own local church to choose his successor. This held for the church of the city of Rome, as for all other churches. The electoral body would, one may suppose, normally have been the presbyters of that local church. Today the Cardinals, in strict theory, are, along with the Pope, the 'three major orders' of the church of the city of Rome; three, because the sway of the bishop of Rome over the churches of his immediate locality (the suburbicarian sees) was such that, for many practical purposes, they had come to be, as it were, chorepiscopi of the Roman bishop. It follows that, since the election of a new Pope is, more basically, the election of a new bishop of the Roman diocese, it is quite proper that his election should be made by the 'college' of Cardinals.

When, however, one is thinking in juridical terms the question arises: what *locus standi* has the diocesan presbyterate during an interregnum? Juridically, the authority of a diocesan presbyterate is a participation (by implicit delegation, I think) in the authority of the bishop. But can a bishop's authority survive his own demise? (Once or twice in the past, Popes have tried to designate their own successors; such attempts have been resisted and have failed.) One may surmise that authority in such a widowed diocese is implicitly derived from the world-wide episcopate with which the local church remains in communion even during an interregnum. If so, then the substance of the thought in this note as it stood in the first edition of this book remains true, but I was mistaken in affirming that the college of cardinals is of (merely) human foundation.]

lege. And it is implied that the authority of the apostolic college, of which the episcopal college is a continuation, was itself not derived from Peter but given immediately by Christ. The college's authority, we infer, is something primordial and essential in the visible Church, while it finds its point of unification in the Pope, and its exercise is subject to the Pope's consent. The episcopal college, then, is not, fundamentally, a reality of the juridical order but of the sacramental order. Juridical consequences flow from the sacramental nature of the Church and its ministry, but the sacramental order retains its ontological priority.[16]

Objection may be made against the importance and value of the council's teaching on the episcopal college that, in the end, the 'last word' still remains with the Pope. Not only can he 'always freely exercise' his own authority, which is supreme over the whole Church including its pastors; but the college can never exercise its collegial powers without his free concurrence. The objection is true, but it invites us to reflection upon the deepest nature of the Christian religion. The objection is true in the *legal* order. A visible society, if it is to function as such, cannot dispense with law. Nor, *sub specie legis*, can it dispense with an ultimate court of appeal. The British governmental system, in practice, tends towards real democracy; and though we have a monarchy we claim that it is a constitutional monarchy. Yet, without the freely given signature of the personal sovereign, or without the signatures of those freely delegated by the sovereign, no Parliamentary bill has the force of law; nor does it, without such signature,

[16] The constitution affirms that the sacramentally given episcopal functions (*munera*) of teaching and ruling 'can by their nature only be exercised in hierarchical communion with the head and members of the college' (n. 21). Here and elsewhere in this chapter the term 'hierarchical communion' is a substitution for the simple word 'communion' which had been previously proposed. The substitution was made in order to allay the fears of some council fathers, to whom 'communion' seemed too indefinite a term. But, in fact, as the doctrinal commission was aware, the ancient idea of 'communion' implied harmonisation with the Church as a structurally organised body. The phrase 'by their nature' in the above quotation may be taken to suggest that the sacrament of Order is intrinsically and ontologically 'ordered' towards the episcopal college (including its head); somewhat as the sacrament of baptism is intrinsically ordered towards membership of the visible Church.

become an Act of Parliament.[17] But neither the British people nor the People of God derives its life from its constitutional and legal system. Political systems, when they are not sustained, below the legal level, by a measure of goodwill and consent in the members of the political society, either disintegrate or become tyrannies and lose their moral claim to the obedience and co-operation of the citizens. Something similar is true of the Church, provided it be borne in mind that the Church's basic 'political' structure is of divine institution, and that the minimal conditions for the survival of the Church are guaranteed by divine promise. The life-blood of the Church is not its legal structure but the *concordia*, the grace-inspired will of its members to sustain their several rôles in the world-wide communion of charity. The virtue of *concordia* (in Greek, *homonoea*) is one which not only the Church at large, but in a special way the episcopal college, and more particularly the head of the college, is called upon to exercise both in general and especially in the exercise of legal 'rights'. But precisely because 'the love of the brotherhood', concord, or Christian charity is not derived from, but rather gives rise to, law, there can be no precise legal safeguard against legalism.

When the Constitution on the Church comes to speak about the doctrinal authority of the Pope or the episcopal college, it points out (n. 25) that this teaching is given according to revelation, which – by divinely guaranteed transmission – 'is holily preserved and faithfully expounded' in the Church. Tradition is not a private source-book in the keeping of the magisterium; it is the common inheritance of the whole Church, and the function of the magisterium is to help in its preservation and to declare its contents and implications. In order to do this, the magisterium has to use suitable means to inform itself of the content of tradition (*ibid.*), and this may entail a 'consultation of the faithful'. It will certainly entail the use of such methods of investigation as prudence may dictate. Hence there can be no doubt that a Pope who attempted to define an article of faith without making use of such

[17] Much of the real hostility to the modern papacy derives from the existential (and largely contingent) character of the papacy of modern preconciliar times. There seems no reason *in ordine rerum* why the future development of the existential papacy should not be on lines analogous to the development of

means would commit a grievous sin. But there is no 'legal' sanction by which he can be prevented from committing such a sin – any more than law can compel the British sovereign to sign a parliamentary bill. In the end, the Church lives by conscientious charity rather than by law.

Not all difficulty is removed by these considerations. The Pope, after all, is a man, and men are morally fallible and also liable to insanity. It is not altogether satisfactory to suppose that the normal results of our human imperfection will, in the case of the Pope, regularly be obviated by God's miraculous intervention. *Miracula non sunt multiplicanda praeter necessitatem.* There is good theological support for the view that, in extraordinary circumstances, the Church is not entirely helpless in the power of a wicked (or insane) Pope. It is, indeed, certain in law that 'no one can judge the first see'. But it can be held that, by the sin of heresy or schism, a duly elected Pope would, in fact, cease to be Pope; and that, if such circumstances arose, 'the Church represented through an ecumenical council by human convocation' could declare that 'the first see' was void and take steps for its replenishment.[18] To demand that law should foresee and make provision for every abnormal situation is to relapse into legalism. Those who construct 'arts of poetry' are continually liable to be made ridiculous by the work of some subsequent poet who 'breaks the rules', but indubitably creates poetry.

At least one major, though rather technically theological, question remains to be considered here. Vatican II clearly teaches, echoing Vatican I, that the Pope has supreme universal authority over the Church. It also teaches that the epis-

---

monarchy in England from its autocratic origins to its constitutional adulthood. Such a development would, in fact, bring the papacy into closer harmony with the Roman primacy as it existed in pre-Constantinian times.

[18] H. Küng, *Structures of the Church*, p. 278. The Constitution on the Church, following current canon law, lays it down that it is a prerogative of the Roman pontiff to summon, preside at, and confirm ecumenical councils. This legal prescription must not be pushed too far. In the early Church councils were, in fact, convoked by emperors. The life of God's people does not derive from law, and a procedure which in normal circumstances would be both illegal and schismatical should not be inhibited in extraordinary situations by a law which takes no cognisance of them. As regards a Pope's possible insanity, it should be remarked that only the 'human acts' of a Pope can claim validity. An insane act is not a human act.

copal college (which includes the Pope as its head) has full and supreme authority over the universal Church: 'The order of bishops . . . in which the apostolic body continuously survives, together with its head the Roman pontiff, and never without this head, is also a subject of supreme and full power in relation to the universal Church.' Are we to infer that universal power over the Church is the appanage of two entities, 1. the Pope, 2. the college (including the Pope)? Are there *two* 'subjects of supreme power' in the divine structure of the Church? At first sight, one would be inclined to say yes; and the use of the word 'also' (*quoque*) in the passage cited would seem to confirm this view. There are, however, grave difficulties against it. It would mean that an identical full authority over one single body was held simultaneously by two different moral persons – and it is not at all certain that this is philosophically possible.[19] There are, it may be suggested, no known parallels in the created order. In the Holy Trinity there are three who are 'Lord' over a single universe, but then they are one in nature – which cannot be said of the college and the Pope.

We have already seen that there was a preconciliar theory that the authority of the bishops (in ecumenical council) was a derivation from that of the Pope. But the constitution nowhere appears to favour this solution; the only natural way to interpret it is to say that the power which the bishops exercise collectively as a college is the *munus* which they received, not from the Pope but by their sacramental consecration directly from Christ.

The most satisfactory solution of our difficulty is precisely the reverse of the one just considered. It seems best to say that just as the Pope, when acting in and as head of the college, is lending his (necessary) co-operation to his fellow bishops and thus enabling the college to exercise its intrinsic powers, so, when he is acting personally without 'existential' co-operation of the rest of the college, he is nevertheless acting *for* the

[19] The two Roman consuls each held *imperium*, according to the accepted theory. But either could veto the acts of the other, which prevented logical chaos, though it may not have conduced to practical efficiency. The episcopal college cannot veto the acts of the Pope; and its own decisions always include his consent.

college and as its head. And as the individual bishop represents that 'portion of the Lord's flock' of which he has been given charge (*ecclesia in episcopo et episcopus in ecclesia*, as St Cyprian puts it), and as the bishops in ecumenical council 'represent the entire Church' (Zinelli, speaking in Vatican I), so the Pope, acting as Pope, always 're-presents' the episcopal college and therefore the universal Church.[20] As St Thomas says of the sovereign, *personam gerit communitatis*. The Pope is never to be excluded from the college or order of bishops, nor from the People of God, of which he is a member by baptism and which it is his rôle to serve: *servus servorum Dei*. The truth about the Pope in relation to the apostolic-episcopal college may be summed up in the words of the explanatory note (referred to in the footnote). The college, while always existing, 'only acts – with a strictly collegial action – at intervals, and only "with the consent of its head". The words "with the consent of its head" are used, lest one might think of *dependence* as though on someone *extraneous* to the college; the term "with the consent of" suggests, on the contrary, *communion* between head and members and implies the necessity of an *act* proper to the head'. Thus the note appears to hold

[20] I should therefore take the word *quoque* in the passage cited above as having a literary, not a theological, significance. The section of our constitution dealing with the episcopal college was, in its final form, introduced by the Doctrinal Commission to the council fathers by an 'introductory explanatory note'. The note points out that the college always involves its head, who in the college preserves intact his rôle of vicar of Christ and pastor of the universal Church; 'in other words there is a distinction not between the Roman pontiff and the bishops collectively, but between the Roman pontiff by himself (*seorsim*) and the Roman pontiff together with the bishops'. The terminology here is not altogether happy. In particular, the word *seorsim* conjures up the image of a Pope in lonely isolation. I do not consider that this language, understood in the light of the intention of the context (which is, to exclude any idea of a college existing or acting *without* the Pope), can be used to disprove the thesis that the Pope, even when acting without the formal collaboration of the other bishops, is still acting as their head, mouthpiece, and organ. The next sentence of the note runs: 'Because the chief pontiff is the *head* of the college, he can do certain things alone which the bishops can in no wise do, e.g. summon and direct the college, approve norms of action, etc.' It is interesting that the Pope is here said to be able to perform these special acts not on the basis of some non-collegial authority but precisely 'because he is the head of the college'. It should be added that the text of this 'explanatory note' was never debated or emended in the council; nor was it ever ratified by a conciliar vote. It has, however, great weight, owing to its provenance, and because it was in the light of its explanations that the section on the episcopal college received an overwhelming majority of conciliar votes.

that the Pope, in all that relates to the college, whether as acting within it when it is 'in act', or bringing it into act, is identically both vicar of Christ and head of the college. I simply suggest that the affirmation is convertible: in all his acts as vicar of Christ the Pope acts as head of the college. Theologians will remark the basic rôle played in the thinking underlying this note by the notion of 'communion' (*koinonia*). This term and notion tend, in the documents of Vatican II, to occupy territory which, in recent centuries, has been occupied rather by the more juridical notion of 'society'.

To sum up, the constitution teaches that, as regards his intrinsic powers and status as endowed with the 'fullness' of the ministerial priesthood, a bishop is fully equipped by sacramental consecration. In order to exercise these powers, he must be accepted into the communion of the episcopal college and its head. As a member of this college, he shares its full authority over the universal Church. But just as the individual bishop cannot use his sacramentally given powers except in this communion, so the college cannot use its corporate authority unless its non-papal members are in communion with the Pope.[21]

From the ecumenical point of view, I hope that the second Vatican Council's teaching on the ministry, as primarily a service done not only to God but to the Church, the People of God in its universal fellowship, by a 'college' of bishops in which the apostolic college survives, a college which derives its knowledge of doctrine not from its own private sources of information but from the life of the Sacred Tradition in the whole body of the faithful, will have gone some way towards realising Dr Ramsey's idea of a true development of doctrine. It presents an episcopate, and within that episcopate a papacy, 'which acts as an organ of the Church's general consciousness and authority in doctrine';[22] and this papacy 'focuses the unity

[21] The idea of the bishop of Rome as the necessary centre of communion of the Church is one of the earliest clearly recorded expressions of the doctrine of the papal primacy. It appears in Optatus of Milevis, St Jerome, and the Acts of a Council of Aquileia presided over by St Ambrose – all in the second half of the fourth century.

[22] Cf. the constitution's teaching on the 'infallibility' of the *sensus fidei* 'in credendo' (n. 12). It may be remarked that the application of the notions of *ecclesia docens and ecclesia discens* might profitably be re-examined. It is commonly supposed that the former is materially identical with the bishops,

of the one episcopate'. Something at least has been done to discredit the image of the papacy as exercising 'the external authority of a ruler "ex cathedra" '. And something has been done to restore the balance of the 'institutional' and the 'organic'.[23] Certainly an answer has been made to Döllinger's complaint, quoted by Dr Ramsey: '(By the new Vatican doctrine) the episcopate of the ancient Church is dissolved in its inmost being.' Vatican II has 'restored' the episcopate (in image and practical effect) to an extent which may even prove embarrassing to some who have not received 'the fullness of the ministerial priesthood'. Similarly, if my interpretation of the council's teaching about the Pope is correct, it seems to repudiate the suggestion that he is, for Roman Catholics, 'not a member of the Church at all, but an external authority to which the Church is subjected' (Mascall, quoted above). Dr Mascall 'found no difficulty in accepting' the Catholic views that Christ conferred upon St Peter a primacy over the Church and over his fellow apostles; that this authority was transmissible to his successors; and that his successors are the bishops of Rome (*The Recovery of Unity*, pp. 197, 201). But he held (before Vatican II) that the current Roman claim involved further an assertion that the Petrine-papal primacy means 'the absolute supremacy in governing and teaching the Church which is commonly claimed by popes and expounded by Roman Catholic theologians at the present day'. He quotes Mgr (later Cardinal) Ch. Journet: 'The Church has no power . . . to control the destiny of him who, once validly elected, is no vicar of hers but vicar of Christ . . . No one on earth can touch the Pope' (*The Church of the World Incarnate*, I, p. 425), and proceeds: 'It is, I think, clear that an authority of this kind is something that is different in essence . . . from anything that can be found in the early Church; for we are faced here with the Pope

and the latter with the rest of the Church's membership. It seems possible that, in fact, the whole Church is, under different and correlative aspects, both *docens* and *discens*. That the bishops have a peculiar magisterial rôle as representing the apostolic college cannot be denied. On the other hand, in modern ecumenical councils, including Vatican II, some prelates who were not bishops had not only a consultative but a deliberative vote in doctrinal issues.

[23] Ramsey, *The Gospel and the Catholic Church*, p. 172.

not as the supreme organ or instrument of the Church's authority, but as the possessor of an authority contrasted with and dominant over any other authority that the Church contains' (*The Recovery of Unity*, pp. 205f.). We have, however, been arguing that Vatican II presents the Pope as precisely the supreme organ or instrument of authority, first of the episcopal college, and then more widely of the whole Church, which he 'personifies'. I should, of course, agree with Cardinal Journet that the Pope – like and beyond other bishops, who 'rule particular churches as vicars and legates of Christ', *Lumen Gentium*, n. 26 – is vicar of Christ; but I should not wish, with him, to deny that he is also vicar of the Church. And when the same eminent theologian says: 'No one can touch the Pope', I should again agree with him, but after making a distinction: it is conceivable that one who has been validly elected Pope might subsequently, for instance through heresy or schism or by becoming habitually insane, cease in reality to be Pope; in such a case the Church can 'touch him' to the extent of declaring the primatial see vacant and proceeding to a valid election. The papacy only exists in the communion of the bishop of Rome, in faith and sacraments, with the whole People of God of which he is a member. I have indeed pointed out that, in normal circumstances, there is no legal remedy against a Pope's abuse of his powers. I suggest, however, that – as in the functioning of the British political system – there are remedies in the moral order, and I will now add that situations are conceivable in which it would be the duty of the Church to apply such remedies. Moral control may be more valuable than legal control. And when I am told by Dr Mascall that I am committed to 'unquestioning obedience' to the Pope (*op. cit.*, p. 209), I reply with Newman: 'Conscience first.'[24]

[24] It remains to observe here that the council has taken occasion, in n. 25, to expound a term in Vatican I's definition of papal infallibility which has, in fact, been misunderstood. Vatican I defined that papal definitions of doctrine concerning faith and morals, granted that they fulfilled certain carefully stated conditions, are 'of themselves, and not from the consent of the Church, irreformable' (Denz. 3074). This, our constitution explains, means that such definitions 'stand in need of no approbation on the part of others, and admit of no appeal to another tribunal'. In other words, it does *not* mean that the doctrines thus defined have any other origin than from the Sacred Tradition as it lives in the whole body of the faithful; the Pope is not an oracle. And it

If we now cast our eyes back over the ground covered in this chapter, it must be admitted that it has been a rough and craggy journey, beset with legal niceties and theoretical distinctions. The council was engaged, in the third chapter of *Lumen Gentium*, in a reaffirmation of a traditional notion of the Church (on earth) as essentially a sacramental reality, and it had to contend with a strongly juridical and legal view of the Church which had found its way into the theological manuals, could appeal to western canon law and especially to eminent exponents of that law, and was in a certain measure the basis of the current practice of the Roman curia, as it certainly coloured the mentality of important curialists. What one may call the argument of the chapter is necessarily, in consequence, conducted to a large degree in legal and juridical terms. The view of the Church which it was sought to enlarge and deepen appealed to no less an authority than the first Vatican Council. The council had, therefore, to show how the doctrine of Vatican I could be incorporated in its own larger view. It had in effect to distinguish that doctrine from what it held to be an exaggerated, even erroneous, emphasis in some contemporary exposition of it. This could not be done without skilled theological swordplay.

What matters, in the end, is the successful achievement of the council's intentions. It has left many questions open. It is even possible that some theologians will try to show that it did not mean what I have claimed it did. I give it, nevertheless,

---

does not mean that the Church's subsequent consent can be dispensed with. On the contrary, as the constitution points out with particular reference to the infallibility (again under certain conditions) of the episcopal college, such consent, or rather assent, will never be absent, since the same Holy Spirit is at work both in the teaching authority and in the Church as a whole, to guide them together into 'all truth' (cf. n. 25). The Pope's infallibility, like that of the college, is in reality not a private thing (*non ut persona privata sententiam profert, ibid.*), but the infallibility of the Church herself; it is *her* grace-gift (*charisma, ibid.*) inhering in a singular way in the Pope as her organ. We may say that it is an eminent *participation* of her infallibility. There are not three infallibilities, of the *sensus fidei* in the body of the faithful, of the episcopal college, and of the Pope. There is a single infallible Church ('the gates of hell will not prevail against her'), exercising her infallibility, according to circumstances and the guidance of the Holy Ghost, in three different modes. When the episcopal college, or its head the Pope, defines a doctrine, it or he does so as the organ and mouthpiece of the Church, giving utterance to 'what all have thought', but none so precisely 'expressed'.

as my opinion that the chapter points the way to a theology of the visible Church and its hierarchical structure which, because it is true and truly traditional, may become helpful in the ecumenical dialogue with East and West alike. The council has not denied the place of law and jurisdiction in the Church. But it has given the primacy to charity and sacrament; and it allows us to see law and jurisdiction as flowing from charity and sacrament and, ultimately controlled (but, of course, not legally controlled) by them.[25]

[25] Dr Mascall (*op. cit.*, p. 208) writes: 'Whereas the episcopate is a sacramental function of the Church, the papacy is a juridical and administrative one, which is imparted by the administrative act of election.' He points out that one who is not yet a bishop may be elected Pope, and that such a one, according to canon law (can. 219) 'obtains by divine law, immediately upon his acceptance of his election, full power of supreme jurisdiction'. This is a nice point. I have wished to see the episcopal college as the full external manifestation of the intrinsic implications of the sacrament of order. The episcopal college comprises the bishop of Rome as its head, and – I have wished to contend – it is as head of the college that he has his own universal authority. In other words, I have wished to argue that the papal primacy is itself part of the intrinsic implications of the sacrament of Order. And my position is apparently contradicted by the fact that 'by divine law' a Pope *who is not yet a bishop* (though of course bound to become one) already holds the 'full power of supreme jurisdiction'. Perhaps a reply might be worked out on the following lines: It is of divine law that the Church be preserved from schism. The danger of schism would be proximate if the authority of a validly elected Pope could be called in question. Hence it is of divine law that such a Pope, even before his incorporation into the episcopal college by episcopal consecration, receive the obedience which is due to him in virtue of his election and *intuitu futurae consecrationis*. I acknowledge, however, that the matter requires further investigation at a theological level. The question was, in fact, raised by two conciliar fathers, with reference to n. 21: When a layman or a presbyter is elected Pope, what powers has he before his (episcopal) consecration? The Doctrinal Commission replied that its text referred to ordinary situations and did not consider such particular cases; the elected Pope becomes, immediately upon his acceptance of his office, head of the Church by the will of God and it is supposed that he has at least the intention of receiving consecration (B. Kloppenburg, 'Votes et derniers Amendements', in *Vatican II, L'Église de Vatican II*, ed. Baraúna, p. 151). Suppose, however, that the new Pope, after accepting office, pertinaciously refuses to be consecrated bishop? One may imagine that he would thus constitute himself a wilful schismatic, and could be declared by the bishops to have vacated his office.

[The last sentence in the Apostolic Constitution *Romano Pontifici Eligendo*, 1975 (cf. note 15, *supra*, p. 90) may reflect Paul VI's recognition of the problem posed by the Code of Canon Law promulgated in 1917, when it stated that as soon as an elected candidate has accepted the office of Pope he assumes 'full power of universal jurisdiction, even if he is not yet a bishop'. *Romano Pontifici* states: 'After accepting, one who is already at the time of his election a bishop, is there and then bishop of the (local) Roman church and at one and the same time the true Pope and the head of the episcopal college and he thereby acquires full and supreme power in relation to the universal Church and can exercise that power. But if the one elected is not a bishop, let him forthwith be ordained bishop (*Quodsi electus charactere episcopali careat, statim ordinetur Episcopus*).' It may be inferred that, in the case of a candidate who is not a bishop, his ordination to the episcopate is part and parcel of his being made Pope; and that if he refused ordination the election would *ipso facto* be void. In that case, Dr Mascall's objection, however pertinent to Canon Law as current when the objection was published, does not hold against the present established procedures for filling the vacancy created by a Pope's death (or resignation). Paul VI's reformed procedures at this point represent a reaction from abstract juridicism towards a genuinely sacramental understanding of the Church: jurisdiction depends on sacrament, not *vice versa*. Note that the traditional homage paid by the Conclave Cardinals to a new Pope is, in the case of a candidate who is not already a bishop when elected, *postponed* until he has received episcopal consecration (*ibid.* n. 89); this postponement doubtless symbolises the truth that, despite election, only a bishop can be a Pope.]

Note: Already before the council K. Rahner (in *The Episcopate and the Primacy*, pp. 76ff.) could speak of a dilemma which 'in the case of the relationship between the primacy and the episcopate can only be resolved by recognising the college as such to be the prior entity, not subsequently composed of individuals already possessed of their own authority before entering the college; and that the primacy of the Pope is a primacy *within* and not *vis-à-vis* this college'. And speaking of the *apostolic* college he says: 'Only if Christ founds a college which as such has an authoritative head and yet as such possesses real power deriving from himself, so that from the outset Peter can never be thought of without the other apostles, nor the college without Peter, is an apostle really an apostle of Christ, come of Christ and Christ's own mission.' And *ibid.*, p. 78: 'Our only recourse is to conclude . . . that Peter has his unique authority in so far as he is constituted head of this college from the outset . . . (p. 79). Peter is Peter, in so far as he is head of this college. . . . Ontologically and juridically, then, the apostolic college with Peter as its head forms one entity. The college cannot exist without Peter, nor he without it. One could say that Peter is the divinely ordained head of the Church in so far as he is head of the apostolic college, which he rules while ruling the Church with it. "With it", not "through it". . . . Peter's whole function is to be head of the college.' And, reverting to the episcopal college, the same author says: 'It is the (ecumenical) council itself that acts when the Pope acts, by reason of his supreme jurisdiction, because the Pope, precisely when he acts *ex sese*, acts not as a private person but as Pope, that is, as head of a college of bishops *iuris divini*' (p. 86). Rahner next turns to the magisterium of the bishops and the Pope, only to maintain that this problem, too, depends on our concept of the Church's basic constitution: 'One society can contain only one supreme authority; a double supreme authority seems a metaphysical absurdity from the outset. . . . Two supreme powers (powers, that is, from which there is no appeal to a higher court in this world), if they are really two, can only rule two distinct bodies. . . . The question to ask . . . is the following: Is the . . . assumption . . . correct, . . . that the infallibility of the Pope when he defines "alone" is in no way also the infallibility of the college of bishops?' And he suggests that 'an act of the Pope "alone" and an act of the (ecumenical) council are only different forms and modes of the activity of the college of bishops' (p. 95). 'The Pope's full jurisdiction over the whole Church and over all her members is precisely what is meant by "head of the college of bishops" translated into concrete terms' (p. 100).

Karl Rahner was one of the most distinguished of the theological experts advising the Doctrinal Commission of Vatican II.

5

Ecumenism

Constantly, since New Testament times, it has been a Christian conviction that outward unity among believers is a normal consequence of redemption, and that schism between Christians is a result of sin. There was, throughout antiquity and up to the time of the Reformation, a consensus that the Church on earth not only ought to be, but is, visibly one, and that this unity is permanently guaranteed by divine assistance. Faced with the existence of other Christian bodies from which his own was separated, the Christian held that these other bodies were 'outside the Church'; and he would be swift to mention that 'outside the Church there is no salvation'.

Such was the view held within the Great Church of the third and fourth centuries, from which all our existing forms of Christianity can trace their descent. The Great Church, it was held, was the one ark of salvation, the only refuge from the deluge of divine judgment. But it was also the view normally held in the ancient 'schismatical' bodies – Novatianists, Donatists, what you will – which have since died out. They, too, held that visible unity was of the *esse* of the Church; but, of course, they believed that their own body was the Church, and that the Great Church was a false pretender. All would have echoed Origen's cry: 'My desire is to be truly ecclesiastical' – i.e. a genuine son of the Church, with which Origen identified the Great Church.

The suggestion has recently been made that St Augustine wavered on this cardinal point of ancient ecclesiology, or at least that he made theoretical concessions which were inconsistent with it. A hundred and fifty years earlier, St Cyprian, objecting to the practice of reconciling to the Church those baptised in schism without 're-baptising' them, had argued: Where there are valid sacraments, there the Church is; but schismatics are outside the Church; therefore, sacraments administered by schismatics are invalid. St Augustine, in his dispute with the Donatists (who denied the validity of the sacraments of the Great Church) found himself at odds with Cyprian, and maintained that schismatics could administer valid sacraments. But Augustine did not draw the conclusion that therefore schismatical bodies form (separated) parts of the Church; he agreed with Cyprian and virtually all Christian antiquity that the Church does not subsist in a number of separated communions. It remains true that the admission, which has become general in western Christendom, that valid sacraments can be found in more than one communion sets a problem for theological developments which have become overdue.

The nature of the Church on earth was not originally at the centre of the Reformation disputes. Their consequences, however, included the fragmentation of western Christendom, and this, in turn, gave rise to new theories about the Church, including – in some quarters – a denial that the Church is necessarily a visible unity, and sometimes to a denial that she is a visible entity at all. On the Catholic side of the Reformation controversies there was a reaction towards a rigidity if possible even more narrow than before. Meanwhile, the Orthodox Churches, not directly affected by the Protestant Reformation, simply maintained their old position: the Orthodox communion is the true Church of Christ, from which both Catholics and Protestants are divided by schism.

In modern times, the whole world position of Christianity has been changing from that inherited from the Middle Ages. Medieval Christendom was a solid geographical and human block, surrounded by Islam and barbarism. The medieval synthesis of religion, politics and culture made it easy to identify being Christian with being fully human – a supposition which at first seemed to be confirmed when discovery opened up America, Africa, and Asia, disclosing what was taken to be a low state of culture among the non-Christian inhabitants of these regions, who were regarded simply as savages. (Jesuit attempts to reconcile Christianity with the great cultures of China and India were eventually frustrated by the action of Rome.) The conquistadores opened the way for the missionaries, and the latter brought with them not only the gospel but a western culture which had been more or less inadvertently regarded as a necessary part of a package deal.

The breakdown of 'colonialism', together with a juster appreciation of cultures other than that of Europe, has made Christians more aware alike of the distinction between 'the faith' and 'Europe' and of their own minority situation in face of the total experience and population of the world. Despite their doctrinal and other differences among themselves, they are acquiring a sense of sharing with one another a common conviction and a common faith peculiar to themselves. This sense has, of course, been enormously intensified by the major historical phenomenon of anti-religious Communism, and, in the last few years, by the growing clamour of irreligious humanism.

Already before the first world war, the problems raised by rival Christian missions in non-European countries had given birth first to practical difficulties and then to a sense of guilt, and thus the Ecumenical Movement was born. After nearly forty years, at Amsterdam in 1948, the World Council of Churches came into existence, giving a new institutional expression to ecumenical aspirations. The membership of the World Council includes most of the great Protestant bodies, the Anglican communion, and some of the eastern Orthodox Churches. But a number of the more extreme evangelical bodies stand aloof, and the Catholic Church has never sought membership.

In fact, the Catholic Church was for many years very reserved in its official attitude to the Ecumenical Movement as a whole. A general suspicion that the movement entailed a measure of doctrinal indifferentism or at least compromise combined, to cause this reserve, with a particular notion that the movement was in some way implicitly committed to the view that no existing Christian body could claim simply and exclusively to be the Church founded by Christ – and this represents a claim which the Catholic Church had traditionally made for itself. However, it should be noted that, although eastern Orthodoxy makes a similar claim for its own communion, some of the eastern Orthodox Churches have for a long time succeeded in combining this claim with vocal membership of the World Council of Churches. And for more than ten years the World Council itself has made it clear that it neither stands for nor excludes any particular ecclesiology and does not require any member-Church to renounce any of her own claims.

The first signs of a thaw in Rome's attitude came with a very cautious Instruction issued by the Holy Office a few years after the last world war. Soon after that there came into existence an unofficial but permitted international conference of Catholic theologians interested in the ecumenical problem. And at length, before the opening of the second Vatican Council, John XXIII set up at Rome, but outside the framework of the curia, the Secretariat for forwarding the Unity of Christians, with Cardinal Bea at its head. This Secretariat assumed a unique position in Vatican II itself. It was not created as a conciliar commission, and its original membership was of the Pope's own choosing; yet it functioned as an extremely influential commission of the council. It had been made responsible for inviting, and entertaining, official observers from other Churches. But after the withdrawal of the abortive draft document on the Sources of Revelation, it made its influence felt, mainly through Cardinal Bea, in the early drafting of *De Divina Revelatione*.

It is beyond my scope here to recount the long and chequered story leading up to the acceptance and promulgation, on 21 November 1964, of the Decree of Ecumenism. Nor need I summarise its contents.

The importance of ecclesiology in the Ecumenical Movement, and the difficulties which can flow from a rigidly determined ecclesiology are obvious. Professor Greenslade, writing from personal experience of ecumenical dialogue, says of the question of the nature of the Church: 'Participation in the movement forces precisely this consideration almost daily upon one, with an urgency and in a manner not perhaps familiar to members of the Roman Catholic Church.' And he adds, with reference to a Catholic critic of his own ecclesiology: 'I am bound to conclude that there are facts which he is not facing, facts of the utmost importance since they consist in what – as we believe – Christ has done and is doing through his Holy Spirit.'[1] Replying to the same Catholic critic, Bishop Tomkins argues that 'schism *within* the Church does not preclude the idea of schism *from* the Church, nor necessarily imply . . . a purely "invisible" Church'. These quotations may introduce our examination of Vatican II's ecclesiology so far as it relates to ecumenism. But first, I remark that the Decree on Ecumenism explicitly sees in the movement the operation of the Holy Spirit, something therefore that 'Christ is doing through his Holy Spirit'; something, in other words, of the utmost importance.

Both *Lumen Gentium* and our Decree restate, as was to be expected, the Roman Catholic Church's peculiar claim for itself, which has been the theme of treatises on the Church ever since the Reformation. The Catholic position is based on two convictions: 1. that visible unity, or full communion between all its parts and members, is of the *esse*, not merely of the *bene esse*, of the Church as established by Christ; 2. that this unity is centred in the apostolic and episcopal 'college' with the successor of St Peter (the bishop of Rome) at its head. The early history of the principle that, as the Council of Aquileia (A.D. 381) puts it, 'the rights of communion derive from Rome' or from the bishop of Rome may be studied in the history books; it may be remarked that the dispute between modern Catholics and Orthodox concerns the question whether this centre of communion is of divine origin or is merely an ecclesiastical or canonical creation.

The problem, and it is not an easy one, is, granted this unchanged and unchangeable Catholic position, how to make Catholic participation in the Ecumenical Movement not just an exercise in Christian courtesy but a positive and constructive contribution. No one, it is true, on engaging in ecumenism is expected to begin by denying or sacrificing his own basic convictions; though he must not insist on these as the

[1] *Schism in the Early Church*, 2nd edition, p. xv.

starting-point of dialogue. But these specific Roman Catholic convictions are certainly an obstacle to easy dialogue. Can the Catholic ecclesiology be enriched and qualified without being surrendered?

We may approach this problem by asking, in the light of the council documents: Who, when we consider men individually, belongs to the Church?; and again: What can we say of the non-Catholic Christian Churches as Churches or Christian communions; is there any sense in which they also 'belong to the Church' as collectivities?[2]

The chapter on the People of God in *Lumen Gentium* develops its thought between two complementary ideas. It begins by stating, in biblical language, that 'whoever fears God and does what is right is acceptable with him' (n. 9; cf. Ac 10:35). This is a principle of the widest application, and a later reference to those who, through no fault of their own, have not yet come to an expressed acknowledgment of God (n. 16) suggests that it can take within its scope professed atheists who 'strive to attain to a (morally) good life' (*ibid.*) ; in doing which, the council points out, they are in fact – though they do not recognise it – helped by divine grace. The other governing idea of the chapter follows immediately: 'It has pleased God to sanctify and save men, not singly and without any mutual connexion, but by constituting them as a people which should acknowledge him in truth and serve him with holiness' (n. 9).

Thus human salvation moves between, involves, two poles. Subjectively, it requires – of adult human beings – that 'they fear God and do what is right'. They must be men who rule their lives by their conscience; and, as moral theology points out, a genuine conscience is always to be obeyed, even if, inculpably, it is misinformed – there are those who judge themselves conscientiously required to profess atheism. But there is an *objective* aspect of salvation.[3] Man cannot save

[2] I have examined these questions at greater length in 'Les Chrétiens non-catholiques et l'Église', in *L'Église de Vatican II*, Vol. 2, ed. G. Baraúna, pp. 651–68.

[3] That salvation has an objective aspect is common ground among Christians. 'For us men and for our salvation' the Son of God was incarnate, died, and was raised from the dead. This aspect is already adumbrated in deutero-Isaiah's teaching that Israel has a divine mission to the Gentiles. It has priority over the subjective aspect, inasmuch as it was 'when we were yet sinners' – i.e. before we 'feared God' – that Christ died for us.

himself; salvation is a gift from God, and God was free to give it the form and content which seemed good to him. He chose, in fact, a social form, and the chosen content is summed up in Christ and his new covenant. Salvation has thus been incorporated into and entrusted to the Christian People of God, the Church; and we have already seen that the council teaches that the Church 'subsists in the Catholic Church, governed by Peter's successor and the bishops in communion with him' (*ibid.*, n. 8). Hence we are told (n. 14) that 'Those could not be saved, who though they were not unaware that the Catholic Church was founded through Jesus Christ as necessary, yet refused to enter it or persevere in it.'

It may be relevant here to point out that there is a strong vein of intransigence running through the Bible. The people of Israel is contrasted with 'the Gentiles that know not God' and, in fact, is addressed by God through the words of his prophet: 'You only have I known of all the peoples of the earth.' Doubtless God is the creator of nature and of man, and is the Lord of all history. But, for this 'intransigent' vein of thought, it would hardly be too much to say with the ancient Rabbis that the whole divine purpose in creation and history reaches its end in Israel, to the welfare and destiny of which all else is subordinate and contributory. This intransigence is carried over into the New Testament. Jesus is the Messiah promised to Israel, and his Church is the spiritual (true) Israel. 'There is no other name under heaven given among men by which we must be saved except the name of Jesus Christ of Nazareth (Ac 4:12); and it is as a Christian speaking to Christians that the author of the first Epistle of St John can say: 'We know that we are of God, and the whole world is in the power of the evil one' (5:19).

There is, it is true, another line of thought to be found in both Old and New Testaments, a line which may be called universalistic. But it is based on intransigence. Israel – in the New Testament the Christian Church – has a mission to bring light, indeed salvation, to all mankind. But it is the light and redemptive grace of the God of Israel, of Jesus Christ: 'God was in Christ reconciling the world to himself, not counting their trespasses against them, and entrusting to us the message of reconciliation' (2 Co 5:19). Because God's whole purpose of man's salvation is summed up in Christ, the function of the Church is indispensable: 'Everyone who calls upon the name of the Lord will be saved. But how are men to call upon him in whom they have not believed? And how are they to believe in him of whom they have not heard? And how are they to hear without a preacher?' (Rm 10:13f). And once a man has believed he still has to be baptised: 'Repent, and be baptised every one of you in the name of Jesus Christ for the forgiveness of your sins; and you shall receive the gift of the Holy Spirit' (Ac 2:38).

Thus, on the supposition that the Roman Catholic Church is the unique Church of Jesus Christ, the historical embodiment of his messianic and eschatological people, the 'intransigent' vein in the *De Ecclesia* is fully justified. But it has to be theologically reconciled with the 'universalistic' implications of the affirmation that whoever 'fears God and does what is right' is acceptable with God.

We may begin by considering a particularly interesting group of unbaptised persons, bearing in mind that *Lumen Gentium* teaches that 'Christ alone is the mediator and way of salvation, and becomes present to us in his body, which is the Church. He himself by emphasising the necessity of faith and baptism in express words (cf. Mk 16:16, Jn 3:5), has thereby confirmed that necessity of the Church, into which men enter through baptism as through a door' (n. 14). The group we have to consider is constituted by the catechumens, those who have been moved by the Holy Spirit, and by an express act of will seek to be incorporated in the Church, and are, in fact, being prepared for baptism. Catechumens were a familiar feature of the ancient Christian scene, as they still are in missionary countries. Of them the constitution says that 'already Mother Church encompasses them as her own with love and solicitude' (*ibid.*). The language is rather vague, but still we have here a group of unbaptised persons whom the Church recognises as 'her own'. Implicitly, I suggest, the council accepts the very ancient and uncontradicted conviction that catechumens, though actually not yet baptised, are yet in such manner related to the Church 'the instrument of the redemption of all' (n. 9) that, if they die before baptism, they are held to be saved. As a group (for no one can judge the interior dispositions of any individual) they are thus regarded as men in whom salvation, that is to say Christ, is already present and efficaciously operative. Externally, they have not yet passed through the 'door' of baptism; but in reality they are already, in some sense, 'inside' the ark of salvation. In them the Church already transcends its own visible limits; in them baptism, not yet externally received, is already operative. They are a privileged case, because they already have an explicit desire for baptism and so for incorporation in the Church; but they are a decisive case, since they show that lack of material or external incorporation into the Church does not prove that one is not, in the vitally important sense that determines salvation, already 'within' it.

In n. 16 the constitution considers the situation of a large mass of other unbaptised persons, who, however, differ from catechumens because, unlike them, they lack any explicit desire to be baptised. Such are non-Christian Jews, Moslems, followers of other religions, and, as already noted, professed atheists or agnostics. All are classified here as 'those who have not yet accepted the gospel', and they are said to be in various ways related to God's people. And it is said, in general, of all who are in inculpable ignorance of Christ's gospel and Church, but who 'seek God with a sincere heart' and seek to fulfil in act his will, which they recognise through the imperative of their conscience, that they can attain eternal salvation. This implies a notable, but not novel, extension of the theological notion utilised in the case of catechumens. Theology is, of course, familiar with the idea that a desire of receiving a sacrament may do duty for actual reception, in cases where the latter is physically or morally impossible. Indeed, in the instance of the sacrament of penance, it is acknowledged that contrition, including a genuine intention of sacramental confession, brings immediate remission of sin, while leaving intact the obligation of actual sacramental confession when a suitable occasion offers. There is thus no special difficulty about catechumens with their explicit desire for baptism. Where, however, this explicit desire is absent, either through ordinary ignorance of the traditional Christian faith, or through a conscientious non-reception of its teaching, we have to fall back on what is known as an 'implicit desire' of the sacramental means. A person who genuinely 'fears God and does what is right' would obviously wish to become a Christian if he recognised this as God's will; it *is* God's will, and he wishes to do God's will; hence, he may be said to desire implicitly what he rejects explicitly. He is like a man who fails, through no fault of his own, to recognise the friend whom he genuinely loves. The implication of the council's positive attitude to all these groups of non-Christians is, that in them also Christ is (anonymously) at work, and that in them also the Church, *extra quam nulla salus*, is transcending her own visible limits.

Obviously, then, the constitution had to take a still more positive line about non-Catholic Christians; about those who 'being baptised, are honoured with the name of Christian, but do not profess the complete faith or do not maintain the unity of communion under Peter's successor' (n. 15).[4] There are many links which unite the Church to these: not only baptism, important as it is because it actually incorporates into Christ (and the Church is Christ's body), but the Bible as the norm of belief and life, and – not to speak of Christian zeal and devotion – there may be other sacraments, too; and in general there is a 'certain communion in prayers and other spiritual benefits, nay a union in the Holy Spirit' (n. 15).

The question of non-Catholic Christians is, we may say, posed in this passage of *Lumen Gentium*. It is here given only a very vague and exiguous answer. More, however, can be gleaned from the Decree on Ecumenism. Schism – a word which the decree avoids, as it does the word 'heresy' – is, in itself a sin; it is a sin against the charity which binds Christians internally and externally with all their fellows. But the decree states explicitly that, while there may have been sin on both sides at the origin of our modern divisions, those who are today *born* in separated Christian bodies are not to be accused of this sin of division; in fact, the Catholic Church embraces our separated brethren with reverence and love. 'For

[4] Explicit mention is not made of, e.g., Quakers, who do not include sacraments in their idea of 'essential Christianity'. Obviously, they are to be 'classified' somewhere between catechumens and those who 'do not know of the gospel'. Their faith in Christ would lead them to baptism, if they understood that it is the 'necessary' door to the Church, and the way in which Christ wishes us to be incorporated in his mystical body.

those who believe in Christ and have duly received baptism are established in a certain *communion* with the Catholic Church, albeit not a perfect communion' (n. 3).

The notion of communion, and the distinction between perfect and imperfect communion, may be said to be fundamental to this decree. It is a notion firmly embodied in the New Testament: 'That which we have seen and heard we proclaim also to you, so that you may have fellowship (*koinonia*, communion) with us; and *our fellowship is with the Father* and with his Son Jesus Christ' (1 Jn 1:3). It appears to signify that kind of association which is involved in common possessions.[5] In this general sense, we may say that the common land of a medieval village was a material reality, shared as a possession by each of the families, and constituting a link between the personal lives of all the villagers. To possess something is to be *constituted in relationship with* everyone to whom that thing is a reality, and *especially* to everyone who, like you, possesses it. Thus there is born the reality and idea of a commonwealth.

A primitive expression of the idea of Christianity as communion was the pooling of material possessions in the early Church in Jerusalem: 'The company of those who believed were of one heart and soul, and no one said that any of the things which he possessed was his own, but they had everything in common' (Ac 4:32). The experiment seems to have been abortive, though it has been continued or re-enacted in the 'religious communities' of later Christianity. But the 'goods' which believers possess in common are, of course, above all the spiritual 'goods' which Christ communicated to the apostles (*De Divina Revelatione*, n. 7). They are summed up in the gift of the Holy Spirit, whereby Christ himself, God's supreme 'gift' to man, is made sacramentally present in and through the Church. The common possession of these spiritual goods sets up a communion between believers. And, by a natural development of linguistic usage, the Church herself comes to be called a 'communion' (St Augustine speaks of *communio sacramentorum*, a phrase which emphasises that the sacraments, as signs conveying what they signify, are the visible means of communion); and again the eucharistic meal is called

[5] The Greeks had a saying, which puts the thing in reverse perspective: The possessions of friends are common to each.

'Holy Communion', since in it we become 'one body', the body of Christ.

Within this general notion of 'communion' the decree makes a distinction between 'perfect' and 'imperfect' communion. By perfect communion it means the total sharing of the whole sacramental reality of Christianity by those who are 'fully incorporated into the society of the Church', those, that is to say, 'who having the Spirit of Christ, accept its complete structure and all the means of salvation established in it, and are in its visible organism (*compage*), joined with Christ who rules it through the supreme pontiff and the bishops – joined in him by the bonds of the profession of faith, the sacraments, ecclesiastical government and communion' (*De Ecclesia*, n. 14).[6]

Before discussing imperfect, or incomplete, communion, it is well to emphasise the unique feature of perfect or complete communion: it involves a common experience made tangible not only in friendly sympathy, external good works, and common witness to the gospel, not only in a positive mystical relationship to Christ the head of the Church, but in actual worship and shared community life, above all in the sharing of a common eucharistic table. Every Christian knows by experience that his links with the other members of his own 'communion' are unique, as compared with those that bind him to other Christians, even though in the sphere of theology and in apostolic concern he may be closer to the latter than the former. This uniqueness has a doctrinal depth. The Bible teaches that it is by sharing in 'one bread' that we become one body; this sharing is diminished where there is not complete communion. The ancient Church branded schism as the setting up of 'altar against altar'. One of the profoundest motives of the ecumenical movement is the wish to recover this full eucharistic communion of all with each and each with all. Imperfect communion, as we shall now proceed to say, is real

[6] It should be obvious that the term 'perfect communion' does not involve a claim that the Catholic Church, as she existentially exists, is morally perfect – such a claim would, of course, be absurd. The term is an improvement on the familiar term 'perfect society', used to describe a society which is *sui iuris* for all purposes involved in its intrinsic *raison d'être*. A nation-state is a perfect society in this sense; a trade union is not, because it is subject to the overriding law of the state within which it exists.

and valuable. But the measure of its reality is the ache at its heart for full communion.

Such being 'perfect communion', it is obvious that Christian communion can be imperfectly realised in a number of modes. Unbaptised believers, for example Quakers, are united to those baptised by their common faith in Christ, their common veneration of the Bible, and their common inherence in the Christian tradition as a reality of the historical order. At the other extreme we have, for example, the Christians of eastern Orthodoxy, who are united to Catholics in the apostolic succession, the Eucharist and the other sacraments; thus they 'are joined with us in the closest relationship' (*De Ecumenismo*, n. 15). Between these limits, there are all those who by baptism are united with each other and with Catholics through the sacrament of 'incorporation into Christ' and are therefore properly acknowledged by 'the sons of the Catholic Church' as their 'brothers in the Lord' (n. 3). Besides faith and baptism, there are also, of course, many other 'common goods' which deepen communion and enrich it both as reality and as idea.

It must be observed that such common possession of authentic elements of the total Christian treasure does not merely unite various groups among themselves; it unites the members of each group with those of all the other groups, including the group called the Roman Catholic Church. Perfect communion, in other words, has a real extension in imperfect communion, and once again we see how the Church transcends her own visible limits; once again we appreciate the cautious statement: 'The Church *subsists in* the Roman Catholic Church' – which falls short of a sheer material identification of Church and Catholic Church.

From consideration of the relation to the visible Church of individuals who are in 'imperfect communion' with her, it is possible to pass on to consider the situation of the separated Christian bodies as such. Any failure on the part of the decree to do so would have had most unfortunate results, since the ecumenical movement has taken the form of a convergence of Christian groups, not merely of individual Christians. The step had not been taken in *Lumen Gentium*, but is taken in the decree: 'The separated Churches and communities, though we believe that they suffer from deficiencies, are by no means destitute of significance and importance in the mystery of salvation. The Spirit of Christ does not refuse to use them as means of salvation, means whose effectiveness is derived from that fullness of grace and truth which has been entrusted to the Catholic Church' (n. 3). This statement, I think, has no parallel in previous official pronouncements of the Catholic Church, and it deserves to be carefully scrutinised.

Christianity is a mystery of communion. Every authentic Christian 'element' is, in its measure, a 'unifying' factor, a factor which produces communion, fellowship, between those who alike acknowledge and live by it. The separated Christian bodies are therefore – from the Catholic point of view – to be seen as ambivalent. As 'separated' they may be said to exist in virtue of a rejection of some element of the total gift of God in Christ to his Church. But as 'Christian bodies' they are, in fact, built upon Christian elements, and are alike cause and effect of the acceptance of such elements by their own adherents. A secular nation-state, however 'Christian' its laws and *mores*, is 'built' on natural foundations. But a Christian church is built upon 'supernatural' elements, elements accepted as deriving from the gospel. They must therefore be considered to be themselves – doubtless in varying degrees – supernatural. And as such they play a positive part in the divine design of man's supernatural redemption and salvation, *as that design takes concrete shape amid the sins and imperfections of mankind.* In an ideal order there would be no separated Christian bodies, but only one visible universal Church, and towards this ideal the Ecumenical Movement may be said to be moving. But in the actual historical order, where sin and error have intervened, the actual salvation of actual men is being promoted by the Holy Spirit both in and by the Catholic Church and in and by other bodies.[7] Hence the decree, while firmly

[7] The decree refers to the non-Catholic Christian bodies as Churches and communities. Some have seen an invidious distinction here. The council was in something of a dilemma. Modern non-Catholic practice speaks of 'the Churches' without discrimination. Catholic precedent, however, confined the use of the title 'Church' to the Catholic Church herself (and her dioceses, each a church within the Church) and to those eastern Christian bodies which, though estranged from Rome for many centuries, have an undoubted continuity of full sacramental and especially eucharistic life, carried on from before communion with the West ceased. By speaking of 'Churches and communities' the decree bore witness to this Catholic precedent, but it did not clearly

maintaining that the Catholic Church is 'the general aid of salvation' in which 'all the fullness of the means of salvation can be attained', boldly speaks of the separated bodies (without distinction) as 'used by the Holy Spirit as means of salvation'.

At this point a Catholic might wonder whether the council was not in danger of slipping into the 'branch theory' of the Church. If there are numerous Christian bodies, each divided from the others, but all genuine Christian communions, means of salvation – and some of them, at least, besides the Catholic Church, entitled to be called 'Churches' – then is not the one Church to be conceived as the sum of these bodies? But the council had no intention of countenancing this theory, long ago denounced as an error. The theory is excluded by the council's explicit teaching. In *Lumen Gentium* we learn that the Church has been given, in perpetuity, by Christ a ministerial or hierarchical structural principle; and that this, again by Christ's institution, is expressed in the apostolic-episcopal college, of which the reality is essentially bound up with the full communion of each member with all the others. (A bishop can exercise his sacramentally given functions of teacher and ruler 'only in *hierarchical communion* with the head and members of the college', n. 21; he is 'constituted a member of the episcopal body by virtue of sacramental consecration and hierarchical communion with the head and members of the college' (n. 22).) This doctrine is presupposed in the Decree on Ecumenism, and is implicit in its teaching that 'perfect communion' is to be found only in the Catholic Church. The 'branch theory' is not constructed to safeguard this truth. Yet it seems inescapable that the decree forces us to acknowledge, outside the visible unity of the Catholic Church, not only

---

indicate which bodies it would refer to as Churches and which as 'only' communities. Behind the linguistic distinction there may lurk a theological consideration. The Eucharist is the heart, centre, food, and growing-point of ecclesial communion at its fullest: 'The bread which we break, is it not a participation (*koinonia*) in the body of Christ? Because there is one bread, we who are many are one body, for we all partake of the one bread' (1 Co 10:16f). Hence, it seems natural to speak of a 'Church' where there exists a Eucharist which we can unconditionally recognise as such. Such *unconditional* recognition can be more easily given to eastern Orthodox Eucharists than to some others. [It is also possible that the drafters had in mind that some Christian bodies prefer not to be called 'Churches'.]

'vestiges' of the Church, not only individuals who, especially if they are baptised, have some communion with the Church and, if incorporated in Christ, are in some degree incorporated in his mystical body which is the Church, but Christian communions of an ecclesial character which, at least if they have 'the genuine and complete substance of the eucharistic mystery' (*De Ecumenismo*, n. 22) (which is the food of the mystical body, and of which the unity of the mystical body is, says St Thomas, the *res*) can truly be called 'Churches'.

There is a field for further theological investigation here. We seem driven to say that the Church, existing in its integral fullness in the Catholic Church, exists also, by self-transcendence, in bodies out of communion with the Catholic Church. We shall mean by 'out of communion' that they do not enjoy 'perfect communion'; but we shall admit that they have with us, and we with them, a communion which is very real, which can increase, and which is ontologically ordered, by the elements which constitute it, towards perfect communion. Our resulting ecclesiology may lack something of the clarity and definiteness of views associated with the name of Bellarmine; but it will have gained in richness and nuance, and in recognition of the mysteriousness of Christianity, not easily framed in precise human language. Perhaps we could say, with a distinguished Orthodox theologian, 'We know where the Church is; it is not for us to judge and say where the Church is not.'[8]

Our examination of the decree has shown that the notion of 'communion', while fully traditional, is yet flexible. In this respect it has a great advantage, for the ecumenical dialogue, over the description of the Church as 'a society'. A society is something whose edges are essentially sharp. You belong to it so long as you recognise and are recognised, in a juridical sense, by its governing authority; otherwise, you do not belong to it. Communion, by contrast, exists wherever there is common possession, whether of material or spiritual riches. There is a primordial communion between all men through their possession of a common specific (and rational) nature.[9] There

[8] P. Evdokimov, *L'Orthodoxie*, p. 343.

[9] It is often said that this sharing of a common rational nature by all men creates a universal human society. I prefer to avoid this phraseology. There

is a closer communion between men of a single culture or single political system. There is a certain communion between all who recognise the existence of a holy creator God. But there is obviously a much greater 'communion' between all those who acknowledge Jesus Christ as the redeemer of mankind. And this is still more true of Christians who, having been truly baptised, are thereby marked with a common seal of incorporation into Christ – a sealing which we believe to be indelible in this life. On the other hand, since all must agree that Christ gave a total endowment of spiritual means to his Church, there must remain a marked difference between forms of Christian communion based on the common sharing of only part of this totality and a 'perfect communion' in the totality of the Sacred Tradition.[10]

It may be almost superfluous to enlarge upon the value, for ecumenical dialogue, of such an ecclesiology of communion. Its importance is that it approaches the whole question of the Church and her nature as visible on earth, from a basis which does not presuppose, on the part of those taking part in the dialogue, an acceptance of the belief that the perfect com-

is no universal authority, at the natural human level, that can at present give that cohesion which I think necessary to constitute a society; the 'authority of conscience' is not external but internal, and – since men's conscientious judgments vary – can be divisive. But it seems true to say that the possession of a common human nature makes men potentially a society, and that it is a dynamic factor making for a universal society. However, in the actual historical order it seems doubtful whether this potentiality can be realised except with the help of a universal *supernatural* society – the Church.

[10] F. D. Maurice, in his important work *The Kingdom of Christ*, builds his ecclesiology on 'signs of a spiritual society'. He enumerates various signs: baptism, the creeds, forms of worship, the Eucharist, the ministry and the Bible. And he argues that these signs are all present in the Church of England. Maurice's 'signs' correspond to our 'common spiritual goods'. Like them, they tend towards communion. While a Catholic would say that Maurice did not grasp the whole idea of the structured episcopal college, one can read with admiration his clear sense of the universality of the episcopate: 'The overseers or bishops of the Christian Church have felt themselves to be emphatically the bonds of communication between different parts of the earth. The jurisdiction of each has been confined within a certain district; but, by the very nature of their office, they have held fellowship, and been obliged to hold fellowship, with those who lived in other districts. . . . This episcopacy has not been merely an accidental addition to, or overgrowth upon other forms of priesthood. In those countries where it has been adopted it has been the root of all other forms, and has been supposed to contain them within it' (*op. cit.*, pp. 98f). The *De Ecclesia* similarly sees the presbyterate as a participation of the priesthood held in fullness by the bishops.

munion exists on earth – or that it is identical with the Roman Catholic Church. Just as it enables Catholics to recognise other Christian bodies as genuinely Christian communions, linked with the Catholic Church by all that is held in common between them, so it enables non-Catholics to acknowledge the Catholic Church as a Christian communion, closely linked to them by the same constitutive elements. Behind this common agreement, or rather beyond it, there remains, of course, disagreement about the actual existence here and now, or the identification, of the perfect communion. But if ecumenical dialogue is directed towards visible Christian unity, it is implied that a perfect communion either *can* exist on earth, or at least is the ideal which must govern ecumenical endeavour. The Catholic, like the eastern Orthodox, in holding that what can exist does exist, and has a divine guarantee of perpetual existence, can claim that he holds to a 'realised' eschatological conception of the Church. But he can respect and co-operate, in thought and practice, with those who hope from the future for what he believes God has guaranteed in the present.

A view of the Church whose sole recommendation was that it could help the Ecumenical Movement might arouse suspicion. But the ecclesiology of communion is, in fact, intimately related to the general view of the Church inspiring the documents of Vatican II, and particularly *Lumen Gentium.* We have already seen that the Constitution on the Church represents a move away from a rather narrow juridical outlook whereby the nature of the Church is deduced from the nature of the papal primacy. This constitution offers an ecclesiology which seems to be basically sacramental. The mystical body of Christ is given substance in human history by sacramental signs; and the visible Church herself is not only a sign of human unity but a sign and instrument of divine salvation; it makes present and active within history the redemptive incarnation of the Son of God. And the centre and climax of this whole sacramental order is the Eucharist, 'whereby the Church continually lives and grows' (*De Ecclesia*, n. 26). As the Constitution on the Liturgy puts it, it is through offering 'the immaculate Victim', Christ, and with him themselves, to God in the Eucharist that the faithful 'are daily consummated into unity with God and among themselves' (*De Liturgia*,

n. 48). Thus the climax of sacrament is also the focal point of communion. When St Thomas, as already mentioned, describes 'the unity of the mystical body' as the *res* or fruit of the Eucharist he is echoing the Christian tradition in its purest form. 'Church' and 'communion' become one thing in the mystery of the Eucharist. Holy Order is itself a sacrament; but it is a sacrament subservient to the mystery of the Eucharist and therefore to communion. Since communion, in its perfection, takes shape as the existential common or social life of believers gathered round the altar, the bishops, in virtue of their sacramental status, have an authority which has a partial expression in juridical terms. But this juridical element in the Church, seen in the wider vision of the ecclesiology of Vatican II, is not creative of the Church. The Church is daily created or re-created in and by her sacramental life, and the juridical element in her government is there to prevent that sacramental life from anarchy and disintegration. In short, though it is true that *ubi episcopus, ibi ecclesia*, it is still more deeply true that *ubi Eucharistia, ibi ecclesia*. And this means that the local Church, centred in the Eucharist – which can only be celebrated as a space-time event – is, as has been said, one of a number of 'cells, each of which contains the whole living mystery of the one body of Christ'.[11] The world-wide communion is 'a communion of communions', not some sort of army in which all power is delegated from above and each platoon has significance only as bestowed on it through its subordination. It is at the local level of the eucharistic fellowship that the People of God actually lives and that Christ is made present through that People.

We have seen that the decree approves the idea that every Christian – and, we may add, every Christian ecclesial body – finds communion with the Catholic Church through sharing in the gospel blessings. It is proper that this communion should find external expression. This will come about through genuine fraternal charity among Christians, and more specifically through ecumenical dialogue. But there should be other expressions of the already existing unity of Christians. As the decree indicates, there should be mutual respect and a common

[11] T. F. Stransky, *The Decree on Ecumenism, a New Translation with a Commentary*, p. 27.

effort in the witness we all bear to the Christian faith and hope. And there should be common Christian co-operation in the broad field of social-economic and, indeed, cultural action (n. 12). The point is taken up in one of its aspects in the Constitution on the Church in the World of Today, where it is said to be desirable that Catholics should actively and positively co-operate, to play their part in international fellowship, 'both with the separated brethren who, like them, profess gospel charity, and with all men who thirst for true peace' (n. 90). A more delicate theological issue arises concerning 'praying together'. The decree acknowledges the value of this on suitable occasions, but speaks with caution of a particular form of it: '*communicatio in sacris*' (n. 8). The term is not defined in the decree. T. F. Stransky, a staff member of the Secretariat for Unity, states that the decree uses it directly to refer to participation in the sacramental life of other Churches, especially in eucharistic services; indirectly, to refer to the sharing of any form of prayer offered by or with members of other Churches.[12] Such common worship, especially if it is liturgical, and above all if it is eucharistic, presents difficulties in ecumenical practice which are now notorious. The liturgy, above all the Eucharist, by its nature 'signifies unity'; it normally expresses, and deepens, a unity already present. In early Christianity as already stated, the existence of *altare contra altare* was seen as the very hall mark of schism; and, on the other hand, even catechumens might be dismissed from Mass before the beginning of the Great Prayer. Thus many have felt, and the feeling is particularly strong among the eastern Orthodox, that it would be something like profanation to hold 'joint Eucharists' before external unity is attained. On the other hand, the grace flowing from the Eucharist is a grace of charity, a grace therefore making directly for unity; so that it could be urged that 'joint Eucharists' would be most effective ways of forwarding ecumenism. The decree therefore states that '*communicatio in sacris*' is not to be considered as a means of indiscriminate application with a view to restoring Christian unity; and leaves the decision in particular cases to the competent authority.

[12] T. F. Stransky, *op. cit.*, p. 41, n. 9.

Ecumenism is, in itself, an affair of practice based on theology rather than of pure theology. Are there any theological grounds for hoping that practical ecumenism, inspired by prayer and taking shape especially in dialogue, may, in fact, culminate in Christian unity? It seems that there are. Dialogue, as we have seen, seeks to operate from a basis of shared convictions and to extend the area of such common convictions through a process of clearing up misunderstandings and communicating insights. Behind the dialogue, however, there will usually be divergent convictions, and these may comprise: 1. truths held by faith on the one hand, but not accepted by another or other parties to the dialogue; 2. tenets which are neither 'of faith' nor necessary corollaries of what is held by faith; and of these tenets some may be erroneously supposed to be 'of faith'. Faith, however, results from a supernatural enlightenment of man's natural powers whereby he is enabled to assent to, and hold by, divine revelation and its content. The precise or 'formal' object of faith is truth revealing itself, for which, and for which alone, it has a natural affinity. It would seem to be strictly impossible to give the assent of faith to something which is not actually true and not given or implied in divine revelation; though it is plainly possible to withhold the explicit assent of faith from something which is actually revealed or implied by revelation, while giving a genuinely 'faithful' assent to other aspects or contents of divine revelation. In the latter case, we shall have to speak about 'implicit faith' and we could compare the situation of a man who has an 'implicit' desire for the baptism which he explicitly refuses. Now the ecumenical dialogue is calculated to communicate insights, and thus to bring the participants to a recognition of aspects of divine revelation which they had overlooked, or to which they had given insufficient attention. It is also calculated to clarify the distinction between what we really 'believe' and what we only hold by opinion. It can lead therefore to mutual enrichment in the apprehension of divine revelation and mutual purification of the articulated faith. It sets the participants, in other words, on convergent theological courses. Doubtless, the achievement of Christian unity will be God's work, not men's; but ecumenism can pave the way to it, and 'dispose' us for the reception of this great and hoped-for grace.

The actual practice of the ecumenical dialogue may be helped by a sentence added during the fourth session of the council, which has been described[13] as possibly the most important change made in the text at that stage: Catholic theologians, in comparing doctrines, 'should bear in mind that there is an order or "hierarchy" of the truths of Catholic doctrine, since these truths are variously linked up with the foundation of the Christian faith' (n. 11). This sentence must not be misunderstood. It does not mean that, of the articles of faith, or among defined doctrines, there are some which are unessential; nor that some are only probably true. You cannot be a Catholic on the basis of a selection of Catholic doctrines excluding some which you, or others advising you, think to be 'unimportant' or disputable. All doctrines, in other words, are equally necessary. But they are not equally important. The doctrine of man's redemption by Christ is not more true than the doctrine of indulgences; but it is vastly more important. When doctrines are viewed in their aspect of being equally necessary they are seen, as it were, two-dimensionally. But the world to which they belong is three-dimensional, a world of perspective.

The importance of this distinction between truth and varying importance is obvious as regards the ecumenical dialogue, in which it should quickly become apparent that most of the more important truths are held in common. This is only to be expected if the criterion of importance is the closeness of the link between a doctrine and the 'foundation of the Christian faith'.[14] It may be of even greater consequence that the acceptance of the distinction could have profound effect on Catholicism as existentially lived. We have already seen that the council, without in any way denying the 'juridical' element in the Christian totality, has shifted the emphasis from this element to the sacramental aspect of the body of Christ. Such

[13] T. Stransky, *op. cit.*, p. 64, n. 30.

[14] How is that 'foundation' to be designated? The first proclamation of the faith was presumably 'Jesus is risen'. Very early too, were such 'confessions' as 'Jesus is the Christ', 'Jesus is Lord'. The decree wisely abstains from further precision.

shifts of emphasis can change the quality of a religion as actually lived – and can increase or diminish its existential credibility.

6

Eschatology and History

The progress of biblical study and the development of a biblical theology have brought many gains to twentieth century Christianity. Not the least of these is what with little exaggeration could be described as the recovery of the eschatological dimension of the gospel. The liberal Protestantism of the nineteenth century was confident that the clue to the meaning of Christ was to be found in his ethical teaching: a doctrine of the brotherhood of man, based upon the common Fatherhood of God, and recommended essentially by its appeal, taking shape in a categorical imperative, to the rational conscience of all men.[1] This way of understanding the gospel produced noble fruits, for instance in Seeley's remarkable book *Ecce Homo*. It could, however, be criticised as imposing on the biblical data an interpretation drawn from modern moralistic concern rather than justified by the original gospel's own historical context. A new direction was given to the understanding of Jesus' own teaching by Weiss and Schweitzer, who familiarised us with the notion of Jesus as 'an apocalyptic

[1] Cf. W. R. Farmer, 'An Historical Essay on the Humanity of Jesus Christ', in *Festschrift for John Knox*: 'The Sermon on the Mount became for Baur the hermeneutical key to other Matthaean texts including the parables. This may reflect the special interest in ethics characteristic of the enlightenment, or possibly even the direct influence of Kant. We know that Kant exercised a considerable influence on Baur and that his Categorical Imperative did center attention in the radical ethical demands of Jesus. . . .'

dreamer', whose ethical teaching was a mere code of behaviour for a brief interim between his own ministry and the end of all things historical through the advent of the eschatological Kingdom of God. For the 'thorough-going eschatologist' the expectation and proclamation of the Last Things as imminent is the sum-total of the real original gospel. Jesus died, in fact, 'to make his dream come true'. If magic is the attempt to constrain the celestial powers to bow to the magician's human will, Christ's self-sought death – anticipating the fanaticism of the Donatist *circumcelliones* – was surely the supreme act of magic.

Thorough-going eschatology relegates the Kingdom of God firmly and wholly to a temporal future. It therefore entails a radical distinction between that Kingdom and the historical Church. As Loisy said: 'Jesus proclaimed the Kingdom, and what actually arrived was the Church'. Theologically, this theory has two disadvantages. It throws into sharp question the reliability of the message of Jesus – since what he proclaimed as imminent has not yet arrived. And it consigns Christianity to a status indistinguishable, as regards basic religious values, from that of the Judaism from which it sprang. Judaism itself lived in expectation of the messianic age and the advent of God's Kingdom; and, if thorough-going eschatology is true, so does Christianity – the only difference being that Christianity has added one rather ambivalent prophet to those whose memory Judaism venerated.

A great deal of work has been done on the New Testament since the publication of Schweitzer's *The Quest of the Historical Jesus* compelled scholarship to treat seriously the challenge thrown down by thorough-going eschatology. Especially Dodd in this country[2] and Cullmann abroad[3] have propounded solutions of the problems which we are here considering; solutions which may be described as realised eschatology. Dodd maintained that wherever we can find traces of the most primitive preaching or *kerygma* of the early Church we find the notion that what Jewish eschatology hoped for has already, in and through Christ, been actualised in history. He holds that

[2] *The Apostolic Preaching and its Developments*. Cf. also, by the same author, *The Parables of the Kingdom*.

[3] *Christus und die Zeit*.

this primitive *kerygma* 'arises directly out of the teaching of Jesus about the Kingdom of God and all that hangs upon it', and that in the Fourth Gospel, with its tremendous affirmation that the word of God 'was made flesh, and we have seen his glory', we have 'the most penetrating exposition' of the central meaning of Jesus's teaching. Similarly, Cullmann holds that the original gospel faces us with the paradox of something which is essentially future, or rather post-historic, and yet has been really, though not completely, actualised in the history of Jesus the redeemer. I believe that this reading of the New Testament evidence is substantially correct – provided that we do not adopt such a thorough-going realised eschatology as to exclude the reality and significance of the Church's hope of a complete and glorious post-historic actualisation of what is given to the Church in this interim period under the veils of faith.

Clearly, if 'the last things' and the reign of God, for which Judaism hoped, can be held to be in some sense realised in the gospel, the relation between the Church and the Kingdom need not be regarded as one of stark mutual exclusion. Since the Church is what historically came of the gospel, there can be a view of the Church which sees its relationship to the Kingdom on the analogy – though only on the analogy – of the relation of Jesus, his ministry, death and resurrection, to the Kingdom. If, on the other hand, Christian eschatology has always retained its note of 'not yet', of something more to hope for, of a realisation in glory answering the realisation in humiliation, of a coming (still to be awaited) of the Son of Man who, in history, 'had not where to lay his head', then we must be careful about any too simple identification of Kingdom and Church, or even of Kingdom and Christianity. A draft document submitted to Vatican I had affirmed that the Church is 'this perfect city which holy writ calls the Kingdom of God'. A similar identification was made in the draft on the Church presented to the fathers of Vatican II in 1962. This draft was the antecedent of our Constitution on the Church; but the latter has extensively and profoundly modified the teaching of the draft.

The constitution *Lumen Gentium* sees the Church as the 'germ and beginning of the Kingdom of Christ and God on earth' (n. 5). But it at once goes on to say that, as she gradually grows on earth, the Church aspires to the perfected Kingdom, hoping and desiring with all her strength to be joined in glory with her King. The image of this aspiring, growing, forward-looking Church, is not that of the 'perfect city', but that of the 'hastening pilgrim', manifesting the mystery of Christ 'in shadow', 'till at the end it shall be disclosed in full light' (n. 8). She makes her way 'through temptations and tribulations' (n. 9), embracing as she does those who are sinners, and being therefore herself 'at once holy and always in need of purification' (n. 8), and strengthened by God to an unceasing task of 'self-renovation, till by way of the cross she comes to the light which knows no setting' (n. 9).

To the subject of the Church's eschatological orientation the constitution devotes its seventh chapter. The eschatology here taught is neither the thorough-going eschatology of Schweitzer nor the thorough-going realised eschatology which has been, perhaps wrongly, attributed to Dodd. 'The Church', we are told, 'will reach its consummation only in heavenly glory, when the time of the restoration of all things shall come and the whole world, along with the human race . . . will be perfectly restored in Christ. . . . The restoration which has been promised and which we await, has already begun in Christ, is carried forward in the sending of the Holy Spirit, and through him proceeds in the Church in which through faith we are taught also about the meaning of our temporal life';

> Already then, the ends of the ages have come upon us (cf. 1 Co 10:11) and the renovation of the world is irrevocably established and in a certain real manner anticipated in this age; for already on earth the Church is marked with true, though imperfect, holiness. But until the new heavens and the new earth come to pass, in which righteousness dwells (cf. 2 P 3:13), the pilgrim Church, in its sacraments and institutions, which belong to this age, bears the figure of this time which passes away and lives her life among creatures which to this day groan and travail and await the revelation of the sons of God (cf. Rm 8:9–22).

What are the deeper theological implications of an eschatology which accepts a real anticipation in history of the Last Things, both in the incarnation of the word of God and in a Church which is the sacrament of his ever-contemporary presence and action in human life on earth? It may be suggested that there is a field for reflection here which has been for long obscured by the reaction upon Christian thinking of our dialogue with Greek philosophy.

Greek philosophy received its basic orientation, as a quest of a unifying explanation of experience, from Thales of Miletus. It reached its high-water mark in Aristotle, whose physics was true to Thales' basic inspiration, though immensely in advance of his conclusions. But in the very measure in which Aristotle sought to understand our experience of being-in-motion he was driven to realise that a genuine intellectual dialectic was driving him, through his very fidelity to experience, beyond the limits of empiricism. 'After Physics' (*meta ta physica*) he knew that he had to consider no longer merely being-in-motion, but 'being as being'. The resultant 'branch' of philosophy is in consequence known as ontology or metaphysics. Here reflection is concerned with an a-temporal sphere and aspect of reality, underpinning the temporal order and giving it, by participation, its measure of intelligibility.

I wish to suggest that the whole of this great intellectual adventure, from Thales to Aristotle, is dominated – with significant exceptions – by the pure unrestricted desire to understand. At its culminating moment, in Aristotle, it had little concern for an historical explanation of human experience, except in so far as each individual life is a history (reproduced in the city) of transition from economic motivations to a quest of super-temporal values. As has often been pointed out, Greek thought tended to see major history as a recurrent unfolding of eternal values which did not themselves share the vicissitudes of temporal change. Time is the moving, revolving, recurring, shadow of eternity. It is not without importance for an understanding of the development of Christian theology that metaphysics has become, in our schools, the propaedeutic of theology. When traditional western theology is accused of propagating a 'non-historical orthodoxy' (Novak), of being 'essentialist' rather than 'existentialist', and of offering a static model of the Church and of human society, the fault, if there is one, has been that the West came under the sway of 'the Philosopher' (as St Thomas Aquinas entitled Aristotle), and of a reflection which, because it was purely intellectual, was also basically a-religious.

The real roots of the gospel, however, are not Greek but Israelitic. The Bible shows a remarkable lack of concern for purely intellectual issues. It bears witness to much hard thinking, but the motivation is not intellectual curiosity, however noble, but the quest of 'answers to those profound mysteries of the human condition which, today even as in olden times, deeply stir the human heart: What is a man? What is the meaning and purpose of our life? What is goodness and what is sin? What gives rise to our sorrows and to what intent? Where lies the path to true happiness? What is the truth about death, judgment, and retribution beyond the grave? What finally is that ultimate and ineffable mystery which engulfs our being, whence we take our rise, and whither our journey leads us?' (Declaration on the Relation of the Church to non-Christian Religions, n. 1). Classical Greek philosophy and the religious message of Israel are both concerned with truth. But while the former seeks truth as a satisfaction of our desire to understand, the latter seeks it as the clue to human behaviour and destiny, and therefore as a guide to action. There is a further difference. Greek philosophy conceives itself to be a man-initiated quest; Israelite religion believes that its own starting-point is a divine initiative: 'now the Lord said unto Abram, Get thee out of thy country, and from thy kindred, and from thy father's house, unto the land that I will show thee: and I will make of thee a great nation . . . and in thee shall all the nations of the earth bless themselves' (Gn 12: 1–3). The divine initiative takes shape characteristically in a 'call', which the recipient conceives as particular to himself, requiring response by action in the unique situation in which he finds himself. Such response is essentially voluntary, and so religion becomes at once a matter of conscience and a matter of actual history with all its particularity and uniqueness. Nevertheless, this voluntary response in a particular situation relates the religious man to ultimate reality, to God himself, and becomes a witness to ultimate truth.

There are two further abiding characteristics of Israelite religion. Since man is – as Aristotle pointed out – a social animal, the divine call implies both a detachment from the social milieu – 'Get thee out . . . from thy kindred and from thy father's house' – and the creation of new social relationships: 'I will make of thee a great nation.' Secondly, since the call is a summons to action, and action is orientated to the future in which its fruits are reaped, the call is associated with a promise – 'I will make of thee a great nation' – and this promise, since its origin is divine, takes on a universal significance: 'In thee all the nations of the earth shall bless themselves.' So deeply is religion intertwined with the full concreteness of history.

The major themes of this view of reality – based, as it is, not on the '*scientia*' that was the object of Greek philosophy but on the 'faith' which assents to a divine invitation – are variously emphasised by the prophets of Israel. The divine call becomes at once a critique of existing historical attitudes and a summons to re-conversion. The divine promise begins, how soon we hardly know, to give shape to what we call the messianic hope. But above all, the historical horizon is enlarged. It is a mark of public events that their context cannot be closely delimited. As world-events brought Israel into the sphere of the warring empires, so this wider history began to be absorbed into the prophetic vision. Great monarchs like Sennacherib and Cyrus were seen as instruments of divine purposes and God's lordship over Israel became a lordship over all human history. The divine premise, too, was seen to have a wider scope and range and to derive fresh colour from the disappointments of the present.

What, however, was most pregnant with possibilities for the future was the gradual realisation that the ultimate explanation of history must be found beyond history. This I suggest is analogous to the internal pressure that drove Aristotle on from the physics to the metaphysics. History even when envisaged as under the sway of divine providence does not explain itself. So, in the centuries preceding the gospel, there was born Jewish apocalyptic, seeking in the beyond the final answers to history's problems and mysteries. It is most important to seize the nature of this beyond. Aristotle's Prime Mover is in an a-temporal sphere of reality. But apocalyptic looks for its answers not 'above' but in what can only be described as a future beyond history, or in a post-historic realisation. One concedes without cavil that the notion of an event that is post-temporal is a paradox, that language and thought seem here to have gone beyond the limits of what is permissible. But the Jews, by and large, were not philosophers. If we want a word for this added dimension in Israelite thinking we can perhaps coin one: what metaphysics is to physics, that metachronics is to history. Metachronics expresses itself in eschatology: the doctrine of the Last Things, or rather of the Last, post-historic, Event.

It was, so far as we can judge, in the context of this apocalyptic rendering of Jewish faith that the gospel first sought its self-expression. But the gospel brought one further development which compounded the paradox of the post-historic Event. As Aristotle's metaphysics, while subsequent in the order of invention to his physics, yet provides the ultimate insights of which physics stands in need and, indeed presupposes; so that gospel proclaims the occurrence, here and now within historical process, of the post-historic event that yet retains its post-historic quality. The explanation that was sought and could only be found beyond history was 'also', because it was an explanation and indeed a presupposition, found within history and gave history its meaning from within. Such is the gospel eschatology, realised in mystery and revelation, and apprehended by faith. It is not surprising that the gospel soon broke through the trammels of a linguistic system which could not contain the dynamic energy of this final development. There were advantages, and also some disadvantages, in the fact that the new language-and-thought system in which it tried to express itself was that provided by Greek philosophy. The gospel and Aristotelianism have strange affinities and analogies; but they are not the same thing. As the product of reason, philosophy is energised from within by the first principles of reason and, behind them, by the unrestricted desire to understand. The gospel, apprehended by faith, finds its first immanent principle in the conscience which 'fears God and does what is right'. Its formal purpose is not to solve the riddles of the understanding, but to provide a meaning for the self-determinations of the will. It does not seek to solve the problems of the pure intellect; it provides the intellect with a new set of problems. And it is faith, not reason, which assures the theologian that his problems are ultimately soluble.

Man is intelligent, but he is not a pure intelligence. His experience is rooted, through the body and its senses, in a world of matter in motion which becomes, through his self-determination, a theatre of history. Caught in the process of a moving universe, his very thinking is historically conditioned. Faith, by which he 'freely commits his whole self to God' as revealed in the gospel, is itself an act or habit temporally conditioned. And the Church is a fellowship of believers. The Church is thus, in its concrete actuality an historical, durational, reality, both giving and receiving meaning from its historical context. That context, since the Church is catholic, universal, is the total human history. And because thus historical, both the Church and the Church's context are basically eschatological, plunged in the metachronic dimension of reality.

Among the many dynamic tensions of the second Vatican Council, the tension between this historical, or as some would say existentialist, view of the Church and her doctrines, and the 'essentialist' view of 'non-historical orthodoxy', was something which was liable to crop up at any moment. It could affect decisions even when the spokesmen in debate were not fully aware of their own motives. One such decision led to taking not, as in *Mystici Corporis*, the notion of the mystical body of Christ but that of the People of God as the motif of the Constitution on the Church. When the Church is viewed as the body of the glorified Christ, it is seen indeed in its essential quality. But when it is viewed as God's people, it is seen in its actual historical existence, in its pilgrimage through actual time. The tension was liable to become acute when, partly for ecumenical reasons, it was sought to embody in the statements of the council a confession of the Church's sinfulness. The reaction of the essentialists was sharp and immediate: we confess in the Creeds that the Church is 'holy'; how then can we admit that she is stained with sin, *semper reformanda*? The same tension was at work when it had to be decided whether the council should describe the relations which would hold between the Church and a statically Christian civil state, and not rather the relations which actually hold between the

Church and a total complex of social relations in an ever-changing world. This tension is latent – some would say unresolved – in the juxtaposition of the hierarchical view of the Church, of her unchanging basic structure, with that of the Church as energised, rendered dynamic, by the charisms or grace-gifts of the Holy Ghost who is no respecter of persons or of office. This charismatic aspect of the Church is what makes her, while unchanging in her essence, unpredictable in her history. *Les portes de l'avenir sont toujours grand-ouvertes.*

When, lastly, we remember that, for Christian faith, the post-historic end of history is already mysteriously anticipated in the incarnation of the Word of God, we come to realise that the latent implication of the council's documents, namely that hierarchical structure and juridical institution are, in the Church, subordinate to sacramental reality, is itself an affirmation of the historical and metachronic against the essentialist, ultimately philosophic or metaphysical, view of the Church.

The category of the sacramental affirming an actual presence in the 'age of the Church' of the historical events in which Christianity originated is a sub-category of metachronics. The presence and action of Christ in the Church and her sacraments is a metachronic presence and action of the Last Thing already incarnate in and as Jesus of Nazareth; it is the sacramental presence here and now of an historically past reality which really but mysteriously anticipates a consummation that is post-historic. So the Church chants, in praise of the greatest of her sacraments: *O sacrum convivium, in quo Christus sumitur, recolitur memoria passionis eius, mens impletur gratiae, et futurae gloriae nobis pignus datur.*

Here a certain caution is no doubt necessary. Theology operates within the horizon of faith. And faith, while truly a grace-gift of God, is a self-determination of man as conscientious. But the believer remains intelligent, and intelligence, within its own domain, brooks no extrinsic control. A gospel which is truly catholic, intensively as well as extensively, is bound to respect this autonomy of the intellect. There were occasions in the council when it might seem that a progressive element was in hidden or explicit revolt against scholasticism. If scholasticism means the system of thought recoverable from the records of medieval western Europe, this revolt is explicable. Such scholasticism was not a pure product of pure intelligence operating on Christian data; it was infected with the contingency of its own historical context. And in the somewhat degraded form in which it has come down to us in theological manuals it could seem to be too Greek to be comprehensively Christian. Meanwhile, man's post-medieval intellectual history is not to be neglected. Above all, through the modern applications of scientific historical research and study the data for theological understanding and eventual synthesis are immensely more abundant than all that was available to St Thomas. But dissatisfaction with the medieval theological synthesis must not give rise to a rejection of the ideal of a theology which can bear the scrutiny of the understanding. For the intellect, history itself is a challenge calling for explanation; and every explanation tends towards system and synthesis. Every Christian scholasticism that has or will come into existence is a homage alike to faith and to reason; no actual scholasticism that has or will exist can claim the finality of faith and dogma.

Theology, however, is not faith but an explication and systematisation of reality as penetrated by divine act and illuminated by the divine revelation which faith directly apprehends in the sign of revelation. Christian faith discovers the clue to all human history and experience in a particular cluster of interrelated historical events, each of which has a context which is ultimately the whole of history, and the whole of the subjacent material substructure of history. In this cluster of events it apprehends the irruption of the superhistorical (taking of necessity in this irruption the figure of the post-historical) into history and as a particular history. Professor Dodd at this point refers to Kittel's notion of 'the scandal of particularity' – 'how can we now take seriously a view which selects one particular episode in history, and declares that it possesses an absolute and final quality distinguishing it from all other events?'[4] This episode is declared not only to have an absolute and final quality, but to have a universal relevance

[4] *The Apostolic Preaching and its Developments*, p. 88.

throughout history, both that history which preceded it and that which will follow it to the end of mundane time.

Here it should be observed that if the divine act which gives meaning to history and human life in history is to be itself, as it must needs be, historical, it must inevitably be 'particular'; for everything that is historical is particular, unique, unrepeatable. To hold this particularity of Christ to be unacceptable is, in the end, to deny that God can establish personal contact with human beings in their full historical reality. Christianity, at least, has taken seriously the Israelite faith that God is the Lord of history and therefore the Lord and creator of history's material *suppositum*. It has taken seriously the Israelite conviction that God can and does address a word of power and revelation to man historically conditioned. God spoke by the prophets; and when God spoke the world was made.

We have already seen that an historical event, which is to say a significant event, both gives to its context, and receives from it, an element of meaning. The New Testament is so steeped in the conviction that the events of our salvation are of absolute and universal significance that, in two culminating passages, it identified Jesus of Nazareth with the divine word which created the universe: 'He is the image of the invisible God, the first-born of all creation; for in him all things were created, in heaven and on earth, visible and invisible, whether thrones or dominations or principalities or authorities – all things were created through him and for him. He is before all things, and in him all things hold together' (Col 1:15–17). 'In the beginning was the word . . . all things were made through him . . . and the word became flesh and dwelt among us, full of grace and truth; we have beheld his glory' (Jn 1:1–14).

One may doubt whether theology has given enough attention to the implications of these passages. It seems insufficient to say that they are evidence of the belief that Jesus was divine, true though this is. There is a further question: is there any reason why creation should be attributed in particular to the second Person of the Trinity, whereas it is a theological axiom that all the works of God '*ad extra*' are common to the three Persons? To explain this attribution by the fact that the divine Word is the expression of God's wisdom, as the divine

Spirit is the expression of divine Love, appears inadequate for two reasons. First, it draws on a Hellenic concept of the divine Logos, though the roots of the New Testament notion of the word of God seem to be rather biblical than Greek. Secondly, is creation any less a sign of divine love than it is of divine wisdom?

One may therefore suppose that the attribution in question springs from the sense of a connection between creation, salvation, and the *Eschaton* (Last End). A medieval question, whether the incarnation would have occurred if man had not fallen, and St Thomas' reply that we have no evidence to show that it would, has perhaps made such a suggestion unpopular. The medieval question itself, however, seems to express an adventure into the unreal field of impossible hypotheses. In considering an ideal system of cause and effect, regarded as immune from free agency, it can be informative to consider a variation in the supposed data and its effects on the whole system. Such intellectual exercises are meaningless when the system considered includes the action of free agents. And on the other hand, our two texts of scripture might be held to give just that support in tradition which St Thomas desiderated for the view which he rejected.

What kind of connection could there be between creation and salvation – other, of course, than the obvious one that salvation presupposes creation? We have to avoid any theory which would disregard the distinction between grace and nature. This is a distinction in the ontological order and is certainly valid. But we are concerned with the existential order. The suggested connection would consist in an extrinsic orientation of the actual created order towards the events of salvation and the *Eschaton*. We may suppose that the whole created order, including the order of created grace, springs from a single divine decree, is the expression of a single divine intention which will be fully realised in that final consummation when he, 'who must reign till he has put all his enemies under his feet' is himself 'subjected to him who put all things under his feet, that God may be everything to everyone' (1 Co 15:25–28). This *Eschaton*, this final consummation, 'last in execution' of the constituents of the divine purpose, would have been 'first in intention', so that the actual existence of nature, as distinct from its ontological essence, would have been pregnant from the first with the intention of salvation and the *Eschaton*. And thus, we may remark, the history of salvation, which like all historical events both gives and receives meaning from its context, would be set in a cosmic context which would have a pre-established harmony with it. And once again we should conclude that the metachronic is not only the post-historic consummation which gives an ultimate meaning to history but is the presupposition of history and of the theatre in which history has to be played out.[5]

Theologically, the council may be said to bear witness to a shift of emphasis from a static model of the Christian reality, and in particular of the Church, to a dynamic model. Such a change of emphasis does not entail a rejection of the truths enunciated at an earlier stage of theological development. The second council of the Vatican, like all previous ecumenical councils since the first, was conscious of an inheritance from the Church's dogmatic past which it was commissioned to preserve and to carry forward. The change of emphasis, however, was real, and implicit in it was the adoption of a framework of thought other than that which had given birth to the static model. The great fathers of the Church, and after them the medieval schoolmen, utilised in the service of Christian truth the thought-scheme that lay to hand in Greek philosophy. Christianity has been well served by that thought-scheme. But a study of patristic exegesis of the scriptures would suggest that it was not entirely apt for the interpretation of the history of salvation. What is extraordinary about this patristic exegesis is the frequency with which we can see

[5] If our suggestion is theologically acceptable, it may offer a clue to the very real problem of the salvation that is possible for those who have never had the gospel announced to them. Salvation presupposes supernatural faith, and faith's object has two aspects: 'formally', it is the truth of God self-revealed; 'materially' it is the 'sign' of that truth which, for a Christian, is the gospel itself, in fact is Christ himself, mediator and fullness of divine revelation. By what 'sign' does the unevangelised man apprehend the truth of God self-revealed? Since 'there is no other name by which one may be saved' except the 'name of Christ', this sign needs to be in some way a participation of the Christ-sign. And, if creation has no ultimate existential meaning except that given to it by the *Eschaton* which is Christ consummated, then all human experience is necessarily 'Christological' in its ultimate significance; and any human experience can, *per se*, serve as a sign of God self-revealed.

it to have been mistaken in itself, coupled with the correctness of the resultant doctrinal whole, as far as it went. It was almost as though the fathers were constructing a Mercator's Projection of Christian truth, a plane-surface map of a reality that was three-dimensional. I venture to think that it is the modern science of historical interpretation and criticism that has made it possible for our generation to realise better than its predecessors that the gospel yields more of its mystery to those who think in terms of history and eschatology – incarnational eschatology – than to those who think in terms of Aristotle.

The council's shift of emphasis was perhaps more instinctive than reflective. The historical, existential, way of looking at experience is in the air which we all breathe today, and the remarkable willingness of the council fathers to listen to the best available theologians and exegetes meant that they were breathing in this atmosphere even when unaware of the fact. Perhaps it is in the Constitution on the Church in the World of Today that the existential model of the Church comes most fully into its own. Already in the *proëm* of this document the council speaks of the 'fellowship of Christ's disciples' as made up of men and experiencing its own intimate union with the human race and its history, and claims to 'have before its eyes the world of men or the universal human family together with the totality of things amidst which it lives: the world, the theatre of the history of the human race, bearing the marks of man's industry, his disasters and his victories'. It is no ideal Church, but the actual community of believers, whose sincere co-operation with the human race is here offered for the task of establishing a universal brotherhood. And it is of no textbook world, but of the actual, contemporary, suffering and aspiring world that it is said – in the Introduction of the constitution – that Christ is the key, the centre, and the goal of all its history.

The same shift from 'essence' to 'existence' may be seen in the council's treatment, later in this constitution, of marriage and the family. The Church's – or her theologians' – treatment of marriage has often been presented in terms of human nature, and there has been a tendency to concentrate attention on the biological side of that nature. In contrast with this approach, the constitution moves towards a theology of marriage which lays stress rather on the human persons existentially involved in marriage and the family, than on the bodily nature called into play in the marriage act. It speaks of 'the conjugal, family fellowship' as 'a fellowship of love', and of the 'intimate union' of husband and wife, and the 'mutual self-giving of two persons' which constitutes this union. And while it is clearly affirmed that such conjugal love, among its ends, has that of disposing husband and wife to co-operate with God in the increase of the human family, the council shows its sense of the fully personal nature of the marriage union when it speaks of the 'human and Christian responsibility' with which this rôle of parenthood should be performed. Such conscientious responsibility will lead them to form 'a right judgment' about the size of their family, a judgment to be formed by 'objective criteria derived from the nature of a person and of personal acts'; here, it will be observed, the concept 'nature' is introduced, but its direct reference is not to man's physical constitution but to his being a person. These objective criteria will be interpreted, for the Christian, by the teaching authority of the Church. All this shows a vision of the Church and her sacraments as constituted by, and in turn constituting, the history of man as an actual family of actual persons.

7

Objective and Subjective

One of the powerful impressions made upon an adult western convert by his new religion is the extreme 'objectiveness' of what is sometimes called the Catholic System. Now at last, he feels, I possess, or rather am possessed by, a faith which I have not invented for myself; the Catholic System stands over against me with the massive reality of a great mountain range, outside myself though entering into my experience. There is a sense in which it matters very little whether I personally believe in it or not. It is there in spite of me; it existed before me and will continue after me. My private judgment could never attain to results of such transcendent stability. *Quot homines, tot sententiae*; but the word of the Lord, expounded and spoken by his Church, endures for ever.

Having accepted the system, ready-made, coherent, multi-dimensional and rather detailed, the convert may be tempted to suppose that the answers to even his most personal and particular problems may be found on the right page of the right book, or by consulting a director or 'someone in authority'. Catholicism is a religion of authority; and the right response to authority is, he thinks, obedience. Can one have too much of either? Certainly, the convert feels, he has had too little of both in his past life; and he is not always sufficiently alive to the danger of proceeding from one extreme to the other.

If, in what follows, I may seem to be criticising the religious attitude portrayed, or perhaps caricatured, by such a convert, I want first to draw attention to the immense religious values implicit in this Catholic objectivity. Our own countrymen are perhaps too prone to assign full objective reality above all to sticks and stones – one remembers Samuel Johnson's refutation of Berkeley – and, in the second place, to stocks and shares; while religion is considered to be a matter of private taste, need, or intuition, a chosen self-orientation of the human person rather than the supreme reality, offering itself to man as concretely and massively as do the objects of sense experience and of natural science. Such a tendency, if pushed to its limits and uncontrolled, is not only debilitating but disastrous to religion itself, and certainly to the Christian religion. So pushed, it would reduce the history of salvation to the status of a myth to be accepted or rejected according as it seemed to give expression to the temperament of the individual. The age-long strength of Christianity has been its insistence on the objective and real truth of the gospel message and its presuppositions. It began by asserting, and has ever asserted, that Jesus of Nazareth – who died under Pontius Pilate – has been raised from the dead. As St Paul says, taking the full consequences of such realism: If Christ be not risen, then is our faith vain. It was this realism that brought the gospel into an inevitable confrontation with Greek philosophy, which was equally, in its own way, concerned with objective truth and reality. The Church could not consent to see her gospel placed on the same level as the Graeco-Roman mythology, which had never given much trouble to the philosophers and had little to fear from them.[1]

In modern times the emphasis on the objective reality and truth of Christianity has been accentuated among Catholics as a reaction to what they took to be a subjectivist tendency in Protestantism. The Reformation was born when Luther, refusing compliance with an ecclesiastical requirement, explained 'that he could not do otherwise' than refuse. Not that

[1] I have suggested elsewhere that Arianism, by condoning the worship of Christ while denying that he is in the full sense God, would have reduced Christianity to mythological status. The Fathers of Nicaea were perhaps dimly aware that Christian realism cannot despise metaphysics.

he was physically incapable of compliance, but that he claimed to recognise an interior obligation of his conscience forbidding obedience. The subsequent movement of protest took shape in a criticism and rejection of the 'traditions' inherited from the Middle Ages, and of the authority of the ecclesiastical officialdom which defended these traditions. From both the traditions and the ecclesiastical authority appeal was made to the content and authority of scripture. The Catholic Church, however, also claimed the authority of scripture for its general positions. Who, then, in this conflict of interpretation, had authority to determine the meaning of scripture? It was the same problem as had been raised by Arianism: how do we know which interpretation is correct? Protestants were driven to proclaim the right of free enquiry into the meaning of scripture, and in some cases, perhaps, the right to follow one's own judgment of that meaning. Such a judgment did not, of course, preclude giving due weight to the convictions and intuitions of other believers and other students of the Bible; and it was stated or implied that the judgment must be a result of the enlightenment and direction of the Holy Spirit. But such divine guidance would, in the last resort, be given interiorly to the conscience; it would not be externally mediated by ecclesiastical authority, the magisterium. Ultimately, but at two very different times, extreme positions were reached in the virtual monopoly accorded by Quakers to the Inner Light, in abstraction from all authoritative dogma or doctrine, and in the Liberal Protestant rejection of the notion of supernatural biblical inspiration. There followed an epidemic of ever-fresh and mutually contradictory expositions of the essence of Christianity.[2]

Protestants may well object that the above is a caricature of their real standpoint. What concerns us here is, not whether it is true, but that it was the impression gained of Protestantism by the Catholics of the Counter-Reformation. Catholics came to think that Protestantism was not only schismatical and heretical but the very apotheosis of subjectivism. Against its supposed dangers, the objectivism and authoritarian character of Catholicism were strongly underlined. In particular,

[2] On the close connection between the Reformation rejection of 'tradition' and its critique of ecclesiastical authority, cf. Ratzinger, 'Revelation and Tradition', in K. Rahner and J. Ratzinger, *Revelation as Tradition*, pp. 26–31.

theology itself, instead of being the function of the individual's faith in search of a more reflective understanding of the Christian mystery, became a sort of clerical preserve and an organ of ecclesiastical authority. Moral theology, for example, which might have developed as an instrument for the education of the faithful, became mainly a *directorium* for confessors; in the result the manuals of moral theology became repositories of a sort of moral algebra which, to a superficial reader, might seem to prescind altogether from the concrete realities of existence and to render superfluous the interior illuminations of the Holy Spirit.[3] Dogmatic theology, meanwhile, secure in the certainty of its own objective and unchanging bases, seemed to be retiring into a world equally remote from the real concerns of the contemporary world. Relations between 'Church' (really the ecclesiastical authorities) and 'state' (civil governments) were expounded on the assumption that the medieval synthesis known as 'Christendom' was the ideal and only normal basis for such relations; and when the theologian was compelled to survey, or the ecclesiastical politicians to find a *modus vivendi* with, the actualities of modern life, a supposedly 'hypothetical' set of maxims, a sort of *Interimsethik*, was

[3] All such statements require qualification. The English Benedictine spiritual classic, *Sancta Sophia*, compiled by Serenus Cressy from the writings of Augustine Baker, who lived in the aftermath of the Council of Trent, contains a section entitled: God by His Holy Inspirations is the Guide and Director of an Internal Contemplative Life. The basic principle of this section is that 'in all good actions . . . God alone is our only master and director; and creatures, when he uses them, are only his instruments'. It is inferred that 'all other teachers whatsoever, whether the light of reason, or external directors, or rules prescribed in books etc., are no further nor otherwise to be followed or hearkened to, than as they are subordinate and conformable to the internal directions and inspirations of God's Holy Spirit, or as God invites, instructs, and moves us to have recourse to them' (p. 68). It is characteristic of the period in which this book was first published that the section ends with a chapter answering the objection that its teaching is prejudicial to external authority. The argument of this chapter is resumed in Cressy's preface to the whole book, pp. 11–19, where note especially the contention that it would be disastrous to give up teaching the truth about divine inspirations on the ground that this truth has been abused by 'the frantic spirits of this age': 'Shall we tell them that there are no inspirations at all? We shall, in so doing, betray the Christian religion. Shall we say, though there be inspirations, yet they are never to be marked, never obeyed nor complied withal? Besides the ridiculous falseness of the assertion, which will expose us to their most just contempt and hatred, they will overwhelm us with unanswerable texts of scripture and passages of the holy fathers' (p. 18).

devised – to be discarded, it was hoped, one day when the world woke from up its Protestant and Liberal dreams and returned to medieval sanity.

A volume could be written on the factors, some intrinsic and some extrinsic, which paved the way to a change of theological emphasis in this field of 'objective and subjective' in Vatican II. From early in the nineteenth century there were Catholic laymen and priests who sought an accommodation with the forces making for modern democracy. Theologians like Newman in this country and Scheeben abroad were feeling their way to a more living theology. The Thomist revival, initiated by Leo XIII, directed the professional theologians back to pre-Reformation modes of thought. It was followed by a revival in patristic studies and a renewal of biblical scholarship and biblical theology. Meanwhile, the sway of liberalism in the world was being challenged by the authoritarianism of communism and national socialism. It began to seem more important to fortify the individual conscience against the demands of illegitimate authority than to inculcate obedience to an authority claiming to be legitimate. And perhaps we should not underrate the influence of a growing interest in mystical theology with its stress on the 'personal religion' of the believer and its instinctively felt need to safeguard this from unwarranted intrusions from outside, even from such as emanated from ecclesiastical authority.[4]

The council's shift of emphasis can be illustrated in various subject-matters. In sacramental theology, post-Reformation Catholic thinkers have insisted strongly on the fact that the sacraments are efficacious *ex opere operato*: the validity of sacraments is conditioned not by the moral dispositions of the recipients nor by those of the ministers, but simply by the intentional and correct 'positing', on the part of a qualified minister, of the sacramental sign. Provided, for instance, the Eucharist is celebrated by an ordained priest who intentionally and correctly performs our Lord's command: Do this in remembrance of me, it is a valid Eucharist whatever the moral

[4] English readers can see this motive at work in Von Hügel's writings, especially *The Mystical Element of Religion and Eternal Life*.

condition of the priest or his congregation.[5]

The Church has, of course, always wanted her children to celebrate the Eucharist with great devotion and reverence, with grace-filled hearts and with minds deeply conscious of what is going forward. And as a first step she requires them to attend the Eucharist on Sundays and certain other holy days. Nevertheless, it is striking that the Constitution on the Liturgy, while of course taking the *opus operatum* aspect of the Eucharist and the other sacraments for granted, lays great stress on the liturgy as something done in common by the faithful: it is an outstanding means whereby 'the faithful give a living expression of, and make manifest to others, the mystery of Christ and the true nature of the Church, which is both human and divine, visible but endowed with invisible properties, fervent in action and devoted to contemplation, present in the world but as a pilgrim' (*De Liturgia*, n. 1). And of the Eucharist in particular, it states that in order that it should have its full efficaciousness, 'it is necessary that the faithful should approach the sacred liturgy with good dispositions, apply their minds to the words they utter in it, and co-operate with divine grace, lest they receive it in vain. Therefore their pastors must see to it not only that the laws for a valid and lawful celebration of the liturgy are observed, but that the faithful take part in it with full knowledge, actively and fruitfully' (n. 11). Such 'conscious and active participation' is required by the very nature of the liturgy; and it is 'the first and necessary source whence the faithful derive a truly Christian spirit' (n. 14). Similarly, the constitution *De Ecclesia* speaks of the faithful as offering in the Eucharist the divine victim and, along with this victim, themselves to God (n. 11). They are not to be mere passive spectators and beneficiaries of an *opus operatum* but active co-operators in an action of the Church which has this *opus operatum* at its heart. Christ himself is present and active in the liturgy, and especially in the eucharistic sacrifice, in which 'the work of our redemption is performed' (cf. the Mass of the Latin Rite for the ninth Sunday after Pentecost). But Christ, in his liturgical action, 'always associ-

[5] For an amusing polemic against what F. D. Maurice thought to be the 'Romish' theory of *opus operatum*, cf. *The Kingdom of Christ*, ed., 1958, vol. I, pp. 282–8.

ates the Church, his beloved spouse, with himself' (*De Liturgia*), n. 7). The Eucharist, validly and legitimately celebrated, is the growing-point of the Church and of her unity. In each 'fellowship of the altar', however small and poor, 'Christ is present, and by his power the one holy catholic and apostolic Church is gathered together. By participation in the body and blood of Christ we tend to become that which we receive' (Leo M., *Serm.* 63) (*De Ecclesia*, n. 26). Here we have a picture of the whole Church epitomised and subjectively alive in the group of the local faithful. The same interest in the subjective life of the Church emerges in the teaching on the 'charisms' or grace-gifts of the Holy Spirit which, while given for the 'renewal and further up-building of the Church', are principles of individual action in no way tied to institutional office. We have already suggested that this 'charismatic' life of the Church, the grace-motivated Christian living of all its members in whatever field of human activity, is the dynamic aspect of that life. This fully personal, responsible and creative activity of the People of God is the intended end-product of the whole sacramental structure of the Church. We may say, in fact, that *opus operatum* is given in order to promote *opus operantis* (cf. *De Ecclesia*, n. 12).

For another illustration of the council's concern with the subjective side of the Christian totality we may consider what has happened, in its documents, to the ancient and permanently valid maxim: *extra ecclesiam nulla salus*. In the past, a very objective interpretation has been given to this maxim, although never without qualifications which were capable of considerable development. St Cyprian gave a strong expression to the objective interpretation. But the early Church admitted the possibility of salvation for catechumens who died before baptism and for unbaptised martyrs. St Augustine took Job as an example of a saint who lived – and presumably died – outside the visible limits of the People of God. Pius IX disclaimed the notion that anyone would be punished for the mere fact of inculpable non-adherence to the visible Catholic Church. And there was a tendency in modern theology before Vatican II to admit a moral, as distinct from a legal, presumption that apparently conscientious non-Catholics are 'in good faith', in other words are not personally guilty of rejecting the means of salvation. But it could be said that all these efforts to make the maxim more elastic started from the consideration, that, objectively speaking, salvation belongs normally to those who adhere visibly to the visible Catholic Church – and who live up to the requirements of that status. The Constitution on the Church, on the other hand, in its chapter on the People of God, opens its discussion of salvation by a primary affirmation that 'whoever fears God and does what is right is acceptable to God' (n. 9). Only after laying down this principle does it proceed to teach that the objective means of salvation are given by God in the People of God, that is, the Church. This inversion of the traditional order of thought may be taken as a shift of emphasis from objective to subjective. Salvation is, for the individual, radically dependent rather on subjective good intention that on external ecclesiastical allegiance. Important as adhesion to objective truth and its sacramental and institutional embodiment is, it is less important than a good will to adhere to truth and to seek ever fuller truth. In the end, subjective conscientiousness is of greater value that objective correctness. There is nothing revolutionary in this new emphasis. Moral theology has long since established the principle that one's own serious judgments of conscience, even if inculpably mistaken, must always be obeyed. And it is obvious that such obedience cannot merit divine punishment. It is further certain that, for those who have reached moral adulthood, there is no middle path between salvation and damnation; and there seems therefore no escape from the conclusion that all who obey their conscience will receive from God the supernatural help they need in order to attain to heaven.

It may here be recalled that, since the maxim *extra ecclesiam nulla salus* still holds good, the above considerations demand a re-examination of the 'limits' of the Church.[6] As we have

[6] The Constitution on the Church, with a plain allusion to the maxim, states: 'Those men could not be saved who, while not unaware that the Catholic Church was established by God through Jesus Christ as necessary, nevertheless refused to enter it or to abide in it' (n. 14). This is a perfectly sound practical interpretation – oddly expressed, because the charitable composer of this statement was loath to admit that anyone could, with his eyes open, reject Catholicism if he knew it to be 'necessary'. But the practical interpretation invites, but does not offer, a theological explanation.

seen, a basis for an enriched theology of the Church and its range is given in chapter I of the Constitution on the Church, which clearly affirms that the Church is both a visible reality and a spiritual one, but avoids a sheer material identification of the two aspects of this one reality, and instead of saying that the Church is the Catholic Church affirms that she 'subsists in the Catholic Church'. Are we not bound, in the end, to acknowledge that sanctifying grace can, and presumably often does, enrich men who are not visibly within the Roman Catholic body, and that the Church is present wherever sanctifying grace is present: *Ubi Spiritus Domini, ibi Ecclesia*?

A short passage from the Constitution on the Church in the World of Today will further illustrate the council's attitude to conscience, and the primacy accorded to it:

> In the recesses of his self-awareness man discovers a law, which he does not give to himself, but which he ought to obey. Its voice, ever summoning him to love and do what is good and to avoid what is evil speaks, when need arises, in his heart's ears: Do this, or avoid that. In fact man has a law written in his heart by God, obedience to which constitutes his very dignity; and according to this law he will be judged. Conscience is man's most secret centre (nucleus) and his shrine; in it he is alone with God, whose voice is echoed in his interior. By conscience is made known, in a wonderful way, that law which is fulfilled in the love of God and neighbour. It is by fidelity to conscience that Christians are linked with the rest of men in order to search out the truth and to solve in truth the many moral problems that arise in the life of the individual and of society.

On this passage it may be remarked that the notion of law, in the moral order, has two aspects. As John Coventry[7] has pointed out, many men are convinced that there is a right and wrong that is not simply a subjective set of preferences to be tailored by me to my own requirements; there really is an 'ought' and an 'ought not' from which I cannot escape and which I did not fabricate for myself. They feel the need of a morality binding on man as man. When the word 'law' is used in this context of thinking, the prime interest is probably in the binding, imperative, character of this morality. And it is this aspect which is emphasised in the first part of our quotation from the Constitution on the Church in the World of Today. In the recognised binding force of the moral imperative

[7] 'Christian Conscience', in *Heythrop Journal*, April 1966.

man – even if he could not thus describe his predicament – in fact, comes 'face to face' with God himself. The other aspect of 'law' is the notion of a code of behaviour – as, for example, the Ten Commandments, which do not merely tell you that you should do what is good and refrain from doing what is evil, but give you further some indication of the sorts of actions that fall into these two categories: Thou shalt not kill, Thou shalt not steal, Thou shalt not bear false witness. Of this aspect of 'law', as law is found and recognised in the untutored heart of man, the constitution is content to say, for the moment, that it is by this interior law, 'written in his heart by God', that man recognises the duty to 'love God and his neighbour'. Fr Coventry, in the article referred to above, similarly says: 'One can frame a few moral principles that are universal logically . . . such as love God, love your neighbour.' He points out that these extremely general and indeed universal principles 'cannot solve moral dilemmas' – what does the love of God – and/or the love of neighbour – prescribe *hic et nunc*?

It is important to observe that the conscience spoken of in this passage from the constitution is not a specially Christian perfection of man. It is, on the contrary, something by which Christians are linked to the rest of humanity. In particular, the Christian who obeys his conscience, the 'conscientious' believer, is linked to every man 'who fears God and does what is right'. It is on this ground of conscience, above all, that John XXIII in his two great encyclicals sought to build a co-operation between Christians and 'all men of good will', and that the constitution addresses itself to all men. This is the foundation of 'dialogue' in its widest possible sense, no longer now only between Christians, or between all who believe in the God of Abraham, or between Christians and other religious persons, but between all who are willing to accept the conditions of dialogue, which are sincerity, mutual respect, and a genuine desire for the common good. If we are to call this emphasis on the 'inside', rather than the objective content, of the moral act 'subjectivism', then we may say that it is this subjectivism which has enabled the Church of John XXIII and Vatican II to take a step forwards from the noble but almost melancholy intransigence of a Pius XII.

We must further observe – and it is here that the link

between the subjective and objective occurs – that it is conscience that moves men, individually and co-operatively, to 'search out the truth' and 'in truth to solve the many moral problems that arise in the life of the individual and of society'. In telling us that we should 'love and do good and avoid evil', conscience raises for us the question 'what is good and what is evil?' Subjective as it is, it presupposes and – in virtue of its unconditional demand upon us – demonstrates the objectivity of the true, and especially of the morally true. Thus, if it is true that there is no way of passing over from 'is' to 'ought' without a surreptitious *petitio principii*, it is certain that there is a licit passage from 'ought' to 'is': knowing that I ought to do what, in my circumstances, is right, I am certain of the existence of my circumstances (and obliged to determine them with sufficient accuracy for my moral needs); certain, too, of objective moral truth (and bound to investigate its principles or norms). Hence the constitution can add: 'Therefore the more that right conscience prevails, so much the more individuals and groups escape from blind caprice and strive to be conformed to objective norms of morality.' Moral progress and a firmer grasp of moral objectivity go hand in hand. There is a kind of preordained harmony or convergence of subjective moral rectitude and objective moral truth. But this is a general law, liable to every kind of actual divergence. As the constitution says: 'Often enough one's conscience makes a mistake as a result of invincible ignorance;[8] it does not therefore lose its dignity'. The same 'cannot be said for one who has no concern for the quest for the true and the good, one whose conscience is by degrees almost blinded as a result of habitual sin' (n. 16).

Theology is eminently a practical science. One practical influence of 'subjectivism' can be seen in the council's attitude to religious freedom. Traditional Catholic emphasis on objective truth has led to a situation in which it could be plausibly argued that in principle the Church claimed liberty for herself

[8] 'Invincible ignorance' is a technical term for inculpable ignorance of the facts or norms relevant in a given moral situation. Thus a non-Catholic who is inculpably unaware of the claims of the Catholic Church, or of their truth, is 'invincibly ignorant' of his obligation to become a Catholic. The obligation remains objectively real; subjectively it is non-existent, because inculpably not perceived.

and her members, but refused it to non-Catholics. In a modern world devoted to the rights of man and the ideal of democracy, few impressions could have been more prejudicial to the good name of the Church. The impression was firmly founded on explicit, and sometimes authoritative, Catholic affirmations. A maxim regrettably current among Catholics was that 'error has no rights'. A distinguished English convert stated that while the Church, as a minority group under a régime of toleration, claimed to enjoy the blessings of toleration, she would abolish toleration wherever she managed to win control of civil affairs.

The Declaration on Religious Freedom (sub-titled: 'The right of the person and of groups to social and civil freedom in religion') was one of the more hotly debated and contested documents of the second Vatican Council. Opposition to it was based partly on the fact that a series of nineteenth-century papal statements had castigated 'freedom of conscience' as understood in the terminology of that century, and all its consequences. Here was classic ground for debate between maximalisers and minimisers in the matter of the teaching authority of the Church and the Pope. More deeply, the debate was between those who emphasised objective revealed truth and those who laid stress on the dignity and rights of a human subject as possessing the God-given duty to govern his behaviour by an interior light.

A first paragraph implies that the council intends to take a fresh look at the Church's 'sacred tradition and doctrine'. The term 'sacred tradition' here should perhaps be particularly remarked, as suggesting a distinction between the genuine gospel tradition and all other inherited attitudes. A hint of what is coming is then added in the statement that from these sources of genuine tradition and doctrine the Church continually draws *new* but not contradictory inferences.

After this brief introduction, the declaration affirms that God has revealed the way of salvation to men, and that, in fact, the true religion subsists in 'the catholic and apostolic Church'. Thus the teaching of the Constitution on the Church is succinctly recalled; and it is further added that men are obliged to seek the truth, 'particularly concerning God and his Church' and, when they have found it, to embrace and maintain it. And in the succeeding paragraph we are told that the declaration intends no derogation of the traditional doctrine concerning the moral duties of men and of societies towards the true religion and the unique Church of Christ.[9] Woven in with these 'intransigent' affirmations we find a sentence in which it is stated that the duty to seek, embrace, and hold firm to religious truth is a matter of *conscience*, and that it is only in virtue of its own nature as truth that truth lays its claim upon the conscience – a quiet rejection of any idea of illegitimate pressure, whether on the part of false philosophies and religions or by the Catholic Church itself.

The fundamental affirmation of this declaration is given in a single sentence: 'This Vatican Council declares that the human person has a right to religious freedom' (n. 2). This sentence is followed immediately by a statement of the meaning to be attached to the term 'religious freedom', namely that 'all men ought to be immune from compulsion, whether by individuals or by social groups or any human power, so that in the sphere of religion no one is compelled to act against his conscience and no one is prevented from acting according to his conscience in private or public, alone or with others, within due limits'.

This right to religious freedom, we are told, is really founded in the very dignity of the human person as made known to us both by the revealed will of God and by reason; and it should become a civil right within the general juridical ordering of human society.

It is to be observed that the council is not fully consistent in its interpretation of the term 'human dignity'. In the Constitution on the Church in the World of Today we are told, as we have seen, that a man whose conscience errs in good faith does not, because of his error, lose his human dignity: 'this cannot be said of one who is indifferent to the quest of truth and of the good'. However, the general context within which this sentence occurs seems to base man's dignity not on the good

[9] This assertion springs from a momentary assumption by the council of the 'objective' point of view. Objectively, the Catholic Church and her teaching are a divine gift to mankind. A divine gift makes inherent and overriding claims on the conscience – but of course, existentially, the obligation to respect those claims depends on one's subjective recognition of them.

use of his endowments as a rational, free and moral person, but on those endowments themselves, as viewed prior to the use actually made of them. We could perhaps say that man's dignity is ontological before becoming existential. His basic worth is intrinsic; but it imposes upon him the task of actualising it in his life: 'man's dignity requires that he should act according to his conscience and free choice, that is to say personally and by internal motion and persuasion, not by blind interior impulse or under mere external constraint. Of such dignity man takes possession when . . . he pursues his end in the free choice of the good. . . .' In other words the dignity of man resides first in the fact of his spiritual endowments, and secondly in the good use made of these endowments.[10]

The Declaration on Religious Freedom bases the right to such freedom not on the good use that men make of their reason, freedom and personality, but on their possession, as human persons, of these endowments. As we have seen, as persons they are under an obligation to seek truth, especially religious truth; and they cannot fulfil this obligation 'in a way agreeing with their own nature' if they do not enjoy 'psychological freedom and also freedom from external constraint'. Hence we are told: 'The right to religious freedom is based not on the subjective disposition of the person but on his very nature. Hence it remains even in those who do not fulfil their duty of seeking and adhering to the truth' (n. 2). The doctrine of this paragraph is of capital importance for the subject in hand, since obviously, if religious freedom were made to rest on the positive moral goodness of the individual, and not on his moral nature as such, it would be open to the state or others to deprive him of his freedom on the grounds that he had failed to respond to his obligations. In defending its position against such an abuse, the declaration uses the term 'subjective disposition' to refer to the voluntary response or resistance of the individual to the message of his conscience. But it should not pass without notice that religious freedom is

[10] There is a Christian analogy in the fact that the baptised believer is both already 'dead to sin' through his baptism and under an obligation to 'put to death the deeds of the body' (Rm 8:13).

here claimed for the person as a subject.[11]

It is obvious to anyone who has studied Catholic practice, and especially Catholic theory, that this doctrine of religious freedom represents an enormous step forward. The Church has from the first been explicit in her claim for freedom for herself and her children in their religious convictions and practices. She has usually based this claim on the fact that she has a divine commission to preach the gospel and to care for men's spiritual welfare. But she has not been so emphatic about the rights to be accorded to the adherents of non-Christian or even only non-Catholic religions, still less about the rights of the groups in which they constitute themselves for religious purposes. The maxim, already mentioned, that 'error has no rights' has been proclaimed aloud when this seemed suitable, and maintained in secret when open affirmation was thought imprudent. And for Catholicism every religious position other than its own is erroneous. It was inferred that, in strict theory, such religious positions, having no right even to exist, should be abolished. However, this extreme theory was tempered by a doctrine of toleration. Toleration means permitting something which in principle would not be permitted, in order to avoid worse evils. Thus the government of a Catholic country with a sizeable non-Catholic minority might be justified in tolerating the minority because to do otherwise would produce evil results worse than the tolerated error itself.

This intransigent theory has been consigned to oblivion by the declaration. True, the claim is made, as always, that the Church has (in the objective order) a special right to freedom, based on her divine origin, message, and commission. But the

[11] For our present purposes we need not linger over the considerations which led the council to affirm the right to religious freedom not only for individuals but for religious groups. Nor need we dwell at length on the limitations on this freedom already suggested by the words 'within due limits'. Obviously civil society has to draw the line somewhere, since most kinds of absurdity and immorality have taken cover under the guise of religion. The limitation posited by the council is 'just public order', or the 'juridical norms, in harmony with the objective moral order' which are necessary for the public peace of the whole civil community, together with 'due care for public morality'. And since the right to impose such limits may itself be abused, a general principle is added: 'The custom of full freedom must be preserved in society; this entails that a maximum of freedom must be accorded to man, and it is not to be restricted except when, and to the extent that, such restriction is necessary' (n. 7).

maxim that error has no rights has disappeared *in toto*. As was pointed out in the council, it is a mere sophistry. Rights inhere not in propositions or systems but in persons. While, then, error has no rights – any more than an idea has a circumference – it remains possible, and the council affirms it as a fact, that a person in error preserves his rights intact. And where a right exists, there exists an obligation on others, and on the civil government, to respect those rights. The notion of 'toleration' does not arise in this context. We are not being told to tolerate error or any other kind of evil, but to respect a right, that is to say a positive good. And this right inheres in the human person as an intelligent and responsible subject. A noteworthy speech by an Italian prelate in the last session of the council, observing the spread of subjectivism today, reminded us that there was much to be said for subjectivism, properly understood.

From this discussion of religious freedom, it is natural to pass on to another matter which aroused hot debate in the final stages of the council. Many, Catholics and others, had been anxious that the council would come out strongly on the subject of modern war, and in particular on the moral questions raised by the hydrogen bomb. There has no doubt been some disappointment that you will search in vain for an unequivocal condemnation by the council of the manufacture and storing of such weapons and of the 'strategy of deterrence'. What the council does say, and with great solemnity, is that indiscriminate slaughter is 'a crime against God and against man, to be firmly and unhesitatingly condemned' (Constitution on the Church in the World of Today, n. 80). Any theologian will tell you that not only a sinful act, but the intention – even hypothetical – to commit a sinful act, is itself sinful; and the council adds a warning of the dangers and evils attendant upon the arms race and issues an emphatic summons to disarmament. I want here, however, to point out one short sentence in the chapter on peace and war, at the end of a paragraph advocating the observance of international conventions on the humanisation of war: 'Moreover it seems reasonable that the laws should make humane provision for the case of those who on conscientious grounds refuse to take up arms, provided they accept some other form of service to the human fellowship' (Constitution on the Church in the World of Today, n. 79). An Englishman may well be surprised at the extreme moderation of this plea for conscientious objectors. But it must be remembered that in many countries, including Italy, such objectors are guilty of an offence against the law, for which they are punishable. Catholic moral theologians have commonly argued that governments, which have the responsibility of embarking on war, are normally better able than their subjects to assess the justice of their cause. The general duty of obeying civil authority is, in the case of war, often combined with a duty of defending one's country. The individual citizen therefore usually may and must obey the summons to fight in a war declared or accepted by his government. The council nowhere explicitly refutes this argumentation, though it is extremely emphatic on the duty of withholding obedience from immoral commands, whatever their source. As regards the conscientious objector, however, it does not enter into the objective rights or wrongs of his position. It merely presumes that his conscience may be subjectively right – that he may be sincerely convinced that it would be wrong for him to take up arms, and it recommends that such sincerity should be respected and not coerced.[12] This is another significant recognition of a certain primacy of the subjective factor in human life.

The same recognition is given in a paragraph of this constitution dealing with responsible parenthood (n. 50). After affirming that parenthood is to be considered as within the sphere of morals (and not, therefore, as merely a biological fact), and that it calls for a 'right judgment' which will take account of the total good of the family, of temporal society and of the Church, the council states that 'it is in the last instance the parents themselves who have to make this judgment in

[12] An obvious objection needs to be considered. The conscientious objector is disobeying the command of legitimate authority. Where disobedience to law is established, there is a legal presumption of guilt. And civil authority is not in a position to probe below such appearances to the subjective intentions of the 'offender'. In this country, however, we have made use of tribunals to assess the sincerity of those who plead conscientious objection. Such tribunals are not infallible, but seem to work fairly well in practice. Most English Christians would probably judge that our system promotes justice and the common good better than one which acted simply on 'legal presumptions'.

the presence of God'.[13] The substance of this sentence is repeated in a later passage (n. 87) concerning the 'population explosion', where civil authority's duty to avert the evils threatened by population increases is limited by the assertion that 'in accordance with man's inalienable right to marriage and procreation, deliberation concerning the number of children (in the family) depends on the right judgment of the parents and can in no way be surrendered to the judgment of public authority'.

A connection may here be suggested between the council's stress on the primacy of conscience and what it has to say about the autonomy of the sciences including under that heading every systematic application of the intellect to our experience. Having laid it down that it is only through culture, that is 'by pursuing the natural goods and values', that the human person attains to a true and full humanity (Constitution on the Church in the World of Today, n. 53), the council enumerates some 'positive values' of modern culture: 'the study of the sciences and precise loyalty to truth in scientific investigation, the need of collaborating with others in technical associations, a sense of international solidarity, a growing consciousness of the responsibility of experts to help and protect men, a desire to ameliorate general living conditions'; and it adds that all this can create a certain preparation for the reception of the gospel message (n. 57). It goes on to say that, since culture springs immediately from man's rational and social nature, it needs a just liberty for its self-development and a legitimate freedom of independent action according to its own principles. It is to be respected, and 'enjoys a kind of inviolability, provided that the rights of the individual and of particular or universal communities are observed – and within the limits of the common good'. The council 'acknowledges this just liberty, and affirms the legitimate autonomy of human culture and especially of the sciences' (n. 59). It is inferred that, again

[13] There follows a reminder to Christian parents that, in forming their judgment on this matter, they should take as their norm 'the divine law' and be docile to the teaching authority of the Church 'which, in the light of the gospel, interprets that law with authority'. A little later, with an obvious reference to methods of birth control, we read: 'The Church's sons may not adopt courses in birth regulation which are condemned by the teaching authority in its explanation of divine law.'

within moral limits, man should be able to seek out the truth and publish his opinion freely. It will be noticed that the freedom here vindicated for culture and the sciences is very similar to that claimed for religion in the Declaration on Religious Liberty, and – like religious freedom – is based on man's rational and social nature. The limits of state control of publications by way of censorship are not clearly expounded. On the analogy of the limits of religious freedom one may suppose that the criteria will be public order and public morality, together with the rights of others who may be affected.[14]

Censorship is a problem not only in regard to civil society but in the Church also. Governmental censorship was a regular feature of seventeenth-century life. In typical modern civil societies in the West it has almost disappeared, although police action may attempt to prevent the circulation of obscene publications and court action, subsequent to publication, can punish public obscenity. The seventeenth-century system has however survived in the Catholic Church; and, in addition, the Index of Prohibited Books was intended to prevent Catholics from reading published literature that was held to be harmful to faith or morals. But it is difficult to see how obligatory censorship can be reconciled with the principle of freedom clearly enunciated by the council. The Constitution on the Church in the Modern World only directly faces the issue in a short sentence which follows a word of encouragement to the pursuit of theology by the laity: 'In order that they may be able to exercise this rôle, the faithful, whether clerical or lay, should be accorded a just freedom of inquiry, thought, and humble and courageous publication of their thought, on subjects in which they have specialised knowledge' (n. 62). Shortly after the council, the Index of Prohibited Books, as a legally enforceable instrument, was abolished by the action of the Holy See. At about the same time the Holy Office had its name changed to 'the Congregation of Doctrine', and its function was

[14] As regards the limits of religious freedom, the council had to choose between 'public order' and 'the common good'. It was felt that the latter term left too much latitude to an unscrupulous government. The reference to the common good as limiting the inviolability of cultural freedom, cited in the text above, may perhaps be taken as indicating intrinsic moral limits rather than the limits of justifiable state interference.

described as being less the repression of error than the promotion of truth.

Emphasis, in Catholicism, on the objective aspect of the total human and Christian fact has usually favoured a similar emphasis on authority, docility, and obedience rather than freedom together with personal initiative in the spheres of thought and action. It must be recognised that there are dangers in the opposite emphasis, not least for a Church which for generations has stressed obedience to a degree that has sometimes seemed to tend towards an atrophy of the moral spontaneity of its members. The emphasis on freedom and personal initiative needs to be safeguarded by a full recognition that freedom requires the immanent control of a well-developed sense of responsibility. Without such control it obviously becomes a source of anarchy in human affairs. But granted a real sense of responsibility, the free person will not only seek to determine the moral indications inherent in his actual situation; he will be ready to look for and comply with the guidance that the common moral sense of mankind can supply, and – if he is a Christian – with the guidance of the Church. A Catholic will recognise the Church's guidance as making demands on his conscience at different levels. He will be docile to the Church's teaching in so far as that purports to expound the gospel entrusted to her preaching; and in so far as the Church shows herself finally committed to a particular formulation of part of the gospel message he will give to this formulation an assent of divine faith. When the Church expounds the content of the moral law, or applies that law to particular human situations that are ordinarily recurrent, he will recognise the summons to practical compliance, a summons that may at times be such as to require of him an act of faith. But he will further admit to himself that the Church as a visible communion bound together by social links requires some form of government, and he will see this requirement actualised above all in the episcopal college and its head, the successor of St Peter. And, since one function of government is to legislate, he will acknowledge that the Church can oblige his loyalty by her laws. There is therefore no necessary conflict between authority and responsible freedom – or free responsibility. In fact, however, abuse of authority or of freedom will produce clashes, which form an element in the drama of a Church endowed with the means to holiness and called to holiness as a body and in its members, yet composed of members who, whether prelates or simply laymen, are all morally fallible and prone to intellectual error. It remains true that the new emphasis on the subjective aspect of human life, on responsible freedom and creative spontaneity, is an emphasis which seems appropriate to an age in which we may hope that man is beginning to attain, at least here and there, to a collective adulthood.

Neither the history of the second Vatican Council nor a realistic study of its Acts suggests that its members were consciously inspired by a single controlling theological principle. It dealt with a great diversity of topics, some doctrinal and others more directly practical. Within the specifically doctrinal area there was at least one matter, that of the position of the episcopate within the Church's sacramental and governmental systems, which had been left over from the first Vatican Council and required particular attention independently of any general modern concern. The council was not closely organised into divergent parties on the model of a democratic parliament, but it was inevitable that conflicting tendencies, progressive or conservative, should declare themselves. As the debates and voting continued, the progressive wing began to secure the voting support of the council's centre. But both a widely held view that the council's Acts should be morally unanimous, and pressure from the Pope to the same end, stood in the way of a total partisan victory. The Acts of the council show the influence of various tendencies and of tensions not fully reconciled. It has to be borne in mind that an ecumenical council is not a theological congress. It may be expected to proclaim doctrine, but its prime concern is not to offer an intellectual synthesis.

If, however, the council did not embody a single human intention, a Christian may believe that, broadly speaking, and after allowance made for human failure to co-operate with grace, the Holy Spirit overruled it to certain broad ends. Of these, we may here summarise something of what has been said on earlier pages by turning once again to the contrast between the sacramental and the juridical, between the subjective and the objective, and between a closed and an open view of the Church.

The decision to take, as the first document for debate, the draft of a Constitution on the Liturgy was a happy one. It is, one may concede, probable that if that constitution could have been revised once again during the final session of the council, when the conciliar fathers had profited by three years of mutual education and had learnt more of their own corporate mind, the result would have been a better document. On the other hand, it was an advantage that the council began its deliberations by facing issues connected with the very centre of the Church's corporate life and the transcendent object of her ultimate concern. Here the Church appeared not primarily as a teacher of propositional truths, still less as a juridical organisation or a system of government, but as performing, through the instrumentality of her apostolic ministry but with the co-operation of the whole Christian community, the 'work of salvation' through sacrifice and sacrament, which are the focus of all liturgical life. At this central core of the Church's sacramental life Christ himself 'is ever present to his Church' and associates her with his own priestly task.

The Constitution on the Church finds its keynote in the statement that 'the Church is in Christ as it were a sacrament or sign and instrument of an interior union with God and of the unity of the whole human race' (n. 1). Attached to the sign which a sacrament is, there is a spiritual grace and efficacy; and the first chapter of this constitution shows how the Church has both a spiritual aspect and an external coherence and unity, so that she 'subsists in the Catholic Church' – a visibly united 'complete communion' of human beings governed by the successor of St Peter and by the bishops in communion with him, while at the same time the spiritual realities which this outward sign signifies and conveys are found, in varying measure and conditions, wherever men 'fear God and do what is right'. In the important third chapter of this constitution the council at last takes up the particular issue bequeathed to it by the first Vatican Council. It seeks its understanding of the episcopate, as also (it may be argued) of the relations of the bishops with one another and with their visible head, in episcopal consecration viewed as the fullness of the sacrament of holy orders. The authoritative and juridical functions of the episcopal ministry, as of all ministry within the Church, are thus subordinated to the sacramental idea.

We found this notion of sacramentality necessary for a fuller appreciation of the council's teaching on the transmission of divine revelation. Revelation was not primarily a disclosure of truths that can be expressed in propositions. Rather it was the significance of divine actions in history and was totally recapitulated in the Word made flesh, in Christ who is at once the mediator and the fullness of revelation. But while propositions can be transmitted by ordinary historical processes, the 'transmission' of Christ, in his historical reality, to all times and places is a requirement that cannot be met except by the fact of sacramental presence and sacramental activity.[15]

In reflecting upon eschatology and history we came to the conclusion that sacramental presence and activity form the link between the 'realised eschatology' of the incarnation and the post-historic consummation of human history. The religious approach to experience is deeply historical, because it proceeds with a desire to find a meaning and value in actual human life. But the attempt to 'understand' history leads us, by a dialectical process (analogous to that which carries the mathematician from arithmetic to algebra) to eschatology, meta-history, or metachronics. The very *differentia* of Christianity among the monotheistic religions is its gospel that the *Eschaton* has been mysteriously anticipated in the particularity of the Christ-event, where – by virtue of Christ's sacramental presence and activity in his Church – it is available to, and apprehensible by, faith.

Because, then, Christianity is a religion of sacrament, its native categories are those of history and eschatology. The council's adoption of an historical – some would say existential

[15] It should be remarked that the problem is not peculiar to a Catholic understanding of Christianity. A Protestant, rejecting all authority in religion other than that of the Bible, still requires to find, in the Bible itself, a 'sacramental' presence of his Redeemer. This is so because the faith which justifies is at once faith in God and faith in Christ who died for us. The Protestant turns to the Bible, to 'meet' Christ there. The Catholic does the same, but believes that Christ's sacramental presence in the Bible is one realisation among others of his sacramental presence in his mystical body and in the rites which are known as 'the seven sacraments'.

– standpoint, in preference to the standpoint of philosophical theology, was not just an opportunist concession to contemporary modes of thought. Rather it was due to a deep sense of the Christian mystery and of the inadequacy of an ultimately Hellenic framework of ideas to penetrate more deeply into that mystery.

History, however, by its very nature, is the experience and action of human persons in all their particularity and with all their potentiality for social relationships and communion. Even written history, it is coming to be more widely realised today, can never be purely 'scientific'. While using all the rigour of criticism possible to a scientific approach, it always has an element of personal evaluation in it. Thus it is not altogether surprising that a council concerned with faith, sacrament, and history should have much to say about personal appropriation of the gospel and the more general issue of personal freedom, responsibility, and integrity. All sacraments, the whole sacramental reality are, as a classic Christian dictum reminds us, *propter homines*, for the sake of human persons. The Church herself, while subsisting in a unique complete communion, exists in, and as, associated persons, moved interiorly by the Holy Spirit to a life of individual spontaneity which is at the same time a service of the whole body of Christ.

The profound Catholic conviction, shared by very many non-Catholics, that the Church is meant to be a fullness of communion, has a genuine biblical foundation. But once it is fully realised that the Church exists in persons, the possibility that human sin and error may exert their disruptive effects has to be considered. That the possibility has been realised is evidenced by the past history and present conditions of the Christian religion. The sin and culpable error of which these conditions are the effect cannot be attributed solely to one side of any of the numerous divisions that have occurred, still less to the modern heirs of past divisive movements. Without any infidelity to our faith that the visible structural elements of the Church as founded by Christ survive as a coherent reality in the world today, the gospel warning that we should not judge one another is a warrant, confirmed by experience so far as it goes, that the Church exists also outside the limits of the 'complete communion' made possible by this structure. We know where the Church is; we cannot determine so confidently where she is not; *ubi Spiritus, ibi ecclesia.*

Thus it was that the dialectic of its own theology impelled the council to look not merely inwards upon the Catholic Church's domestic problems, but outwards to the whole Christian world, and to seek to encounter our fellow Christians individually and as communities, with respect and fraternal charity. Already there is a communion between all who acknowledge Christ as the universal redeemer. This communion is of varying levels and depths. It is based not only on a common spiritual outlook but on the shared possession of sacramental or other 'visible' elements of the Sacred Tradition. And, just as it is a Christian logic that turns the Catholic's eyes towards non-Catholics, so the same Christian logic impels all Christians, Catholic and non-Catholic alike, to look forward and move forward to the healing of our divisions.

The Church, however, was not intended to be a 'closed shop'. It is sent with a message to all mankind and is bound to embrace in its charity not only the whole extent of humanity but every depth of human experience and aspiration. It is the sign and instrument of human unity. The council was therefore led to look outwards not only to other Christians and their communities, but to the Jews in their religious aspect, to Islam, and to the other great world religions or ways of the spirit. And beyond the limits of anything that can be recognised as a reflectively religious commitment, it looked out to a-religious humanism and to every indication of actual or possible goodwill. The distinction 'Church and World' can easily be misunderstood, as if it meant two groups of human beings standing over against one another, sundered by the gulf of faith. But the world is made up of all human beings, including believers; and the Church, as we have seen, cannot easily show where she is not. Not only do we believe that the God of our salvation is the creator of the world and of every man. We believe that the redemption wrought in Christ is of universal significance; that it has changed the basic relationship of man, as man, with God. We can suppose, with K.

Rahner,[16] that the 'possibility' of the actual creation as we know it depends on the 'possibility' of the incarnation, and that the Word made flesh is the ultimate source, as it were the transcendent dimension, of man's very existence as man. The Church, in fact, exists to bring a message and means of redemption to a redeemed world; just as we have been taught by St Paul that she exists, in her members, in virtue of a lifelong 'mortification' of that 'old man' which has already been 'put to death' in them through baptism.

It is by subjective goodwill that a man, physically or psychologically remote from the message of the Church, is opened up to the inflow of a grace whose nature and conditions he only dimly apprehends; opened up to a union – actually in the unrecognised Christ – with God whose very existence he may verbally and conceptually deny. Goodwill is a positive disposition towards the acceptance of the nature and consequences of objective morality. We may therefore say that it is orientated, not indeed to an *a priori* discovery of the gospel, but towards a recognition of the gospel as objectively true – however often, amid the complicated cross-currents of our actual experience, the recognition fails, in fact, to occur.

We may, then, say that wherever man responds with conscientious seriousness to his experience, there is a kind of implicit virtual tendency towards the fullness of Christian truth and towards complete Christian communion. On the other hand, the Church tends by her divine commission towards all humanity and towards everything that is human. The depth of man's responsible subjectivity on the one hand, and the Christian gospel and Church on the other, may thus be said to be on converging courses; and as they tend to meet so they tend to embrace each other in a communion of which the expression is dialogue.

What has the Church, in that dialogue, to offer to man? In the enthusiasm of the first discovery of dialogue, some Catholics seem to speak as though the Church were merely man become conscious of himself; and as if her whole message could be reduced to that law of love of neighbour which was given to the Jews and which Christ himself endorsed and universal-

[16] *Nature and Grace*, p. 23.

ised. But so to think would be a betrayal both of the gospel and of man. Essentially eschatological, the gospel directs man's gaze to an end transcending his comprehension and his innate powers. The love of neighbour only takes on its full depth and significance in its conjunction with the 'love of God above all things'. And on the other hand, man was made for no other end than *this* end. 'Thou hast made us for thyself, and our heart is without rest till it comes to rest in thee.' Unable to discover or attain that end by his own unaided efforts, man becomes frustrated and his own moral endeavour falters. With the Roman poet he says: *Video meliora proboque, Deteriora sequor.* And still his conscience, when he listens to it, orientates him towards the undescried goal. The gospel is not simply a noble humanism; it is also a message of divine redemption. And the Church, in bringing that message, is found to be entrusted also with the 'means of grace' which man needs but could never have procured for himself. Man finds himself, finds his peace, and finds his joy, only in being brought by the love of God, the love which is God, to transcend himself in Christ, and thus in God.

8

Liturgy; Church and World; Reflections

The lectures upon which the first edition of this book was based were limited in their scope. They reflected certain special interests which I had taken with me to the council, of which I was a speaking and voting member in virtue of my office as President of the English Benedictine Congregation. I was interested in the uniqueness of the Catholic Church and of her universal mission to mankind; with the relation of the worldwide episcopate to the papacy (part of the unfinished business of Vatican I); with ecumenism; with biblical scholarship and, in consequence, with the issue of biblical 'inerrancy' and the relation of such scholarship to control by the official teaching authorities of the Church; with the relations between philosophy and science on the one hand and the Church's *magisterium* on the other. I ought also to have been interested in the theology of the 'religious life', that is to say the theology related to the monastic and other forms of specially dedicated life; but I confess, to my shame, that this subject was not of great concern to me in 1962, and the council's efforts to provide such a theology still do not strike me as being very satisfying.

A glance at the titles of the sixteen documents emanating from the council will show that there were other aspects of its work to which this book had given insufficient attention. First on the list, chronologically at least, is liturgy. The Constitution on the Sacred Liturgy, introduced at the first session of the council, and the first of its documents to be promulgated (December 1963) is an achievement which has affected ordinary church-going Catholics more, perhaps, than any other of the conciliar documents. Its purpose, to bring the liturgy to the people and the people to the liturgy, is deeply consonant with the ecclesiology of the Constitution on the Church; and it was also important for its bearing on the ecumenical orientation of the post-conciliar Church. Other documents were more directly concerned with the Church's relations to the world in which it lives and of which it forms part: the Declaration on the Church's relationship to non-Christian Religions, and that on Religious Freedom; and more generally, the Pastoral Constitution on the Church in the Modern World. Such documents carry further the outward-looking impulse that is already evinced in the Decree on Ecumenism, and indeed in the opening paragraph of the Dogmatic Constitution on the Church:

> By her relationship with Christ, the Church is a kind of sacrament or sign of intimate union with God, and of the unity of all mankind. She is also an instrument for the achievement of such union and unity. . . . The conditions of this age lend special urgency to the Church's task of bringing all men to full union with Christ, since mankind today is joined together more closely than ever before by social, technical, and cultural bonds (n. 1).

To deal adequately with these further issues would in effect change the nature of this book. I hope to have them in mind as I proceed to an evaluation not only of the first edition of the book but of the council itself.

First, however, I may be allowed to observe that the council was, for me, a great educative experience. Not only did it bring me into contact with Church leaders from every part of the world and with the problems of their regions, thus widening my general horizon enormously, but it opened up for me fresh horizons of doctrinal and theological concern. And here I must pay tribute to the tremendous services rendered to the council by theologians from many countries who were not members of the council but were at hand to advise both members and Commissions. The Theology Commission in particular (of which I was a member from the end of the council's second session) had an astonishing array of first-class theologians to help it in its work. Perhaps I should remark here that their work was indeed indispensable, and yet I feel glad that the determining decisions were taken not by theologians as such but by those entrusted with the pastoral care of the Church, and in particular by bishops with their 'charism' of teaching and their commonsense prudence.

The experience of the council was also an experience of the way in which the Roman Curia influences and to a large extent governs the life of the Church; and it helped one to distinguish the 'Holy See' with its curial organs from the Pope himself, the head of the college of bishops in virtue of his rôle as the bishop of Rome and the successor of Peter. The Curia can be regarded as the 'civil service' of the papacy. It exists to be the instrument of the Pope, and its published decisions and instructions are often at least formally endorsed by the Pope, in somewhat the same way as the work of our British civil service is formally the expression of the intentions of the ministers of the Crown. The analogy is a useful one. A department of the civil service, the Treasury for example, is felt to possess traditions and an ethos of its own, in large measure independent of the particular viewpoints and intentions of successive chancellors of the exchequer; ministers come and go, and when they first arrive in office they have a lot to learn, a lot concerning which the Treasury is seen as the natural source of information. The Curia has in the past been recruited normally from Italy, though since Paul VI there has been an influx, at top levels, of personnel from other countries; and these foreigners have a lot to learn from the high-ranking officials and the general ethos of the particular Congregations of which they are nominally in charge. It is not unreasonable to hold that the second Vatican Council's recovered vision of the inherent powers of the world-wide episcopate as such, and of bishops individually, should lead towards the construction of a new kind of Curia which should be truly international in character and outlook. It should voice the will of the episcopal college, and not only of its Head the Pope. Meanwhile, the present Curia is strangely reminiscent of the officialdom (largely made up, at least in early times, of freedmen) through which the Roman Emperors governed their peoples in an indisputably dictatorial fashion. It is not surprising that the

Curia viewed the council with a certain amount of cynical detachment and sometimes with alarm and hostility. And historians will not forget that the presidents of the conciliar commissions were often Curial cardinals; this was notably so in the case of the theology commission, presided over by Cardinal Ottaviani of the Holy Office, a leader of the 'conservative' minority whose opposition to change was in large measure, eventually, defeated by the increasing volume of council members who were won over to the 'progressive' outlook.

I know of no thorough and thoroughly critical history of the second Vatican Council. Xavier Rynne's chronicle of the four sessions and Michael Novak's book, *The Open Church*, are invaluable introductions to it. But such works have the limitations of journalism and inevitably are liable to miss a great deal of what was going on in the relative privacy of 'the corridors' of the council.[1] I make no attempt to fill the gap that such books have left; and indeed I have neither the knowledge nor the competence to do so. Some readers, however, may be helped by the following few and very general remarks.

Pope John XXIII was seventy-six years old when he was elected to the papacy in 1957. Born in Bergamo in northern Italy of a farming family, he was ordained priest before the first world war, in which he served as an army sergeant. His subsequent ecclesiastical career was in the 'diplomatic service' of the Church. Senior appointments in Belgrade and Ankara were followed by his appointment as Nuncio in Paris after the second world war. A few years before the death of Pius XII he became Patriarch of Venice, a posting that might have been taken as the preface to an honourable retirement. His election as Pope seemed to many to indicate that the conclave had deliberately chosen a 'caretaker government' of the Church, perhaps to bridge the gap till Archbishop Montini of Milan could be elected. The decision to summon a general council of the Church was emphatically John's own. My impression is that it was received with less than universal satisfaction in curial circles, and there was a feeling that the Curia, in the interval between the summoning and the actual gathering of the council, was trying to limit the council's scope for inno-

[1] See also the five-volume *Commentary on the Documents of Vatican II*, ed. H. Vorgrimler, Burns & Oates and Herder & Herder.

vation. No one, however, could dispute the Pope's right to hold a council, and already in the first session the Pope himself intervened to keep open a door of advance which the curialists would gladly have closed: the draft Constitution on the Sources of Revelation was withdrawn by John's personal decision and its replacement, the Constitution on Divine Revelation, was drafted by a new joint commission headed by Cardinals Ottaviani and Bea, the former a champion of 'conservatism' and the latter the President of the 'progressive' commission on Ecumenism.

John XXIII died between the first and second sessions of the council and was succeeded by Cardinal Montini of Milan who took the name of Paul (VI). Paul, like his predecessor, was born in a family of northern Italy. He had spent most of his working life within the Curia, and had become, along with Tardini, one of two 'substitutes' for the post of Secretary of State, Pius XII having preferred, during his last years, to work without a Secretary. Paul VI was thus a man who knew the Curia from the inside and had both admired it and suffered in it. He was highly intelligent, and my impression is that he had assimilated the thinking of such 'neo-thomists' as Jacques Maritain during the thirties, but was less at home with the new wave of Catholic philosophy and theology that sprang from the work of the Belgian Jesuit Maréchal. Of this 'new', but deeply orthodox, thinking there are two outstanding spokesmen: the great German Jesuit, Karl Rahner, and the great Canadian Jesuit, Bernard Lonergan. My personal view is that it is such thinking that can be regarded as the, largely unconscious, inspiration of the second Vatican Council's most original perceptions. Whether or not Paul VI either understood or fully sympathised with this inspiration, he was genuinely a man of Vatican II, and there can be no doubt that he saw it as one of his duties to make that council effective in the remaining years of his own life. He was also determined to hold the Church together in a communion of charity, and to maintain the privileges of the Petrine office to which he had been elected. During the council itself he did not relax his attention to the efforts of the 'progressive' elements, and more than once he seems to have tried to stem the tide that was flowing.

The 'victory' of the progressives still seems to me to be an astonishing historical occurrence. The new theology and the new biblical scholarship, together with features of the new social, cultural and ecumenical concern, must have been welcome at the start of the council to only a minority of the council members; yet by the last session of the council the tide was flowing fully and almost unchecked in a 'progressive' direction. It is permissible to doubt whether the assembled bishops, who had usually attained to their office for reasons remote from a pure passion for theology, always understood precisely what they were sanctioning by their votes, or at least the theological motivation behind the documents they had been debating. (Speeches in the council were almost always delivered in Latin, and a familiarity with the 'tridentine' Missal and a faithful recitation of the Latin breviary do not necessarily amount to a facility in understanding oral Latin communications on subjects undreamt of by the composers of those books of liturgy and devotion.) Perhaps the council is to be seen as an exercise in group dynamics. Certainly, when it was over and the bishops returned to their dioceses, they did on occasion appear like men who had never heard of the decisions to which they had given their assent (by overwhelming majorities) in the council itself. Sometimes they seemed like Nebuchadnezzar, conscious on awaking that he had had an unpleasant dream, but unable to recollect its contents.

Turning now to some of the outstanding lacunae in the first edition of this book, it is noteworthy that there is no reference in its general index to liturgy (the official corporate worship of the Church), though the Constitution on the Sacred Liturgy is listed in the index of references to the texts of Vatican II, and five references to it are then cited. The passages of the book thus referred to are, in harmony with the book's intention, concerned less with the practical changes in liturgy proposed by the constitution than with their bearing on the theological themes of the book. As already indicated, however, the reform of the liturgy was the aspect of the council's work which has most directly affected the ordinary religious behaviour of Catholics; it has also influenced public worship in other Christian churches. The history of this influence falls outside the scope of this book. For us, it is the theology of the constitution that matters, and this (as already illustrated in the chapter on Ecumenism, *supra*) is deeply congruous with that of the dogmatic Constitution on the Church: in the Mass and Holy Communion the faithful are 'consummated into unity with God *and among themselves*' (De Liturgia, n. 48). The word 'communion' is used, in the Christian tradition, in two apparently different connections, both of which may have their origins in apostolic times. We speak of Holy Communion, and for this use of the word we may appeal to 1 Cor 10:16: 'Is it not a participation in the body of Christ?'. The Greek word here translated 'participation' is *koinonia*, i.e. communion, and the same word is used in 1 Jn 1:3: 'That which we have seen and heard we proclaim also to you, so that you may have fellowship (*koinonia*) with us.' And today, just as we speak of Holy Communion, so we speak of the Anglican Communion, of being in communion with the See of Rome, and of excommunication.

The two meanings are in fact closely connected, or so it appears. In the early Christian centuries when a visitor from abroad was admitted to Holy Communion in a local church, this was a public expression of the fact that his local church and the one at which he was a visitor were in official 'communion' with each other. The Eucharist and Holy Communion are the summit of the Church's sacramental life, and the Church is built upon the sacraments.

For many generations, if not centuries, Holy Communion has been thought of in the Church almost as if it were a private affair between the individual communicant and Christ; and the celebrating priest was thought of as performing a rite which was in some sense his personal privilege. The custom of 'private Masses' may have a historical connection with the phenomenon of 'chantry priests' in the late Middle Ages, but it has undoubtedly tended to foster this individualism of attitude to the Mass. And yet, as so often, the renewed emphasis in the Constitution on the Liturgy on the Eucharist as the act of worship in which the faithful are 'consummated in unity . . . among themselves' is a recovery of a truth which was fully recognised by, for example, St Thomas Aquinas, as pointed out in an earlier chapter of this book.[2]

Following on logically from this eucharistic theology the local church, corporately celebrating the Eucharist, is an actualisation of *the* Church of Christ. The diocesan bishop, or the priest who represents him at such a celebration, is thus the representative of the Church and its unity. Thus the Church is not only unified inasmuch as its members are in communion with the Pope; it is unified in each legitimate celebration of the Eucharist – it is multi-centred. It should follow that we are to think of the Church universal not as a communion of individuals but as a communion of communions, and this concept fits in well with the council's realisation that a local bishop is not the deputy or delegate of the Pope but functions in his own right, although he is obliged to be in communion with the rest of the episcopal 'college' and with its head, the successor of Peter.

The Decree on the Missionary Activity of the Church received no attention in the first edition of this book. It is interesting historically because it replaces a draft presented to the council and recommended by Paul VI in his one and only appearance at the council in his rôle as one bishop among others.[3] Despite this recommendation the council Fathers lost

[2] This true doctrine, linking Holy Communion most closely with the unity of the Church, is one reason why the Catholic Church is still so reluctant to offer our separated Christian brethren access to the 'open table' of the Eucharist; if someone wishes to receive Holy Communion at a Catholic altar, it should normally be because he intends to be in full communion of faith and charity, as well as sacrament, with the Catholic Church.

[3] Popes have often, indeed usually, abstained from personal attendance at general councils. This tradition grew up in the age of the first seven such councils, from the first Council of Nicaea (A.D. 325) to the seventh general council in the closing decades of the eighth century. In that period, when councils were liable to be under the influence of Roman Emperors, Popes may have felt that it was prudent to stay away and to be represented by legates, sc as to leave final ratification to themselves in comparative detachment from political pressures. The tradition passed on into modern times. Even the two Vatican councils, though sitting almost within earshot of the Pope (and, as regards Vatican II, able to be watched by him with the help of closed-circuit television), were not regularly attended by him. He would preside at the inaugural and closing ceremonies of a session but would not, except for this one occasion of the draft on Missions, take part in the debates. The rejection of the draft despite the support given to it by the Pope was regarded as shocking in the Curia. It is possible that Paul VI was pleased to find that the council had enough self-assurance to form its own judgment on the matter. Certainly, the Decree as eventually passed was a great improvement on the rather jejune document that was rejected.

little time in expressing their view that the draft was inadequate; the result was the present Decree, a valuable application to the field of 'missionary activity' of the principles laid down in the Constitution on the Church, and enriched by the ecumenical insights that come to find expression in the Decree on Ecumenism. On the whole, the Decree is a very good one. It should be observed that its central concern is missionary activity in the areas of the world that have not, in the past, been effectively evangelised; today, we should probably lay more emphasis on the fact that even in countries that once belonged to 'Christendom', and certainly in Latin America where the Church has functioned for centuries, there is a vast need of the Church's 'mission' to those who are in effect dechristianised.

The Decree lays firm biblical foundations for its recommendations and doctrine: Christ, the Word of God incarnate, not only redeemed the world but wished the message of redemption to be spread throughout mankind. The message is entrusted to the Church, which is therefore 'missionary' (commissioned to spread the Good News) in its essence.

The missionary efforts of the early centuries at length led to the establishment of the Church as the one official religion of Europe. Outside Europe the faith and the Church had indeed spread beyond the boundaries of the Roman Empire. But, especially through the victories of Islam and the Moslem nations, the Church in Europe was cut off from the outlying regions of Christianity and a state of affairs was reached when Hilaire Belloc could coin his famous and regrettable dictum, 'the faith is Europe and Europe is the faith'. One result of this was, of course, that the gospel, whose origins were outside Europe, itself became so deeply intertwined with Europeanism that Europe and the faith were, for many of us, practically indistinguishable, and the recent 'secularisation' of European culture was seen as an unnatural betrayal of the very soul of Europe.

The opening of the rest of the world to Europe came about almost simultaneously with the Protestant Reformation, and there ensued a period of 'colonisation' so fantastic, at least in the claims made for it, that practically the whole face of the globe, excepting China, Japan and the Turkish empire, could be designated on maps divided up among the European Powers and their offspring in North and Latin America. Colonisation was the combined work of trade and politics. But it took Christianity along with it or, in some circumstances, at least allowed Christianity to follow in its footsteps. A great period of Christian missionary endeavour now took shape. It was unfortunate that, as a result of the Reformation, the Christianity thus exported to the rest of the world was one that reproduced, in countries remote from the theological concerns of the sixteenth century, the divisions which had splintered Western Christendom. On the whole, where colonisation was the work of a Catholic country, it was Catholic missions that profited by its patronage; where the colonisers were Protestants, patronage went to Protestant missionaries. But often, in fact, Protestant and Catholic missionaries were competing in the same region. Uganda, for instance, was part of British East Africa, and Anglicanism took a firm foothold there under the aegis of the Church Missionary Society, though there were missions founded also by the Free Churches of this country. But Catholicism also took early root in Uganda. Both Anglican and Catholic converts gave witness by martyrdom to their new faith. And today both Churches are strong in independent Uganda, and thankfully are co-operating in the climate of Ecumenism.

The Decree on Missionary Activity does not forget to mention the desirability of good ecumenical relations and co-operation in the mission field. It also makes two important points. Whereas the Christianity taken to 'heathen' countries by modern missionaries was usually heavily marked with the national or European culture of the missionaries, the Decree points out that the secular cultural integument of Christianity is not part of its unchanging religious meaning, and that when it moves into a new culture it must willingly divest itself of the culture it brought with it and express itself in the culture which it finds in its new situation.[4] This process has been

[4] Change of time, as well as of geography, may create a need for adaptation to new cultural situations. The great Dominican philosophic theologian, Thomas Aquinas, lived in the same areas as his predecessors of the eleventh and twelfth century. But in the lapse of time that area had become infiltrated with Islamic and Jewish Aristotelianism, creating a new cultural challenge which Aquinas met, not by rejecting, but by utilising Aristotelianism in his theology. Today, Lonergan has emphasised very strongly that we are living in a cultural

named indigenisation, acculturalisation, or inculturalisation. A full recognition of the need for it is comparatively recent, and has been aided among Catholic missionaries by the teaching of Vatican II. At an earlier period, a faithful reproduction of the liturgy (in Latin), of scholastic theology and of the 'mores' of Western Catholicism was something of which a missionary could feel proud. Perhaps it is not surprising that, when the Council opened, hardly any of the African dioceses had black bishops, except auxiliary bishops who were subject to the direction of their diocesans.

A second very important point made by the Decree on Missionary Activity is that missionary endeavour should lead normally to the establishment in the missionary territories of complete dioceses. It should not perpetuate the provisional arrangements whereby these territories were under the control of the missionary societies and religious Congregations who had sent the missionaries out, and beyond them were subject to the congregation of the Propagation of the Faith, a department of the Roman Curia. Thus the 'missionary' condition of these territories would be replaced as soon as was prudent by a fully ecclesial status; the Churches of black Africa and of Asia would have parity of esteem with those of Europe, a goal made all the more important by the fact that it has been estimated that the opening years of the twenty-first century will present an African Catholicism which will be numerically larger than that of Europe.

Of the other documents of the Council not mentioned in the first edition of this book most can be regarded as applying, to special areas of concern, the theology expounded in the Constitution on the Church and that on Divine Revelation. One that hardly comes under that description is the Decree on the Instruments of Social Communication. Neither at the time of its acceptance by the Council nor subsequently has this Decree

---

situation which is not only geographically but historically very different from that of Aquinas. Today the culture of Europe and to some extent of the world beyond Europe is deeply affected by the rise of the empirical sciences, of Kantian and post-Kantian philosophy, and of critical historical scholarship, along with the social sciences. Mere repetition of scholastic 'axioms' and a defensive attitude against these modern concerns are not sufficient as a service to the gospel.

been regarded as among the major successes of the council. It concerns itself in large measure with the 'mass media', that is with newspapers, journalism, and radio and television, but it had on the whole a poor reception from professionals in these fields. As has been said elsewhere, 'It seems somewhat ironic that the Church, which is basically concerned with communicating truth and life to the world, and has shown, especially in the period of the council, an awareness of the importance of mass means of communication, issued the slightest document of the Council on the media of social communication' (T. J. M. Burke, S. J., in *The Documents of the Second Vatican Council*, ed. Abbott, p. 317). The fact is that the council Fathers were ill-equipped to deal with this subject and showed a certain lack of interest in it. Perhaps one day the Synod of Bishops will improve on this conciliar text. Communications have become an object of academic attention in their own right in recent years, and the Church, itself commissioned to communicate the Good News which is Christ, the Word of God, will have to learn from the results of this attention.

A major document of the council is the Pastoral Constitution on the Church in the Modern World. There are several references to it in the first edition of this book, but it deserves to be examined in its own right. The other great documents of the council had been prepared for in the pre-conciliar commissions entrusted with the task of presenting to the council draft proposals on such central issues as the theology of the Church, divine revelation, and liturgy; not to speak of the subject of Ecumenism. There was no draft of a document on the Church in the Modern World, and the idea that such a document should be issued emerged only in the course of the council itself. Cardinal Suenens, then Archbishop of Malines-Brussels, brought the proposal before the council a few days before the close of its first session (4 December 1962). Some of the themes of the resulting document had indeed been touched on in drafts from the preparatory commissions on social action and on the Christian moral order. These drafts were never debated as such in the council, but some elements in them are reflected in the Constitution on the Church in the Modern World. The constitution itself was prepared by the two commissions for Theology and the Apostolate of the Laity. The moving forces behind the decision to compose this new document were John XXIII's own expressed desire that the council should turn its gaze outwards to the world, and the council members, Suenens, Helder Camara, Léger (Montreal) and Montini (Milan; later Pope Paul VI). A comparison of the constitution with the two preparatory documents which disappeared from the council as a result of this new initiative will serve to illustrate the difference of perspectives between the Curia-dominated preparatory commissions and the council itself as it learnt to discover its own mind.[5]

The constitution is divided into two parts. The first deals mainly with doctrinal foundations, the second with practical applications. The whole is preceded by a statement on the situation of man in the modern world, a statement which conveys the attitude accepted by the council in surveying the relations between a Church committed to abiding doctrines and a world rooted in history and changing with the lapse of time. Some extracts from this introduction and the preface which precedes it will not be amiss:

> The joys and hopes, the griefs and the anxieties of the men of this age, especially those who are poor or in any way afflicted, these too are the joys and hopes, the griefs and anxieties of the followers of Christ. This community (of believers) realises that it is truly and intimately linked with mankind and its history. . . .
>
> The second Vatican Council . . . now addresses itself . . . to the whole of humanity . . . focuses its attention on the world of men, the whole human family along with the sum of those realities in the midst of which that family lives . . . It gazes upon that world which the Christian sees as created and sustained by its maker's love, fallen indeed into the bondage of sin, yet emancipated by Christ. . . .
>
> The pivotal point of our total presentation will be man himself, whole and entire, body and soul, heart and conscience, mind and will. . . . The Church seeks but a solitary goal: to carry forward the work of Christ himself under the lead of the befriending Spirit. And Christ entered this world to give witness to the truth, to rescue and not to sit in judgment, to serve and not to be served. (nn. 1–4) . . .

[5] For the history and pre-history of the constitution, see C. Moeller's very knowledgeable 'History of the constitution' in *Commentary on the Documents of Vatican II*, vol. V, pp. 1–76.

> Today, the human race is passing through a new stage of its history. Profound and rapid changes are spreading by degrees around the whole world. Triggered by the intelligence and creative energies of man, these changes recoil upon him, upon his decisions and desires, both individual and collective, and upon his manner of thinking and acting with respect to things and people. Hence we can already speak of a true social and cultural transformation, one which has repercussions upon his religious life as well. . . .

Thus mankind is going through a 'crisis of growth' and finds itself faced with strange paradoxes.

> Never has the human race enjoyed such an abundance of wealth, resources, and economic power. Yet a huge proportion of the world's citizens is still tormented by hunger. . . . Never before has man been so keenly aware of freedom, yet at the same time new forms of social and psychological slavery make their appearance. Although the world of today has a very vivid sense of unity . . . it is most grievously torn into opposing camps by conflicting forces. . . . The very words by which key concepts are expressed take on quite different meanings in diverse ideological systems. . . . Buffeted between hope and anxiety . . . [men] are burdened down with uneasiness. This same course of events leads men to look for answers. Indeed, it forces them to do so.

The council goes on to speak of the influence of the mathematical and natural sciences, of technology, of the expanding horizon of historical investigation and of 'planning for the future'. It mentions the demographic problem, and adds: 'The human race has passed from a rather static concept of reality to a more dynamic, evolutionary one.' But it is not content to speak of social problems and anxieties; it turns its attention also to those of the individual person:

> In man himself many elements wrestle with one another. . . . As a creature he experiences his limitations in a multitude of ways. On the other hand he feels himself to be boundless in his desires and summoned to a higher life . . . nor are there lacking men who despair of any meaning in life and praise the boldness of those who . . . strive to confer a total meaning on it by their own ingenuity alone. Nevertheless . . . an ever-increasing number of people are raising the most basic questions or recognising them with a new sharpness: What is man? What is the sense of sorrow, of evil, of death . . . What is the purpose of these victories, purchased at so high a cost? . . . What follows this earthly life?

It is worth remembering that the council was speaking in the middle sixties, at a time when the Cuban crisis had been successfully surmounted, when the Western world was enjoying its brief carnival of affluence, and when that same world, including the Christians in it, was only just beginning to wake up to a recognition of the poverty and unrest of the Third World. Already, however, there were the warning voices, and the philosophy of the absurd, if it had not penetrated to the masses, was alive in intellectual circles. At the same time the hippies were making their mild symbolic protest against the values and the technology of the dominant culture. Now, a decade and a half later, the West is less sure that affluence can advance or even survive much longer; the needs and the menace of the Third World are very much before our eyes even though we avert our mind from them; and incidents like the Russian occupation of Afghanistan have warned us of the fragility of détente. We can read such passages as the above from the Constitution on the Church in the Modern World with a sense of greater actuality than ever.

A document which tried to speak in unecclesiastical language, to speak not just to believers but to all men who might have enough good will to listen, and to speak not primarily in dissent and reproof but in dialogue, was something quite new in the history of official Catholic statements about 'the world'. It is worth remembering that the composition of this document has profited by the interest and suggestions of Christians from outside the Catholic Church, particularly from some who were associated with the World Council of Churches. There was, however, under the influence of Barth, a strand of apocalyptic judgment of the world in some of this Protestant thinking which contrasts, to a certain degree, with the more welcoming, hopeful and 'incarnational' mood of the Constitution. As the preparation of the document proceeded, from the end of 1962 to its promulgation at the end of 1965, the co-operation of expert lay people and of religious Sisters became more marked. The outcome was not only an invitation to dialogue but a result of dialogue.

After the preface and the lengthy and moving introduction the first part of the constitution is a statement of the basic insights of the Church with reference to the human condition. Chapter I deals with 'the dignity of the human person', finding in personhood the originating source of mankind's history, and in the ultimate 'dignity' of the person (under God) the norm for human behaviour – behaviour which is founded in freedom and therefore marked by sin and its consequences. This chapter includes the splendid statement on the dignity of the moral conscience, cited earlier in this book. And seeing in conscience the voice of God speaking to man in the very depths of his personal being, the Constitution moves on to examine atheism, including in that general term not only dogmatic atheism but agnosticism. It observes in passing that the defects of Christians themselves are at least in part responsible for the prevalence of such 'atheism': the God whom atheists reject or to whom they are hostile or indifferent is often only the false image of God that they have learnt from their acquaintenance with 'believers'. And it refers to the ideological atheism of such (unnamed) political systems as that of communist Russia. There were those who wished the council to publish an explicit and strong condemnation of communism, so it is striking that the following passage actually finds its place in this treatment of atheism:

> While rejecting atheism root and branch, the Church sincerely professes that all men, believers and unbelievers alike, ought to work for the rightful betterment of this world in which all alike live. Such an ideal cannot be realised, however, apart from sincere and prudent dialogue. . . . She courteously invites atheists to examine the gospel of Christ with an open mind.

This chapter concludes with a presentation of Christ as not only the revelation of the mystery of God but the full revelation of man to himself, man so unique in his personal dignity and so marvellously called to a destiny beyond his merely human powers. The grace of Christ, victorious over death and evil, works not only in believing Christians but, in an unseen way, in the hearts of 'all men of good will' (cf. K. Rahner's theme of the 'anonymous Christians').[6] Developing the Constitution's own notion of 'evolution' in the created order (a marked contrast to the static picture of the universe and of man's nature that had been inherited from pre-scientific times) we could say that Christ's manhood is the model and the goal towards which all worthy human effort, assisted by the hidden

[6] K. Rahner, *Theological Investigations*, vol. II (Darton, Longman & Todd 1974), p. 237a.

grace that flows from our redemption, is tending. Throughout these chapters the Constitution takes note of the supra-historical, eschatological goal of the created and incarnational order, and it can be said to endorse, if tacitly, Augustine's picture of the *totus Christus*, Jesus *and* his mystical body, but this whole Christ glorified in the life beyond the grave.

Man as not merely personal but also called to live in fellowship, is the subject of the second chapter of the constitution: 'God, who has fatherly concern for everyone, has willed that all men should constitute one family and treat one another in the spirit of brotherhood.' It is thus not accidental that man lives in society; and society and the individual person interact. There is not only a personal 'good' to be attained by each individually; there is a 'common good', and these two goods converge and are ultimately identical.

The third chapter deals with work, or, as it prefers to say, with 'man's activity throughout the world'. It emphasises that all such activity, secular though it may sometimes seem, has a positive contribution to make to the realisation of God's plan for the created order: 'Christians are convinced that the triumphs of the human race are a sign of God's greatness and the flowering of his own mysterious design.' In transforming his environment through his own activity man is at the same time developing his own manhood. It is also emphasised that 'secular' activity has its own autonomy, resulting from the fact that the created things with which it deals have their own 'stability, truth, goodness, proper laws, and order'. There may be a hidden reference to the Galileo affair in the remark in this chapter: 'We cannot but deplore certain habits of mind, sometimes found too among Christians, which do not sufficiently attend to the rightful independence of science.' On the other hand, it is remarked, 'when God is forgotten the creature itself grows unintelligible', and a warning is added that in actual fact human activity is often infected by sin, to such an extent that, in our own day, 'the magnified power of humanity threatens to destroy the race itself'.[7]

[7] The first session of the council took place, in part, against the background of the Cuban crisis. I remember thinking that if a Russian nuclear attack destroyed the council in session, Archbishop-Bishop King of Portsmouth, absent for reasons of health from the council, might find himself Pope.

> A monumental struggle against the powers of darkness pervades the whole history of man. The battle was joined from the very origins of the world and will continue until the last day, as the Lord has attested. Caught in this conflict, man is obliged to wrestle constantly if he is to cling to what is good. Nor can he achieve his own integrity without valiant efforts and the help of God's grace.

And when we are warned 'not to conform ourselves to this world' (Rm 12:2) the meaning of 'the world' here is, 'that spirit of vanity and malice which transforms into an instrument of sin those human energies intended for the service of God and man'. This warning can serve as a reminder that the authors of the constitution were plagued by the ambivalence of the word 'world' in scripture and in subsequent Christian literature. 'The whole world lies, [says the first Epistle of St John] in the power of the evil one.' Nevertheless, God 'so loved the world that he sent his only Son', says the Gospel of St John; and not only did Christ come to reconcile the world to himself, but the world is God's creation, and when he saw it he saw it as 'very good'. In Christian tradition the world is often distinguished from the Church, almost as though you could belong to one or the other but not to both. And then there is the uncertainty whether to mean by 'the world' the whole of creation, or more narrowly the 'world' of men in history. The constitution prefers to see the world as the whole created order, but that order as finding its fullest expression in human history; and it does not encourage the idea that to be of the world is to be outside the Church, or *vice versa*. It is fully aware of the havoc wrought in the world by sin; but it does not pretend that that havoc stops at the door of the Church; on the contrary, the Church herself, as already stated in the Dogmatic Constitution on the Church, is *semper purificanda*, always in need of purgation. Moreover, if the Constitution grants, as it does, that grace and the Spirit of God are operative outside the visible limits of the Roman Catholic Church considered as an institution, and indeed in areas to which the gospel has never penetrated, it becomes uncertain where the limits of the Church's existence in history can be drawn.

The relation of the Church and the world is in fact the subject of the fourth chapter of Part I. It may be sufficient here to remark that, while the constitution suggests ways in which the Church can help the world, it also frankly acknowledges the continuing debt of the Church to the world:

> Thanks to the experience of past ages, the progress of the sciences, and the treasures hidden in the various forms of human culture, the nature of man is [now] more clearly revealed and new roads to truth are opened. These benefits profit the Church, too. For, from the beginning of her history, she has learned to express the message of Christ with the help of the ideas and terminology of various peoples, and has tried to clarify it with the wisdom of philosophers, too. . . . Each nation develops the ability to express Christ's message in its own way. At the same time, a living exchange is fostered between the Church and the diverse cultures of people.

This relation of Christianity to culture is one of the most important issues facing theologians today. At the heart of Christianity is the message from God, a message proclaimed from age to age by the Church. This message is the incarnate 'Word' of God. We have to remember that this Word incarnate was born, like the rest of us, an infant, literally one without speech. He learnt to speak, learnt we may add, humanly, to think in words and concepts and conventions provided by the culture of his people, the Palestinian Jews. This was a particular culture. Palestine was at the time of Jesus' birth a vassal state of the Roman Empire. Before he had grown up it was fully incorporated into the Empire as a sort of sub-province with a Roman governor. But the cultural impact of these political arrangements was minimal. The people continued to talk their Semitic language and to think in Semitic ways. Along with racial unity they were held together by their religion, a unique tradition in the midst of the polytheism of surrounding cultures. The intrinsic intransigence of this ethical monotheism and claim to a revealed covenant with God combined with their racial kinship to give them a powerful sense of identity, and to make them relatively impervious even to the more advanced intellectual culture of the European world, of which they were now politically a part. The same is not true of the Judaism of the dispersion, where exposure to Gentile culture was more immediate and intense. In a great Jewish centre like Egyptian Alexandria there was the seduction, but there was also the challenge, of Greek philosophy. In dialogue with this philosophy the Judaism of the intellectuals of Jewish Alexandria assimilated a great deal as well as offering an alternative higher synthesis. There was 'communion' between the dispersion Jews and the Palestinian, and the great Philo of Alexandria visited Jerusalem just about the time of Christ. Once the Church, less than two decades after the resurrection of Christ, turned first to the dispersion Jews, and then to the Gentiles direct, the Greek philosophic interest, mediated by Hellenistic Judaism, began to pour in and enrich Christian theology, as can be clearly seen in the Epistles of St Paul. This was already an example of the influence of culture and cultural change upon the expression of the Christian Tradition. It helps to explain the contrast between the parables of Jesus and the exalted theologising of the hymn to Christ in the Epistle to the Philippians or the creation-redemption theology of the Epistle to the Ephesians. The Logos christology of the later but still pre-Nicene centuries was a Christian attempt to pursue, further than the Gospel of St John had taken it, the philosophical speculation of Alexandrian Judaism. But in the fourth and fifth centuries the Church, now welcomed into the fullness of Graeco-Roman culture, had to face and express itself through Greek philosophy in its immediate form, no longer merely as mediated by Hellenistic Judaism. That Greek philosophy came before it predominantly in the shape of late Platonism and neo-Platonism. It was centuries later that, for the Western Church, first St Albert and then Aquinas took Aristotle really seriously; in the fourth century Aristotle had been used mainly by heretics who wanted to create difficulties for Trinitarian theology by appealing to his logic.

The second Vatican Council, with its treatment of culture, has at long last officially committed the Church to taking modern science and historical scholarship, with all the problems for exegesis and hermeneusis that the latter entails, as seriously as Aquinas took Aristotle. We are doubtless only beginning to witness the consequences of this.

But the council's positive attitude to 'profane' culture has its consequences also with reference to cultures that are remote from the long Jewish and then European tradition. We shall have to take seriously the indigenous cultures of Africa, India, the Far East, and China. Already the first tentative steps are being taken towards a dialogue with Islam, a faith which is closely connected with Jewish and Christian faith but also strongly linked with cultures that have lost, or never had, a deep connection with European culture. 'Indigenisation' and 'acculturalisation' are ugly words for a very necessary process. Europe (and Rome, which is historically as much European as it is Catholic) will have to leave space for the Christian assimilation of these cultures; and to be patient with the corrigible mistakes that will inevitably be made.

It remains to say that perhaps the deepest hermeneutical problem for Christians is the discernment of the unchanging Word of God from the contingency of its cultural embodiments, remembering that it is only in these cultural embodiments that we can perceive that Word at all.

The second part of the Constitution on the Church in the World of Today deals with a group of more specific and 'urgent' problems. One of these, in fact, is 'Culture' (Part II, Chapter 2), and it will be convenient to add here a few remarks on this subject suggested by that chapter.

'Culture' is a European word, and in the past there has been a tendency to suppose that European culture is the norm and standard of all that is truly cultural, and to judge the 'cultures' of other regions of the earth by the extent to which they approximate to this norm. Matthew Arnold, in *Culture and Anarchy*, singled out the Hebrew and the Hellenic traditions as the joint foundations of this culture; and, as already mentioned, Hilaire Belloc identified Europe and the faith. In consequence of this (largely unreflective) arrogance, political colonialism has been followed not only by economic colonialism but by a kind of cultural colonialism also; and since the task of educating the non-Europeans was often left by governments largely in the hands of the missionaries, this cultural colonialism was actually promoted by them. It seemed obvious, for example, that literacy and numeracy were unqualified benefits to be bestowed on the 'natives'. It is worth remembering that the *Iliad* and the *Odyssey* are in substance the product of a pre-literary culture, and that even in the later stages of their composition, reading and writing were still the attainments of a comparatively small minority of the people. The ancient traditions of Israel will have developed in similar conditions, although writing was known and used, again no doubt by a small privileged minority, for thousands of years in the Near East before it spread to Europe.

A further consideration is the antiquity and refinement of the cultures of India and China. If it was understandable that the natives of central Africa seemed to European discoverers to be embodiments of Aquinas's idea of 'the man of the woods', *homo silvestris*, the same mistake would have been inexcusable if made with regard to the Indians and the Chinese. And yet there may be something unique about European culture: the contribution of Greek philosophy to the culture of mankind is something which, in my opinion, has no real parallels elsewhere, though no doubt claims will be made for the thinkers of India. It has to be added that this philosophic urge was basically the same that created mathematics as a pure science and laid the ultimate foundations of modern science. If one can justly make such claims for the Greeks, it is no less obvious that the development of ethical monotheism in Israel, and its further and unexpected development in the incarnation of the divine Word, give an absolute uniqueness to the contribution of the Jewish-Christian tradition to human history and universal human culture.

Thus, if there remains some lack of unity in the meaning attached to the word 'culture' in the Constitution on the Church in the World of Today, some drifting between the idea of a multiplicity of national cultures and the unity of a single human culture, there is a partial justification for this ambiguity. European philosophy and science, the technology that is the fruit of science, and the Christian gospel have their origins, indeed, in particular national cultures, but they are valid for all cultures. The problem is, and it is not an easy one to solve, to extend their influence while respecting the legitimate traditions, outlooks and indeed 'cultures' of countries other than the European.

A further remark is important in connection with this chapter on culture. It is here that the council finds occasion to remark that just as every created reality has its own internal organisation and autonomy, so the study of these realities has a right to freedom of investigation, theorising and publication; a right which both state and Church should respect. There had been a long history of paternalistic (or less worthily motivated) censorship and restriction on free intellectual enterprise, a history of such restriction both by political authorities and by the institutional Church. Freedom of expression is still controlled in communist countries, and the Church's 'index of prohibited books' only lost its legal authority in the sixties. There remains, of course, a duty for the state to check pornography, and for ecclesiastical authority to see that the official teaching in seminaries and from the pulpit does not contradict the teaching of the Church. But the principle of intellectual freedom is clearly laid down by the Constitution, though its implications still need to be worked out both in the secular and the religious field.

Something must now be said about the first chapter in this second part of the constitution. Its subject is Marriage and the Family. Both human society in general and the life of the individual person are closely linked, the council tells us, with the well-being of the family, which it proceeds to call 'a community of love', a community which, while held 'in high esteem' in many quarters, is yet under many threats today. The council, therefore, proposes to clarify certain points in the Christian doctrine concerning marriage, for the help both of believers and of others who seek to foster 'the natural dignity and superlative value' of the married state.

The constitution finds the root of the marriage partnership in the 'conjugal covenant of irrevocable personal consent'. The word covenant is important. Civil and ecclesiastical law have preferred to speak of marriage as a 'contract' between two consenting parties. This preference is not surprising. For marriage and the family are matters of public concern as well as being the peculiar concern of the parties to the marriage. Public law is ill equipped to deal with such imponderable realities as personal love and commitment in love; it finds it easier to deal with the written evidence of contracts entered into and formulated according to legally enforceable conventions. From the Christian, and ultimately the human, point of view this concentration on the contractual aspect of marriage can be unfortunate. Just as Bellarmine can 'define' the Church in such a way that the holiness of its members becomes apparently irrelevant to its nature, so a marriage, viewed purely as a contract, can appear to be totally without heart and without spiritual value.

The word 'covenant' is borrowed from the biblical tradition. It has been pointed out that, in the Old Testament, the covenant with Abraham is chronologically prior to the establishment of the Law. A covenant is a personal agreement and is founded not on law but on mutual trust. Law enters in subsequently to give precision to this trustful mutual commitment, and to lay down sanctions to protect it. But behind or before legal enactment there must be, for a truly spiritual relationship, the personal commitment of partner to partner, and this commitment is almost hypocritical if it is not itself an expression of mutual love.

Graham Greene, in his short novel, *Dr Fischer of Geneva*,[8] puts into the mouth of his leading character a distinction which is not without importance here. He suggests that 'being in love with' is not the same thing as 'loving', and that the former can exist where the latter is absent. The character in question, speaking of his first marriage, observes that, while he was in love with his wife, the relationship had not matured into a genuine 'love' before the death of his wife. The Constitution on the Church in the World of Today clearly means, when it speaks of the 'covenant' that is at the heart of marriage, a genuine love, as distinct from a mere 'being in love'. In principle, one can cease to 'be in love' with someone; but, again in principle, where there is genuine love the relationship is one of irrevocable self-giving:

> Let me not to the marriage of true minds
> Admit impediment. Love is not love
> Which alters where it alteration finds,
> Or bends with the remover to remove.

Hence the constitution does not need to invoke the terms of a legal contract in order to pronounce the irrevocability of the personal consent which is the constitutive factor of the 'covenant'.

The word 'personal' is of decisive importance in this whole matter of marriage. From the fifth century the Christian tradition has been familiar with the distinction between nature

[8] Bodley Head 1980.

and person, or hypostasis: the council of Chalcedon taught that in Jesus Christ there are two natures, divine and human, but these two natures belong to one and the same person, Jesus of Nazareth. When we ask 'who' someone is we are asking about a person; when we ask what he is we are asking for information about his nature as that nature exists in the flux of history. Man operates within the framework provided by his nature and its context; but his operations, when they are most genuinely his own, are expressions of him as a person. I can love someone's physical charm, intellectual brilliance, powers of imagination, generosity, courage. But if my love stops short at that point, it will disappear if he loses the qualities which I have found amiable. But if I love someone as himself, then my love can survive the disappearance of the qualities and attributes which first attracted me to him. The ideal of married love is a love of persons for each other, a love which is capable of growth and developing maturity, but not strictly of dying.

At a more superficial but very important level the indissolubility of marriage can be defended by reference to the needs of the children of the resultant family. Not all marriages, however, are blessed with children; and children grow up and cease to need the support of their original home. Marriage remains indissoluble, despite this, because the deepest reason for its permanence is the permanence of the mutual commitment of love in which it found its starting-point.

The constitution points out that marriage, so understood, has been raised to a new and sacramental level for Christians, and becomes an expression of that redeeming love that was incarnate in Christ himself: 'Authentic married love is caught up into divine love and is governed and enriched by Christ's redeeming power and the saving activity of the Church.'

Such is the natural and supernatural context in which children of a Christian family grow up; and as they grow, so they too contribute to the family love. Since love is of its nature expansive, such a family becomes a centre radiating the love of God beyond itself to enrich the life of the Church as a whole and of mankind.

Married love, the constitution teaches, 'is uniquely expressed and perfected through the marital act', and, 'the actions within marriage whereby the couple are united intimately and chastely are noble and worthy ones. Expressed in a manner which is truly human, these actions signify and promote that mutual self-giving by which spouses enrich each other with a joyful and thankful will.'

The constitution elaborates on 'the fruitfulness of marriage' in a special paragraph.

> Marriage and conjugal love are by their nature ordained toward the begetting and educating of children.[9] Children are really the supreme gift of marriage and contribute very substantially to the welfare of their parents. . . . Hence, while not making the other-purposes of marriage of less account, the true practice of conjugal love, and the whole meaning of the family life which results from it, have this aim: that the couple be ready with stout hearts to co-operate with the love of the Creator and the Saviour, who through them will enlarge and enrich his own family day by day.

The constitution, however, by no means advocates irresponsible multiplication of children. It teaches that the married couple should recognise and carry out their own responsibility in this area. In place of the rather cold modern term, family planning, the council prefers the expression, responsible parenthood. It remarks that decisions in this area should be made by 'a conscience dutifully conformed to the divine law itself', and they should be submissive towards the Church's teaching office, which 'authentically interprets that law in the light of the gospel'. On the other hand, the constitution recognises that when the method used to avoid having children is that of wholly abstaining from marital intercourse the results can be serious even for the marriage itself. There is thus a problem which the council leaves unsolved. It firmly condemns abortion and infanticide as methods of keeping down the size of the family. It praises conjugal chastity (which does not necessarily mean abstinence). Beyond that, it only affirms that, 'sons of the Church, may not undertake methods of regulating procreation which are found blameworthy by the teaching authority of the Church in its unfolding of the divine law'. Why all this hesitation, and why this vague language which, incidentally, requires careful exegesis in view of the distinction

[9] It must not, however, be forgotten that there can be genuine Christian marriage also in cases where, for reasons of age, there is no expectation or possibility of children.

between the infallible and the non-infallible teaching of the Church?

There is no doubt that among the members of the council there were those who would have wished for a 'liberalisation' of the teaching on birth control made famous by Pius XI's encyclical *Casti Connubii*. There were many others who felt very strongly that the position laid down by Pius XI must be maintained, whether because they would in any case have disapproved of contraception, or because they feared the blow to the teaching authority of the Church if it should be seen to have changed its stance on this matter of vital importance to so many people. In any case, Paul VI had effectively withdrawn the issue from the agenda of the council by announcing (June 1964) that he would create a pontifical commission to examine the question. This did not, we are informed, prevent a last-minute attempt to secure the insertion of an unambiguous condemnation of contraception into the text of this chapter of the Constitution. Such an insertion would have been deplorable, since the council, in view of the existence of the papal commission on the subject, had refrained from a proper debate on the issue. A footnote to the relevant passage ('Constitution on the Church in the World of Today', n. 51 *ad fin.*) somewhat drily concludes: 'With the doctrine of the Church's teaching office in this state, this Holy Synod does not intend to propose immediate concrete solutions.'

On the other hand, there are suggestions in the text as finally approved which could have given occasion for useful developments. Not only is there the admission, noted above, that abstinence from marital intercourse can be dangerous to the whole conjugal relationship, but the 'objective standards' which should decide on methods of ensuring responsible parenthood are, we are told, to be based on 'the nature of the human person and of its acts' (n. 51). Once again we see the personalist orientation of the Constitution; the manuals of moral theology had led many people to suppose that it was not the nature of the human persons but the animal biology of the organs of procreation which determine the morality or immorality of conjugal behaviour.

The issue of responsible parenthood recurs late in the constitution, in a passage dealing with the alleged threat of over-population (n. 87). The council acknowledges that this is a problem gravely exercising men's minds, but it warns against solutions which contradict the moral law (for example, compulsory contraception or compulsory sterilisation, though these examples are not mentioned explicitly); and it affirms that the decision on the number of children of a marriage 'belongs to the honest judgment of the parents' and cannot be left to the judgment of civil governments. At this point the council takes occasion to refer to the investigation of scientific but moral methods of birth control (for example, 'natural' methods).

The passage just referred to comes from Part II, Chapter 5, of the constitution, of which the subject is 'the fostering of peace and the promotion of a community of nations'. The council here urges all Christians to join with all true peacemakers in pleading for peace and bringing it about. It takes the opportunity thus provided to praise those who 'renounce the use of violence in the vindication of their rights' . . . 'provided that this can be done without injury to the rights and duties of others or of the community itself'. The added proviso is a typical example of the way in which a determined conservative minority in the council sought to limit the effectiveness of statements which they found objectionable but could not directly expunge. The issue of non-violence is closely linked with that of conscientious objection, mentioned in the next section (n. 79): 'It seems right that laws make humane provision for the case of those who for reasons of conscience refuse to bear arms, provided however that they accept some other form of service to the human community.' It is to be noted that the council here neither affirms nor denies that conscientious objection to active service in war is *objectively* justifiable. At the time of the council there were countries in which conscientious objection was illegal.

The constitution next turns its attention to 'total war' and the scientific development of methods of material and human destruction. Obviously the 'nuclear deterrent' is particularly in view in this section. The council states that we have to take fresh stock of our views on war, and approach the subject 'with an entirely new attitude'. It is well known that traditional moral theology has long operated with the concept of 'the just war'; a war of defence against aggression, waged with a minimum of necessary violence,and with a reasonable prospect of success. This casuistical approach may have had some colour of reasonableness when wars were fought between professional uniformed armies and with limited weaponry. It is hardly valid when one is contemplating the possibility of a nuclear holocaust. The council therefore declares: 'Any act of war aimed indiscriminately at the destruction of entire cities or of extensive areas along with their population is a crime against God and man himself. It merits unequivocal and unhesitating condemnation.' Since the very possession of such weaponry gives the opportunity for total war and 'through a certain inexorable chain of events' can urge men 'to the most atrocious decisions', the council urges 'all men, especially government officials and military leaders' to give unremitting thought to the awesome responsibility which is theirs. A competition in the building up of such armanents is not, says the council, a safe way to preserve a stable peace: 'The arms race is an unutterably treacherous trap for humanity.' Peace must be born of mutual trust between nations rather than imposed on them through fear of one another's weapons. . . . Meanwhile, arms limitation should be promoted on a bilateral basis.

Some reflections seem to be called for. First, it would seem that the council intended to condemn the use of strategic nuclear weapons (tactical nuclear weaponry was less developed in 1965 than it is today). Secondly, it can be argued that the threat of using such weapons could be justified as a *ruse de guerre*, although the American hierarchy has recently condemned such threatening as immoral. But thirdly, the intention to use these weapons is to be distinguished both from their actual use and from the 'bluff' of threatening to use them. If we accept the council's teaching that total war is immoral, we can hardly avoid condemning the intention of their use. If I intend to commit murder I am not rendered guiltless by the fact that, as circumstances turned out, I did not actually put the intention into act. Not only an unconditional intention to commit murder, but a hypothetical intention to do so is immoral: if my intention is to commit murder unless my demands are met, then that conditional intention is itself murderous and immoral. The central moral dilemma for the great powers today, as I see it, is that they may not intend to execute their threats of nuclear retaliation, and yet are bound to behave in all respects as though they had that intention. This is the case not only for the heads of government but for every officer and man in the armed forces who is in a position in which he has to profess readiness to obey an order from higher authority to 'press the button' of a nuclear attack.

In abstract theory it is of course possible to combine the development of nuclear armaments and the threat of their use with a genuine intention not to use them if one's 'bluff' is called. In actual hard political fact the combination must be extremely difficult (especially as it requires the reflection of that combination in the intentions of all concerned with the manufacture and supply of such weaponry and all who are being trained to use them and particularly those who are trained to receive orders from their superiors to launch the missiles).

In current debate the question of intention seems to be largely overlooked. Arguments are pursued for and against the thesis: 'It would be better to annihilate the human race than to submit to Communist domination.' There are very many who maintain that we must preserve our nuclear capability in order to persuade the Russians to co-operate with us in a process of continuing and at last total nuclear disarmament.

A further point needs to be made. There are those who question the supposition behind the council's condemnation of total warfare, namely that such warfare involves the direct and intended slaughter of non-combatants. Against this supposition, it is claimed that the slaughter of children, the infirm and so on, is an unavoidable feature of even a 'just' war and can be dealt with by the casuistry of 'double effect': my action does not intend its evil results even though these are foreseen; my intention is the just intention of destroying the enemy's fighting capability. It is added that, in modern warfare, not only the uniformed and armed forces but practically every adult able-bodied citizen contributes, directly or indirectly (for example by paying taxes) to the war effort, so that the distinction between combatants and non-combatants needs to be reviewed.

Perhaps one may be allowed a personal comment. There

comes a time when the arguments of theoreticians (among whom I include moral theologians) begin to look grotesque when measured against the existential realities. When we add to our considerations the possibilities of chemical and biological warfare we are faced with a situation of such horrific proportions that one can feel driven to a thoroughly radical proposal. Certainly, it was laudable that the council strongly urged multilateral nuclear disarmament. But as the decades pass the possibility of achieving effective and sufficient results by negotiation appear to be tenuous, and the awful possibility of an unintended crisis developing into a deplorable recourse to the nuclear weapon is always present.[10] Should not Christians be proclaiming openly to our rulers and our fellowmen that we will have no more to do with the whole thing, and that unilateral disarmament is the only constructive way forward? We should have to admit that this might well leave the way open for world-domination by the Kremlin. That possibility must be acknowledged, and we should have to affirm that even that price is not too high to pay for moral integrity. We might of course add, reasonably, I think, that the more universal the theoretical domination of Russia, the less effective such domination is likely to be.

The remaining two chapters of Part II of the constitution deal with economic life and political life. Considerations of space impel me to treat these two chapters with extreme brevity.

As could have been expected, the constitution firmly subordinates economics to morals. It shows little sympathy with economic *laisser faire*. It is also not surprising that it pays special attention to the inequity of the extreme poverty of the Third World compared with the affluence of the industrialised north. It does not seem to have anticipated the problems of the present decade and the decline in those factors which promoted the affluent mentality. Nor has it anything of significance to say about the limited quantity of oil and solid fuels available

[10] The West has an almost pathological fear of the aggressive intentions of the Kremlin. It is worth while to remember that Russia has a similar fear of Western aggression. The danger is acute that these contradictory fears will lead both East and West to total destruction which is surely worse even than the results of aggression.

for future generations. While it speaks rather favourably of technology, provided that it is kept under moral control, it does not foresee the serious problem that will face us as we move into the era of the 'silicon chip'. Similarly, one may regret that the constitution has little or nothing to say about the moral problems of the great multi-national business corporations, and about the 'intermediate technology' advocated by the late Dr Schumacher of *Small is Beautiful*[11] and his followers. More positively, the present chapter of the constitution not only endorses the general approach of John XXIII in his encyclical *Pacem in Terris* and paves the way for Paul VI's *Populorum Progressio*, but may be said to have given a perhaps unintended impetus to the theology of liberation which has been such a marked feature of Catholic thinking in Latin America in recent years. It was also probably influential in moving the Latin American hierarchies in the direction of greater social and economic concern and a certain detachment from the policies of the capitalist and military governments of that sub-continent.

On the subject of politics, it will suffice to draw attention to three points. First, the constitution takes a strong line on human rights and the requirement that political authority should respect these rights in regard to their own citizens. Secondly, the constitution can be quoted as evidence that the authorities of the Church have lost their Victorian distaste for democracy. Thirdly, one passage hints at the possibility, if not desirability, of detaching the institutional Church from a close alliance with political authorities which, in opposition to Eastern communism, have adopted a capitalistic bias:

> The Church . . . employs the things of time to the degree that her own proper mission demands. Still she does not lodge her hope in privileges conferred by civil authority. Indeed, she stands ready to renounce the exercise of certain legitimately acquired rights if it becomes clear that their use raises doubts about the sincerity of her witness or that new conditions of life demand some other arrangement. . . . She has the right to pass moral judgments, even in matters touching the political order, whenever basic personal rights or the salvation of souls make such judgments necessary.

History may look back on the pontificates of John XXIII and

[11] Blond & Briggs 1973.

Paul VI as the period in which the Church began to reaffirm her detachment from established political orders of whatever colour. The effort to do so has laid the Church and the Holy See open to the charge of being unduly 'soft' towards communism and left-wing tendencies generally; but probably this is due to an impression which is almost inevitable when Christians are waking up to the hidden dangers of a close alliance with capitalism and right-wing governments. What has still to be learnt by bishops in some countries is that the cause of Christian morality is not always best served by attempting to gain for this morality the support of secular political sanctions.

9

Retrospect and Prospect

By the end of the council the expectation that it would prove to be a defeat for the advocates of a 'new theology' had been resoundingly falsified. The 'conservatives', despite the intelligent leadership of eminent curialists, could only muster insignificant minority votes against conciliar documents that might have been even more 'progressive' had not the influence of the Pope, exercised largely behind the scenes, been at work to prevent an open split in the leadership of the Church. On the day when the council bade farewell to Rome the Pope himself summed up the meaning of what occurred as the discovery that in Christ theology and anthropology, our knowledge of God and our knowledge of man, are reconciled: in Christ's perfected humanity we 'see God' to the extent that this is possible within the limits of this life. There was much euphoria on that final day.

The thought did occur to me that, in democratic countries, when a government has lost a massive vote of confidence, it is replaced by another more in harmony with the national mood. Would the Pope take any similar step with regard to the Curia? He did two things. He called in a number of non-Italians to head various Congregations of the Curia; but these men were usually inexperienced in the working of the curial machine, and it has often been suggested that, even in a country like Britain, the permanent officials of the civil service have an immense advantage over the 'amateur' politicians whom they are supposed to be serving. Secondly, the Pope reformed the Curia itself; but this was largely an exercise in improving its efficiency, and in concentrating power in the hands of the Secretary of State, through whom the Pope could more effectively exercise his personal authority.

Meanwhile the bishops had returned to their dioceses and were soon immersed in the routine work of administration which imposes such a heavy burden in dioceses with a large Catholic population. How much had they been changed by the experience of the council? They had gone through a prolonged exercise in group dynamics and had found themselves endorsing statements which would have been repugnant to many of them before the exercise began. They were loyally determined to translate into practice the decisions of the council. It is less clear that they had seized its spirit and made it their own. The new emphasis on the functions of national and regional episcopal conferences ensured that practical implementation would go ahead. But old habits die hard, and I have the impression that both at Rome and elsewhere the implementation was conceived as taking place through prescriptive methods more in keeping with the Church before the council than with the council's own spirit. The vernacular liturgy was imposed with alacrity, and it was easy to relax the rules of fasting and abstinence. But too little was done, at least in Britain, to educate the Catholic people and particularly the clergy in the doctrine and insights of Vatican II. Experience has shown that the parish clergy are the key element in any attempt to change the direction of Catholic thought and action, and obviously the clergy in 1965 (apart from the bishops) were still living on the teaching they had received in seminaries untouched by the council; they had not had the experience of the bishops themselves during those four sessions in Rome from 1962 to 1965.

There was resistance to the council, at first largely instinctive and unorganised, later becoming more articulate and pronounced. In a recent study of Catholic attitudes in England and Wales the author, preferring to avoid the popular distinction between 'traditionalists' and 'progressives', speaks of a 'conservation' group, which believes that the witness of the Church 'largely depends upon her changelessness', and a 'furtherance' group, which believes that renewal and adaptation of the Church are good and need to be taken further (D. Miles Board, in *Responses*, 1980, pp. 1f.). It should be stressed that the reference is to attitudes of mind and emotional reactions rather than to organised groupings of the faithful. And it must be borne in mind that a vast number of Catholics simply take what the bishops and clergy offer them, grumble or rejoice, and carry on as though nothing had happened.

Elsewhere in the world, while the Lefebvre movement was beginning to take shape in Western Europe, the Church in Africa and elements in the Church of Latin America were energetically exploring the possibilities for long-overdue change which the Council had opened up for them. There were numerous retirements of white bishops in Africa to make room for black diocesan bishops.

Then, in the high summer of 1968, Paul VI issued his encyclical *Humanae Vitae*, embodying his judgment on the issue of contraception. The document may have been intended to put an end to uncertainty and conflict. In fact, however, it threw the Church into a turmoil of unprecedented emotion and created a 'crisis of authority' which has outlasted the immediate excitements.

As already observed, the question of contraception had been removed by the Pope from the agenda of the council and had been entrusted to the consideration of a Commission established by the Pope himself, a Commission which in the end included a large contingent of cardinals. Theoretically, the Commission worked in private. But in the spring of 1967 its advice to the Pope was 'leaked' and the world became aware that this advice amounted to a proposal to 'liberalise' the Church's teaching on artificial contraception. The Commission suggested that what the Church should condemn as immoral was not the contraceptive act itself but the 'contraceptive mentality' which took advantage of artificial contraception to shirk the responsibilities and vocation of parenthood and make marital intercourse nothing more than an exercise in mutual self-indulgence. It appears that the Report of the Commission was not accompanied by an official Minority Report, although a group of four theologians who had been involved in its debates composed their own strongly-worded dissent from the Council's liberal attitude.

However regrettable the unauthorised publication of the Commission's Report may have been, the accuracy of the 'leak' has never been denied. The Report was advice to the Pope from a body which he himself had established. It had no official standing except as a consultative document and the Church had to wait for over a year before receiving the Pope's official response. This response did not confine itself to the narrow issue of contraception; it spoke more widely about the dignity of marriage and in these respects was in line with the teaching of the chapter on marriage and the family in the Constitution on the Church in the World of Today. It was, however, the encyclical's teaching on contraception that riveted the attention of both the Church and the world in 1968. This teaching is given in the following passages of the encyclical:

> [To be excluded is] any action which either before, at the moment of, or after sexual intercourse is specifically intended to prevent procreation – whether as an end or as a means. . . . It is never lawful, even for the gravest reasons, to do evil that good may come of it – in other words, to intend positively something which intrinsically contradicts the moral order. Consequently it is a serious error to think that a whole married life of otherwise normal relations can justify sexual intercourse which is deliberately contraceptive and so intrinsically wrong.[1]

This is not the place to criticise or defend the moral teaching of *Humanae Vitae*. What matters from the point of view of this study of the aftermath of the second Vatican Council is the powerful repercussions that the document caused. It happened that just at the moment when the encyclical was published the bishops of the Anglican Communion were in session for the 1968 Lambeth Conference, at which ecumenical issues were on the agenda. The position of the Anglican Communion with respect to contraception is that the practice is a matter

[1] The Latin original runs as follows: 'Quivis respuendus est actus qui, cum conjugale commercium vel praevidetur vel efficitur vel ad suos naturales exitus ducit, id, tanquam finem obtinendum aut viam adhibendam, intendat ut procreatio impediatur. . . . Nunquam . . . licet, ne ob gravissimas quidem causas, facere mala ut eveniant bona . . . Quapropter erret omnino qui arbitretur conjugalem actum, sua fecunditate ex industria destitutum, ideoque intrinsice inhonestum, fecundis totius conjugum vitae congressionibus comprobari posse'.

for the individual consciences of the married partners. The encyclical was seen, by comparison, as an illiberal document and perhaps as an indication that, for all the fine ecumenical words that had been heard from the Catholic side since 1965, the papacy was still both obscurantist and authoritarian.

Opposition to the encyclical from outside the Catholic body was matched by dismay within the Church. The encyclical posed problems for bishops, priests and laity, though of course not for all. Episcopal conferences tried to temper the wind of the document to the shorn lambs of their flocks. Some priests openly protested against the papal teaching and a good many of them, if they did not renounce their priestly functions, were disciplined by their bishops. Married Catholics in very large numbers were driven to ask themselves crucial questions about their Catholic allegiance; and it began to happen that priests who were thought to take a lenient view concerning contraception were deliberately sought out in the confessional.

What was basically at issue was the authority of the encyclical: was it possible to withhold assent from its teaching without ceasing to be a loyal Catholic? One of the positive results of the crisis was that many Catholics, aided by theologians, were driven to make a sharp distinction between the 'infallible' and the 'non-infallible' pronouncements of Church authority, including the authority of the Pope himself.

For nearly a hundred years from the definition of papal infallibility by the first Vatican Council in 1870 there had been a largely unreflective tendency among Catholics to accept every doctrinal or disciplinary dictum of the papacy as virtually enjoying the authority of an infallible pronouncement. This authority tended to be accorded not only to the immediate teaching of the Pope himself but to every pronouncement of the Curia and its fringe (e.g. the Biblical Commission). There were of course theologians who knew better; but they had relatively little influence on the mass of the faithful, and not much even on the ordinary clergy. The Pope in practice had come to be looked on as the oracle of God.

Humanae Vitae ensured that the theological question of the extent of papal infallibility became a question for the ordinary Catholic and his pastors. How necessary this was can be seen from the argumentation of the group of four theologians who had dissociated themselves from the findings of the pontifical commission. They argued that to liberalise the Church's stand on birth control would shake the foundations of a magisterial authority which would seem to have contradicted itself, since as recently as the early '30's Pius XI, in *Casti Connubii*, had taught with confident emphasis that all contraception was a great moral evil. The four theologians went so far as to complain, egregiously enough, that if the Pope took the line proposed by his own Commission he would in effect be saying that the Holy Spirit (who guides the Church into all truth) was, in the years 1930–1931, not with the Pope but with the Anglican bishops who had at that date left the issue of birth control to the conscience of the Christian married couples. That this question of the authority of past teaching was a powerful factor in the whole crisis can be seen from some words of *Humanae Vitae* itself. The Pope observes that he could not have accepted the findings of his Commission without questioning them, 'above all because certain criteria of solution had emerged which departed from the moral teaching on marriage proposed with constant firmness by the teaching authority of the Church'. So the issue was at least as much an issue of ecclesiastical authority as it was of marital morality.

The service rendered to the Church in this crisis by theologians cannot be too highly praised. Already in September 1968, when controversy was at its height, Karl Rahner contributed an article to *Stimmen der Zeit*, in which he wrote: 'A bishop must not and dare not act as if the papal declaration were simply incapable of reform and as if any dissenting from it would necessarily imply a basic denial of the Church's teaching authority'.[2]

English readers may also consult a series of three articles of the very greatest importance, contributed by Fr John McHugh to the *Clergy Review* August, Sept., Oct. 1969. Fr McHugh shows that to distinguish between the authority of infallible definitions and all other pronouncements of the Church's authority is not a modern attempt to escape from obedience into licence but was something already worked out by the 'Roman' theologians of the nineteenth century. He

[2] Quotation from *Humane Vitae and the Bishops*, ed. John Horgan, Irish University Press 1972. This volume includes a valuable collection of documents from episcopal conferences dealing with the encyclical.

makes no attempt to claim that *Humanae Vitae*'s teaching has infallible status and he is emphatic that a Catholic who conscientiously and after due reflection and consideration of the authoritative teaching, concludes that he is not bound by this teaching is still a perfectly loyal Catholic and, it is implied, can follow his conscience. So far as I know Fr McHugh's position has never been refuted. It is all the more impressive as coming from one who had no personal difficulty in accepting the papal teaching on birth control as true, and indeed saw difficulties in adopting any other position.

Vatican II had left contraception as an open question. But in the Dogmatic Constitution on the Church it had itself quietly drawn the distinction between infallible and non-infallible teaching. Infallible definitions of ecumenical councils, it says, are to be adhered to with the *obsequium fidei*, and will in fact be received with the *assensus Ecclesiae*. Official teaching that is not infallible, whether of Pope or of bishops, is to be adhered to *religioso animi obsequio* or with *religiosum intellectus et voluntatis obsequium*. It is important to observe that the word *obsequium* is not synonymous with *assensus*. Assent (*assensus*) is a simple 'yes' accorded to an utterance inviting such a response. *Obsequium* is a vague word, meaning something like compliance (which may fall short of assent), respect or deference. When the council speaks of *obsequium fidei* it obviously means nothing less than assent, though not using the word; which, however, it does also use of infallible definitions. *Obsequium intellectus et voluntatis* may be supposed to be something other than assent. Indeed, as used in its conciliar context, it must mean something different; for the council recognises degrees of *religiosum obsequium*; and there can be no degrees of assent: it is either given or it is withheld. The council even requires that *religiosum obsequium* be shown to the teaching of individual (diocesan) bishops by their subjects; such at least can be taken to be the meaning of a passage in n. 25); and I think it is also implied that this *obsequium* is itself capable of degrees of fullness, whereas of course there are no degrees in assent to an exercise of infallibility.[3]

The truth is that an unexpected blessing flowed from Vati-

[3] Those who make use of Abbott's otherwise admirable English translation of the documents of Vatican II should note that Abbott unfortunately translates *obsequium* as 'assent'. This is, to say the least, confusing.

can I's definition of the 'infallible teaching-role of the Pope'. It was obvious that some conditions needed to be laid down for distinguishing infallible teaching from all other teaching; otherwise it might be supposed that a Pope is a perpetual oracle of truth and nothing but the truth, and that when he gives a public welcome to a society of bee-keepers and makes some observations about their craft he is uttering infallible and irreformable truth. The conditions laid down were stringent, though I think they could have been added to; for example, Vatican I does not say, but would presumably agree, that a Pope cannot define infallibly when he is insane or for some other reason incapable of a fully human act; and it should be added that the question of heretical Popes remains on the agenda of theologians and must be assumed to be relevant to the conditions for infallible teaching.

The stringency of these conditions, which could presumably be applied also to the teaching given by bishops assembled in general council, brings it about that the number of occasions on which it is clear and generally agreed that a Pope has spoken infallibly is very small. Undoubtedly there is, beyond the range of specific infallible definitions, a habitual infallibility of the Church as a whole,[4] but such a habitual state of

[4] In order to understand the doctrine of the Pope's 'infallible teaching role' (*infallibile magisterium*) it is fundamentally important to bear in mind that the Pope does not have a *habit* of infallibility. When we speak of faith, hope and charity we may be speaking of particular acts or of abiding habits: we make an *act* of faith when we recite the Creed, but this act is the expression of a habit that colours all our waking hours. The Pope has no such habit of infallibility. A papal act of infallible definition is not the exercise of a habit with which he is constantly endowed, it is the effect of a momentary act of ('charismatic') negative assistance accorded by the Holy Spirit *ad hoc*. Before the Pope moves to the decision embodied in the new definition, and after the definition has been made, he is no more 'infallible' than the rest of us. Papal teaching utterances are not to be distinguished from one another on the basis that some are 'more' infallible than others, but on the basis that some (a very few) are simply infallible, while all the rest are simply *not* infallible.

It may be helpful to suggest, though so far as I know this point has never been officially clarified, that the act of 'definition' is not synonymous with the words in which the papal teaching is expressed but with the basic intention more or less adequately and purely expressed in those words. What is to be believed is what the Pope basically *meant* to teach, and the clue to this meaning is to be sought in the words he used and the total context in which he used them. It is acknowledged today (cf. John XXIII's inaugural address to the second Vatican Council) that the words of a doctrine can be reformed, provided its (basic) meaning is retained.

affairs does not allow us to enunciate truths of faith in precise and considered language. The upshot is that responsible Christians have a wide area of reflection in which they are not constricted by papal or episcopal 'infallibility'.

From the particular issue of *Humanae Vitae*, viewed as a question of authority, we may now turn to the more general questions: How far has the second Vatican Council affected the life of the Catholic Church, and what are the prospects for the future?

The answer to the former of these questions can best be sought from sociologists. I am not a sociologist, and I know no thorough sociological investigation of the problem that interests us. Obviously, the 'reception' of the council has varied enormously from country to country, and from one stratum of society to another. What is true of Holland is not necessarily equally true of Ireland. Reactions in Latin America have not necessarily been the same as those in sub-equatorial Africa. Again, the response of bishops has not always been similar to that of theologians, of religious Orders and Congregations, or of the parish clergy and their parishioners. The Catholic Church is an immense, trans-national and transcultural body of human beings. If, as I shall shortly be proposing, the council offered to the Church a new orientation that can only be compared, in the Church's past history, to the decision to move out from the limits of Judaism to a genuine universalism, then it is only to be expected that its results will take a long time to mature. The council has to be digested and assimilated by the universal Church, and the process will take not years but many decades. But already a generation is reaching adulthood that has no memory of the preconciliar Church, a generation for which compulsory 'fish on Friday', the 'Tridentine' Latin Mass, and strong hostility to Protestantism are either unknown or seem as odd as the crinoline. Whether this new generation can discover its own and the Church's identity in what is offered to them as today's Catholicism is of course another question.

Lacking the help of sociological studies, I venture just a few very tentative suggestions. First, as regards the bishops. Some bishops returned from the council delighted with its unhoped-for achievements. Many others came back with a loyal determination to carry the findings of the council into effect; but their 'conversion' was cerebral rather than total, and their caution in implementing the council was not very different from reluctance. One must also bear in mind that a large number of bishops have died since the council, and an even larger number of new bishops have been created. It would be superficial to assume that the new bishops would be more attuned to the spirit of the council than the elderly men who have died. On the contrary, it was once pointed out to me that at least the old bishops had personally experienced the group dynamics of the council, while the new ones would largely have been drawn from among priests who completed their seminary training (and therefore, in the case of many of them, their theological education) before the council opened. It will be some years before virtually the whole body of bishops will be composed of men who grew up in the postconciliar Church.

The parish clergy have been key figures in determining the fortunes of the conciliar spirit. A parish priest deeply imbued with that spirit can lead his flock to a genuinely conciliar outlook and activity. On the other hand, it is a matter of experience that if, for example, a parish priest is rootedly opposed to ecumenism the best efforts of individual parishioners among his flock will be frustrated. One has to bear in mind that a good parish priest is not by any means necessarily a man who has an enthusiasm for theological exploration.

One of the great failings of the postconciliar period has been the lack of 'adult education' of the laity (I use the term 'adult education' with some distaste, but mean it in the widest sense, not in a narrowly technical one). On the whole, they have not had the council and its work explained to them, and that work has come before them mainly in the guise of changes in the celebration of Mass which have sometimes deserved, and certainly have often earned, the disfavour of men and women for whom Sunday worship had been a point of numinous stability in a world of threatening and unwelcome change. Against this fact, however, must be set the change in the Catholic population at least in Britain over the last thirty years. This change is in considerable measure due to the educational reforms introduced by the present Lord Butler in 1944. Before that date the majority of the population of this country had no 'secondary' education; the 'elementary' schools catered for them till the age of fourteen, and then they left school and forgot their books. The Catholic population in particular, which had a large proportion of lower-income families in it, had but a small representation in the field of secondary education; this education (except in the case of 'scholars') had to be paid for, and the Catholic masses lacked the wherewithal to pay for it. The Butler Act gave secondary education to every boy and girl, and opened the way to university education for all who had the ability and desire for it. The consequence has been that there is now a considerable fraction of the Catholics of this country who need feel no inferiority complex among their equals when the criterion of excellence is a tertiary education assimilated by those of intellectual ability. This has made possible the emergence of an articulate 'public opinion' in the Catholic body of this country, and the development of a loyalty which, while genuine, is also critical. For many in this group the work of Vatican II has been an inspiration and a challenge. Account needs to be taken of them by both priests and bishops. There might, in fact, be a danger that this attention could obscure the importance of the less articulate laity, and even tend to turn the Catholic body in this country into a 'middle-class' one. It will be necessary to bear in mind that, besides those who take up their pen to write letters to the popular Catholic papers, there is the far larger number who may read such papers but would not 'presume' to air their own views in them; and that besides these there are those who read very little except the sporting news, and will usually switch their television sets when what is offered them is serious theological discussion.

Something must obviously be said about the theologians and the biblical and historical scholars. These have, as such, no rank in the structure of the institutional Church. Theology and scholarship are examples of 'charism' rather than of office. In the decades before the council I think it fair to say that theology and biblical scholarship were at a low ebb in the English and Welsh Catholic Church. Catholic theologians and scholars were hardly represented in the universities. What we now call Colleges of Education were then not improperly termed training colleges: an arena for catechetics rather than theology. The seminaries were also catechetical rather than theological in their approach to the study of the Christian *datum*. Things are very much better today, and they were better in some countries even before the Council: in France, Belgium and Germany in particular. Even the United States of America had Catholic universities, though at least one of them was more renowned for its athletic than for its intellectual prowess. It was from Western Europe, excluding the British Isles, that the theological inspiration of Vatican II's so-called 'progressives' emanated; and from the United States it was Fr Courtney Murray who prepared the way for the very important Declaration on Religious Freedom. In Britain we are still catching up with the lead given by other countries; and we are beginning to penetrate the British university world. We should, eventually, have much to contribute, and there is already evidence that our presence in the universities is welcomed. If we have not provided the Church with anything so startlingly novel and pregnant with great possibilities as the liberation theology of Latin America, that may be in part because we are not, as a country, yet living in the acute conditions of social and political crisis of that subcontinent.

* * * *

Among the General Councils that have marked the history of the Church some are of more permanent importance than others. The first of them all (not counting the so-called Council of Jerusalem described in the Acts of the Apostles) was the Council of Nicaea in A.D. 325. Its effect was to ensure that the Church's traditional adoration of Jesus Christ, as deserving such respect as would be idolatry if offered to a mere creature, would continue and have henceforth the backing of a conciliar dogmatic affirmation. The Council of Chalcedon (A.D. 451) expanded the Christological and Trinitarian consequences of that dogma and the associated doctrine that the Holy Spirit is 'personally' (better, hypostatically) an object of adoration. The Council of Florence (A.D. 1439–1445) would have been a moment of the very greatest significance, in the reconciliation of Eastern Orthodoxy with Western Catholicism, had its findings not been repudiated by the Orthodox believers themselves after the termination of the council. The Council of Trent (A.D. 1545–1563) was a council of counter-protest, of retrenchment and reform; it did not strike out new paths of thought and was, like the Counter-Reformation as a whole, retrospective rather than prospective. The Council of Vatican I (1869–1870) is mainly remembered as terminating the long struggle between Gallicanism and Ultramontanism and as canonising the infallible teaching rôle of the Pope.

I wish to put forward the suggestion that the second Vatican Council was significantly different from all these other great councils, and not only because it did not enrich the Church with any new infallible dogmas. It was significant because it was a belated attempt to make the Church and Christianity relevant to the human race in an epoch of unprecedented change in the human condition and man's perception of that condition; and because it opened the way for a renewed and most genuinely Christian understanding of the gospel of Christ, and of the response which that gospel invites from man in his fully historical existence on earth.

What follows is a tentative, provisional, and undoubtedly imperfect attempt to grasp something of the spirit, as distinct from the words, of the second Vatican Council. It is a hazardous undertaking. The only adequate way to grasp the spirit of a great poem is, after whatever preparation, to let the poem say its own thing to us. But the Acts of Vatican II are not a great poem, or even a collection of great poems. They are documents of very varying literary and intellectual merit. Is it possible to discover a spirit animating them, or most of them, and particularly the great Constitutions on Revelation, the Church, Liturgy, and the Church in the World of Today? Is it possible to substantiate the claim that this spirit has a quality of almost evolutionary novelty and is pregnant with the hope of a magnificent future?

I am speaking not of revolutionary but of evolutionary novelty. The distinction is important. A new biological species is both continuous and discontinuous with the species from which it evolves. *Homo sapiens* is not an entirely new creation unconnected with the subhuman species that preceded it chronologically. It is a novelty but a novelty that grows out of what has long been familiar. It is, as Aristotle had said, *animal rationale*. Its animality, inherited from earlier evolutionary history, is essential to its rationality, and *vice versa*. The analogy of the evolution of a new species is of course imperfect. For in human history (of which religion, Christianity and the Catholic Church form part) there is no occurrence of a new species supervening upon the great novelty of *homo sapiens*. A new species, it has been said, is a (new) solution to a concrete problem in concrete circumstances, and 'a solution is the sort of thing that insight hits upon and not the sort that results from accumulated, observable difference'. To the extent that a new species is a solution to a problem, it bears some resemblance to the solutions that human intelligence 'hits upon' to meet the changing problems of human living. But genuinely human solutions to problems do not entail the change to a new species. Man is capable of intelligent enquiry and insight, and enquiry and insights are 'not so much a higher system', which is what a new species is, 'as a perennial source of higher system. . . . Man, then, is at once explanatory genus and explanatory species', and it follows that human history is capable of the most astonishing steps forwards and upwards without ceasing to remain the history of a single species.[5] For a Christian the greatest and, in the religious aspect, definitive step upwards was of course Jesus Christ himself, the second Adam. A Catholic will have no difficulty in believing that the Church, in her unceasing exploration of the infinite riches of the incarnation, can herself make tremendous, quasi-evolutionary steps upwards under the guidance and animation of the Holy Spirit of Christ.

Continuity and discontinuity. An honest appraisal of Vatican II must take account of both elements. It is possible to present the council, by a judicious quotation of extracts from its documents, as either a mere restatement of the self-understanding of the Church in the period immediately before the council, or alternatively as a wildly and dangerously innovating affair, unfaithful to the Church's historical past and, indeed, to the Sacred Tradition itself.

[5] Cf. Bernard Lonergan, *Insight*, pp. 265–67. The incarnation is not the coming into being of a new superhuman species. Jesus is the perfect man, 'consubstantial' with us, as he is, in his divine nature, 'consubstantial' with his heavenly Father.

The truth however would seem to be that the council was extremely careful to be faithful to what it had inherited from the past, and at the same time was bold in venturing out into areas which the official Church had long neglected. If you wish to grasp the difference between this council and its predecessors, you have to pay special attention to what strikes one as novel in the positions which it made its own.

The comparison with 'the first council', the so-called council of Jerusalem as described by the Acts of the Apostles, or rather with the great decision of which Acts makes that event the expression, is helpful. The primitive Church had no intention of renouncing what it viewed as its inheritance from the Jews and the 'Old Covenant'. The very term Church (*ecclesia*) which it chose as its self-designation, was an Old Testament term, and its choice signified that the Christians claimed that their new association was the legitimate representation of the 'Church of God' of Old Testament times. Again, in adopting the title Christ (Messiah) for Jesus of Nazareth, they clearly meant to present the gospel as the actualisation of the great hope of Judaism. The same attitude pervades the New Testament literature. It comes out, for example, in St Paul's description of the conversion of his Thessalonian Christians as the act by which they 'turned from idols to serve the living God', that is to say the God of the Jews. The Epistle to the Hebrews is a classic exposition of the primitive Church's doctrine that all that is of permanent worth in Judaism finds its perfection in the Christian system. It is precisely against this background of a reaffirmation of the traditional faith of the People of God, that the decision to accept Gentiles into the Church without circumcision and without obligation to observe the ritual prescriptions of Judaism stands out as a prodigious novelty. St Paul stresses this novelty, when he declares that 'even if we have known Christ according to the flesh, yet now we know him so no more'. Christ according to the flesh was identical with the Christ of faith; but to 'know him' only according to the flesh was to miss the point of the gospel and *also*, St Paul claimed, of the Old Covenant itself: the true offspring of Abraham were the Christian believers.

We sometimes underestimate the magnitude and the shock of the decision to make Christianity not just a movement within the established boundaries of existing Judaism but a really independent universal ('catholic') religion, and the Church, a 'catholic' Church; we underestimate this shock partly no doubt because we are so familiar with the latter idea, and partly perhaps because the gentle author of the Acts prefers to present a picture of sweetness and light rather than one of conflict and agony. But there are indications in the Epistles of St Paul that Christian 'traditionalists' made life hard for the apostle of the Gentiles. Certainly, if you wish to understand the Christian religion you cannot afford to play down the 'innovations' introduced already in the time of the Apostles.

Thus, in seeking to grasp the spirit of Vatican II we shall not neglect the evident intention, expressed in its documents, to be faithful to the inheritance of tradition. But we shall pay special attention to what it adds to those elements. It is proper to bear in mind that 'traditionalism' is itself an ambiguous word. In the eyes of many opponents of the council, tradition means the stance and current affirmations of the Church as it existed in the middle decades of the twentieth century. But no moment of the Church's history has ever successfully expressed, in its own formulations, rites and laws, the fullness of the Sacred Tradition. The content of the Sacred Tradition is the living Word of God in his historical incarnation, his redemptive acts and sufferings and his resurrection. That content is of inexhaustible richness. No accumulation of human words and gestures can render it in its totality, and usually the Church is exploiting only limited sections of the truths that have been thus expressed. As Alberigo has pointed out, ideas like that of the episcopal college can more or less 'go underground' for a considerable period of time, but are waiting to be recovered when the needs of the Church and the world direct our attention towards them. But, to repeat, the real content of Tradition is Christ himself, transcending all human attempts to 'put him into words' or express him in rites, ceremonies, poetry and art. Tradition thus understood lives not so much in the so-called 'monuments of tradition' as in the heart and mind of the Church, and its life is connected with the gift of the Holy Spirit to the Church as its, so to speak, animating principle. One of the most evident examples of the recovery of tradition by the Council is its reference away from scholastic philosophical theology to a more biblical theology and, in addition, to the patristic tradition.[6]

Earlier in these pages I devoted a chapter, which concluded the contents of the first edition, on 'Objective and Subjective'. In it I argued that while the Church of the Counter-Reformation and succeeding centuries heavily stressed the objectivity of the Christian religion and its embodiment in the constitution, Vatican II gave evidence of a shift of emphasis from the objective to the subjective aspect of human and Christian experience, and I referred to a speech in the council (by Cardinal Pellegrino of Turin) in which we were told that there was much to be said for 'subjectivism properly understood'. At the time of writing the first edition of this book I was already an admirer of Bernard Lonergan's great book, *Insight*, but his lecture entitled 'The Subject' had not then been published. In it he points out that the philosophic idea of the soul is the result of studying human activity and human nature as though they were objects, as external to the student as chemical compounds or plant biology. Such a study leads to a distinction between faculties of the soul, and to an objectivist psychology. What has been overlooked in such study is the human being as subject, as conscious and aware and, by reflection, capable of becoming an object to himself, though never an object in his precise subjectivity. Live human beings are actually subjects, a fact which philosophy would be wise not to overlook. Lonergan likes to speak of the 'existential subject', in order to make clear that he is not speaking of the 'nature' of a subject but of the subject as actually, and always subjec-

[6] In at least one example, referred to earlier in this book, the wearisome insistence on the traditional teaching of Vatican I is due precisely to the intention to introduce and re-emphasise a classical doctrine about the episcopate and the episcopal college which is part of the Sacred Tradition but had been given scanty attention in the documents (as contrasted with the debates) of Vatican I. To take this reiteration of Vatican I's papalism as disclosing the *spirit* of Vatican II and to neglect the teaching which this insistence was framed to make possible, is to distort the truth about the second Vatican Council. Vatican I was indeed the council of the papacy. Vatican II was not; rather, it was the council of the bishops and their 'collegial' authority.Earlier in this book I have drawn attention to Karl Rahner's thesis, which seems correct, that according to Vatican II, the papacy, as understood by Vatican I, is only seen correctly when it is understood, as by Vatican II, within the ambit of the college.

tively, alive. The existential subject is not only a knower; he is a doer, and his doing not only affects 'the world of objects' but changes himself:

> Human doing is free and responsible. Within it is contained the reality of morals, of building up or destroying character, of achieving personality or failing in that task. By his own acts the human subject makes himself what he is to be, and he does so freely and responsibly; indeed, he does so precisely because his acts are the free and responsible expression of himself. ('The Subject', p. 19; re-published in *A Second Collection*, 1974, p. 79.)

Lonergan's understanding of the 'existential subject' coheres with his view of 'the object' and of the relation between objectivity and subjectivity. The object of human knowledge, when that knowledge is fully human, is found not just in material things and sensible events as experienced by the knower; it is found in the content and complications of experience lifted to a higher plane by understanding and affirmed in judgment. Since such knowing is the fruit of man's unbounded desire to know, the object is in the end an 'objective', a goal of a dynamic enterprise rather than something that statically confronts our senses.

The desire of the subject to know has to be seen in the context of the same subject's desire for 'the good' or, to use Lonergan's own term, 'value'. The desire to know is, in itself, unrestricted. When lack of evidence, or a problem situation which for the moment is insoluble, checks that desire, the subject suffers a sense of frustration or experiences a challenge to pursue his investigations still further; everyone wants to know what is on the other side of the mountain which obscures his vision. So too, the desire for value is intrinsically unrestricted; and one value towards which it is orientated is the value of truth, which is the object of the desire to know. The human subject, then, has as his ultimate and controlling objective ('object' not in the sense of something already presented to the senses but as the unknown, unattained, which inspires all his actual thinking and striving) absolute unlimited truth, reality, goodness: 'Thou hast made us for thyself', to quote St Augustine, 'and our heart is without repose until it comes to rest in thee'. But this goal of infinite Reality is necessarily and for ever beyond the native power of the subject to reach. The subject is therefore for ever in a condition of waiting upon a word and an empowerment from the free action and self-disclosure of God; and the Christian gospel is precisely the announcement that this word and help have been given in and as Jesus Christ and the gift of his Spirit. The two levels, of natural desire and supernatural divine revelation, together constitute the dignity of the human subject; and men of good will are by implication[7] recognised by Vatican II as having responded positively to the divine invitation.

The council, however, was not teaching a vague liberal ethic of mindless good will. It takes the message of a divine intervention in history seriously; in other words, it proclaims, as the Church has always proclaimed, the incarnation of the divine Word. It is this incarnate Word which speaks to the heart of every man in all places and ages, before and after the event of the first Christmas day; and it is to this incarnate Word that the man of good will makes a positive response, enabled so to do by the Spirit of Christ, even when this man is not in a position to identify the Word with Jesus of Nazareth.

It seems clear that if, following St Augustine, we agree that there are among those who visibly adhere to the visible Church, some who are interiorly alienated from it by sin, there are others who are not visibly "Catholics' but who are yet, in the deepest sense, at one with the Church because, fundamentally, they follow the light of their conscience; and the light of conscience is always the Word of God incarnate, even when not recognised as such. If such is the true teaching of the second Vatican Council, then the council was in deep harmony with the Sacred Tradition. This teaching provides the basis for all constructive dialogue about fundamentals. I have suggested in Chapter 7 that it surmounts the opposition between objective and subjective, inasmuch as good will is always orientated towards the true and the good, and on the other hand the gospel and the Church are orientated towards the will

[7] 'By implication': doubtless it would be desirable to substantiate this interpretation of the 'spirit' of Vatican II. One might begin by considering the Council's attitude to non-Catholic Christians and their 'churches and ecclesial communities', pass on to a study of the Declaration on the non-Christian Religions; and then generalise.

which is already good (and the will which the gospel is summoning and enabling for 'repentance' or conversion).

At a lowlier but still important level, the spirit of Vatican II suggests a new vision (which is a very old and deeply traditional one) of the Church in its institutional reality. Confronted by the estranged East and the Protestant North-West, the Church in recent centuries has emphasised the primacy of the bishop of Rome as successor of St Peter. But long before the Reformation and the event of A.D. 1054 the papacy was being not only emphasised but, in some respects, over-emphasised. Historically, it looks as though the great impulse towards super-papalism came with the 'establishment' of the Church as the religion of the Roman Empire in the fourth century, coinciding roughly with the transference of the seat of civil power from the city of Rome to Constantinople, the 'new Rome'. The See of Rome already had a great prestige, particularly in the West; and more and more it began to emerge as the one great, actually present, 'authority' in the West, unrivalled either by civil powers or by other ecclesiastical sees. Historians will agree that out of this situation there emerged the 'direct government' of the whole Western Church by the bishop of Rome. In my view it can be argued within the limits of a strictly orthodox theology that such 'papal caesarism', however justifiable as a contingent and temporary remedy for grave evils and dangers in the world and the Church, is not an *articulus stantis aut cadentis ecclesiae*. Vatican II can encourage us to look back behind the year A.D. 400 to the early patristic period and the age of the apostolic Fathers, and to recover the vision of a Church in which the local Eucharist is the centre of communion; the bishop, by whom or by whose co-operating presbyters, the Eucharist is celebrated, is the guardian of the communion and the one whose task it is to keep the local communion 'open' to the other eucharistic communions the world over; and the bishops in their collegiate unity, of which the bishop of Rome is the centre and head, are the seat of supreme authority in the universal Church. What is still required is a genuine recognition that the papal primacy, though universal and immediate, is not 'ordinary' in the sense of being a matter of daily exercise, but 'ordinary' only in the legal sense that it is not delegated to the Pope by any other merely human source of power. When Rome has fully recognised that, and translated it into its own conduct and into the structures supporting that conduct, not only will the ecumenical task, to which Vatican II has called us, be immensely facilitated, but the true genius of Catholic Christianity as a fellowship of mutual respect and love rather than of authoritarianism and obedience, will be disclosed, and the Church's mission to mankind, in all the variety of local cultures, be seen in its true purity.

* * * *

The council covered a wide variety of topics and expressed its spirit in the way in which it treated them. It is usually thought that it failed to deal adequately with the great questions concerning communications in general and the mass media in particular. I do not wish to apologise for this, except to say that the Decree on the Instruments of Social Communication was one of its earlier efforts and the heart of the council members was not engaged in it as no doubt it should have been.

Perhaps a more serious criticism could be that the council has very little to say about personal, as distinct from liturgical, prayer. Of course there is encouragement and respect for personal prayer, and a reference to Christ 'praying on the mountain' implies a commendation of contemplative prayer, more particularly as it is practised by members of contemplative Orders and communities.

The chapter in the Constitution on the Church entitled 'The Call of the Whole Church to Holiness' certainly gives a foundation for a treatment of personal prayer. This chapter is mainly concerned to emphasise that the call to holiness is not a prerogative of those who are also called to the religious life, but concerns every believer: there are not two classes in the Church, a small one of those who are called to real holiness, and a much larger one of those who are not expected to accomplish more than a good average and rather external compliance with the divine law as elevated to a new perfection in the gospel. On the contrary, to be a Christian is to be summoned by God to a goal of holiness which is limitless, and therefore beyond the powers of any of us; we all depend in this matter on grace, but grace is given, and given more abundantly in the measure that we have responded to grace. What distinguishes monks and nuns and other 'religious' from the rest of the People of God (including of course most bishops, other ordained ministers and lay people) is not a different goal to pursue, but a choice of particular means to that end.

Probably as a consequence of this emphasis on a truly traditional doctrine of the universal call to holiness, the constitution in this chapter makes it abundantly clear that ordinary people are called to pursue holiness not only by the faithful performance of their 'religious' duties (taking part in the Mass, frequenting of the sacraments, obeying the Church's regulations on fasting and abstinence) but also by infusing with charity and pursuing with diligence their rôles in secular society. St Francis de Sales would have welcomed this emphasis. But somehow, there seems to be a lack of concern in the constitution about personal prayer, and certainly little guidance as to the development of a life of personal prayer.

The immediate mood of the Church after the council was one of feverish activism. There was so much to be done. There was a new Roman Missal to be prepared and a new Breviary, re-named The Prayer of the Church (and still liturgical in its general style); and these had to be introduced into the practice of the Church and her ministers. At Rome there were Secretariats to be organised (not to speak of the Concilium for the revision of the liturgy). The proposal for a regular Synod of Bishops had to be translated into action. Episcopal conferences had to be set up or, where they already existed, to adapt their modes of procedures to the 'new look'. At more local levels there had to be established diocesan pastoral councils, senates of priests and parish councils. There was an enormous amount of discussion, and there emerged 'conservation' and 'renewal' groups and movements. Meanwhile, the theologians, the biblical scholars and the ecclesiastical journalists were hard at work and enjoying a much enlarged readership. The religious Orders and Congregations were revising their own constitutions and were often rent by interior tensions between those who preferred the old ways and those who were hungry for the new.

Then in 1967 an extraordinary thing happened. At Duquesne University in the United States the Catholic Charismatic Movement, or Catholic Pentecostalism, was born. This movement can be integrated into the vision of Vatican II inasmuch as the Council made efforts (insufficient, in the eyes of some critics) to pay attention to the place of the Holy Spirit in doctrine, theology and action, and it has a pregnant few sentences about the 'charismatic', as distinct from the structural, gifts of God to his Church. The ecclesiology of the council is more open to spontaneity and even novelty in the life of the Church than the manualistic ecclesiology of an earlier date; and there was at least one remarkable speech in the council reminding the members that the future of the Church is always unpredictable, precisely because the Holy Spirit is like the wind which 'blows where it listeth'.[8]

I mention this remarkable movement which has spread far and wide in the Church, not in order to discuss the exterior phenomena connected with it, phenomena that have aroused a good deal of suspicion and some controversy, but because prayer, not only liturgical but paraliturgical and also personal, is of the essence of the movement. There has been a great renewal of interest in prayer and 'in prayer groups' during the last decade, and much of this interest occurs outside the limits of what is called Catholic Pentecostalism. Indeed, it is part of a development which is going on in the Christian world in general, and the prayer groups are sometimes interdenominational.

Nothing could be more traditional than this interest in informal and personal prayer, bearing always in mind that, for the Christian, prayer, while it includes asking God for favours, whether spiritual or temporal, is not by any means confined to this. One may hope that the search for prayer and for direction in prayer will lead many to the great classics of the spiritual life: not only to the Bible but to that massive witness and guide to prayer which is found in the central tradition of the Catholic Church, and is particularly exemplified in the post-Reformation literature from St John of the Cross and St

[8] For a useful study of 'charismatic renewal' in the Catholic Church reference may be made to René Laurentin, *Catholic Pentecostalism*, Darton, Longman and Todd 1977, and Doubleday and Co., New York, 1977.

Francis de Sales, by way especially but not exclusively of some great French Jesuit writers, down to the eighteenth-century Jesuits de Caussade and Grou (the latter of whom, though French, had come to England from revolutionary France and became the Spiritual director of the Weld family at Lulworth Castle, dying in 1803).

In conclusion, one may turn to two English authors for a framework in which to place the second Vatican Council and its consequences. Newman distinguished in the Church three rôles or functions, the prophetic, the regal and the sacerdotal. Von Hügel, in turn, and in dependance on Newman, spoke of three 'elements' of religion: the institutional, the intellectual and the mystical. And these three elements tend to develop in chronological sequence, the second and the third subsuming but not abandoning the first. The institutional element is reflected in the vision of the Church given by Counter-Reformation ecclesiology. The intellectual element inspires theological reflection and theological development. The mystical element is the deeply personal life of the believer, profoundly prayerful but fruitful also in many-sided activity. It may not be altogether misleading to view Vatican I as a council of the institutional element, and Vatican II as opening the way for the intellectual element. Let us hope that, as the Church gradually assimilates the teaching and is captured by the spirit of Vatican II, it will be the theatre, and be recognised as the authentic witness, of the mystical element in which the essential life of the Church and of every believer comes to flower and fruit. We need, however, to bear in mind that the intellectual element of religion is permanently tributary to the institutional element and becomes rootless if detached from it; while the mystical element runs wild and eventually withers if it loses contact with either or both of the other elements.

Index of References to the Texts of Vatican II

Index Excluding Texts of Vatican II